SELF-DEFENSE AND BATTERED WOMEN WHO KILL

SELF-DEFENSE AND BATTERED WOMEN WHO KILL

A New Framework

Robbin S.Ogle and Susan Jacobs

Westport, Connecticut
London

Library of Congress Cataloging-in-Publication Data

Ogle, Robbin S., 1960–
    Self-defense and battered women who kill : a new framework / Robbin S. Ogle
and Susan Jacobs.
      p. cm.
    Includes bibliographical references.
    ISBN 0–275–96711–5 (alk. paper)
    1. Justifiable homicide—United States. 2. Self-defense (Law)—United States.
3. Abused women—Legal status, laws, etc.—United States. 4. Abused women—
United States. I. Jacobs, Susan, 1945– II. Title.
    KF9305.O34 2002
    364.15'2—dc21   2002019623

British Library Cataloguing in Publication Data is available.

Library of Congress Catalog Card Number: 2002019623
ISBN: 0–275–96711–5

First published in 2002

Praeger Publishers, 88 Post Road West, Westport, CT 06881
An imprint of Greenwood Publishing Group, Inc.
www.praeger.com

Printed in the United States of America

The paper used in this book complies with the
Permanent Paper Standard issued by the National
Information Standards Organization (Z39.48–1984).

10 9 8 7 6 5 4 3 2 1

Copyright Acknowledgments

The author and publisher gratefully acknowledge permission for use of the following material:

From Rosen, R.A. (1993). On self-defense, imminence, and women who kill their batterers. *North Carolina Law Review*, 71, 371–411. Used by permission of the *North Carolina Law Review*.

From Schopp, Robert F., Sturgis, Barbara J., Sullivan, Megan (1994). Battered woman syndrome, expert testimony, and the distinction between justification and excuse. *University of Illinois Law Review*, 45. Copyright to the *University of Illinois Law Review* is held by The Board of Trustees of the University of Illinois.

TO BOB AND CAROL
THANKS, RSO

Contents

Acknowledgments   xi

1 An Overview   1

Introduction   1

Overview of the Chapters   7

The Test Case as Originally and Traditionally Tried   8

    Traditional Case   8

    People v. Beasley, 622 N.E. 1236 (Ill. App. 5 Dist. 1993) 8

        Facts   8

        Expert Witnesses   19

        Lay Witnesses   23

        Jury Instructions 23

        Prosecutor's Opening Statement 25

        Defense Counsel's Opening Statement 25

        Prosecutor's Closing Argument 25

        Defense Counsel's Closing Argument 26

        Sentencing   28

2   A Review of the Relevant Literature   33
A Brief Overview of History: Social and Legal Issues   33
Battering   37
    Individual/Biological Perspectives   38
    Socio-Cultural Perspectives   38
    Family Violence Perspectives   39
Social Science Research on Women Who Kill   44
Battering Homicide   45
Existing Theories on Women Who Kill   49
    The First Theory: Homicidal Behavior Among Women   49
    The Second Theory: Postpartum Depression or Psychosis   50
    The Third Theory: Battered Woman Syndrome   51
Interaction Theory   55
Conclusion   56

3   Battering as a Slow Homicidal Process: A Social
    Interaction Perspective   69
Introduction   69
The Theory   70
    Battering Issues in Realistic Social Perspective   72
        Socialization Differences   72
        The Physical Size and Strength Differential   73
        Misconceptions about Social Resources   74
    The Battering Cycle as a Slow Homicidal Process   77
    Putting It All Together in a Theoretical Framework   80
Conclusion   84

4   The Law of Self-Defense and the Battered Woman   93
Self-Defense Generally   100
Self-Defense as a Justification   101
Traditional Elements of Self-Defense   106
    Reasonableness   106
        By What Standard Do We Measure Reasonableness?   106
        The Objective Test   108
        The Subjective Test   111

The Blending of Objective and Subjective Tests 113

Reasonableness and the Model Penal Code 117

Imminence 120

What Is a "Threat of Imminent Harm?" 121

Is "Imminent" Harm the Same as "Immediate" Harm? 123

Imminence Is Closely Related to Reasonableness 128

Law of Self-Defense Is Advanced by Reliance on Proof of Necessity 129

Law of Self-Defense Is Advanced by Allowing Contextual Evidence 132

Expert Testimony to Establish the Context of Abuse 132

Use of Expert Testimony to Establish Reasonableness of Defendant's Belief in the Necessity of Self-Defense 136

Use of Expert Testimony to Dispel Myths about Battered Women and Battering 138

Use of Expert Testimony to Show Typical Emotional and Behavioral Responses of Battered Women 141

Expert Testimony Is Generally Not Admissible to Establish Defendant's State of Mind 142

Lay Testimony to Establish the Context of Abuse 144

Instructing the Jury on Self-Defense 147

When Self-Defense Instruction Is Refused in Battered Woman Cases 147

When Self-Defense Instruction Is Given, It Generally Tracks Statutory Language 150

When Self-Defense Instruction Is Given, It May Include Specific Reference to the Battering Relationship 153

The Battering Relationship May Be Considered Along with Every Other Fact in Determining Self-Defense 153

The Battering Relationship May Be Considered to Determine Whether the Defendant Honestly Believed She Was in Imminent Danger 154

The Battering Relationship May Be Considered to Determine If the Defendant Acted Reasonably 155

Conclusion 159

5 The Traditional Test Case Revisited   167

People v. Beasley (1993)   167

   Facts   167

      Socialization Differences   168

      Physical Size and Strength Differences   170

      Isolation   171

      Resources   173

      Control   176

      Escalation of Violence   178

      Jury Instructions   183

**6 Application of These Theoretical Ideas to Gay and
Lesbian Battering *by Anne Garner and Robbin S. Ogle***   185

What Is Same-Sex Domestic Violence?   186

Myths and Stereotypes Regarding Lesbian and Gay Domestic
Violence   187

Literature Review   188

Application of Ogle and Jacobs' Perspective to Lesbian and Gay
Battering and Battering Escalation   196

   Three Elements That Influence the Battering Interaction   196

      The First Element   196

      The Second Element   198

      The Third Element   199

   The Battering Cycle as an Interaction Process   201

Conclusion   204

Acknowledgments

Any authors who have written a book will likely tell you that they can not possibly thank everyone who made a contribution to their research, developmental thinking, or final product. However, we would like to thank those who made major contributions and without whose assistance this book would never have come to fruition. First, we must thank Sheila Beasley for being willing to share her ordeal and some of the most difficult moments in her life. We hope that we have done justice to her story and that its use will be of assistance to others facing the same ordeal in the future. We also must thank Nancy Gore for her support, friendship, excellent input on the topic, and tremendous editing skills. Without her assistance we believe this book would never have been useful to others. We are also grateful to Alissa Lauer and Clifford Lee who assisted enormously with the collection and organization of case law. Any errors in analysis are those of the authors and should not be attributed to them. Our thanks also go to Heather Staines at Greenwood Publishing Group for her patience and efforts on our behalf. Chapter 6 of this book is an experimental chapter where the new theory is applied to gay and lesbian battering homicide. This chapter would not have been possible without the knowledge of the literature and efforts of Anne Garner. Our thanks go out to her for her willingness to help write a chapter in this book. We want to thank Whitney L. Shockley and Christian A. Nolasco for their graphics skills resulting in the wonderful illustrations in the text. Finally, we would like to thank our families and the University of Nebraska at Omaha for allowing us to pursue this lengthy project and providing support and prodding as needed.

Chapter 1

An Overview

INTRODUCTION

Since this book provides a new theoretical perspective on battering and its escalation to homicide, it seems reasonable to begin with a brief discussion of our view on theory and how it is developed. Criminologists have long been trained to develop and use the most parsimonious explanation possible for any phenomenon. In our opinion, this has led to an overreliance on simplistic or partial explanations developed out of the quantitative analysis of limited individualized variables. But the social world is very complex. This often makes theory look like a leap away from reality rather than an explanation for it. For that reason, laymen look at criminological theory and question its applicability to the real world. Theory should not be confined only to parameters previously examined in quantitative research. Just because we do not presently know exactly how to test something quantitatively does not mean that we should resist the progression of theoretical ideas. Social scientists such as Durkheim, Weber, Parsons, Sutherland, Merton, and Foucault have demonstrated repeatedly the value of thinking beyond our current ability to test. Clearly, quantitative analysis changes on a consistent basis as well. New theoretical ideas challenge us as criminologists to develop new quantitative and qualitative methods that bring us closer to understanding our social world.

The development of new theoretical perspectives in the social sciences is both absolutely necessary and extremely difficult. This is so because social science focuses on the study of the two most variable things in the world: people and society. These two phenomena change constantly, requiring social scientists to create evolving perspectives that often demand thinking outside the confines of traditional ideas. New theory requires the examination of existing research in a new or different way, always with an eye to what we do not presently understand and to changes in social reality. This examination allows us to ask questions that we have overlooked in the past. It also provides us with the opportunity to examine the applicability of other perspectives that might contribute to an integrated theoretical explanation. There is some disagreement among criminologists concerning the value of theoretical integration; however, proponents consistently point to the need to move criminological theory forward or risk stagnation in the field. Liska, Krohn, and Messner (1989) indicate that there are "considerable opportunity and need" to pursue both integration and elaboration in criminological theory (p. 9). They point to the particular need for theoretical integration that takes an "end to end" approach. This approach utilizes micro-level concepts of one theory explaining "day to day experiences of people" to elaborate or extend the explanation provided by a macro-level theory that describes "the social and demographic structures of small- and large-scale social units" (p. 9). Liska et al. (1989) note the significance of both large- and small-scale integration efforts, meaning that it is acceptable and even preferable for theory development to involve the melding of two complete theories (assuming their assumptions are not completely counter to each other) and smaller-scale integration involving the borrowing of concepts and propositions from different theories to create a new approach.

The new theory in this book was developed in this way. We looked at the information obtained from a mass of quantitative research presently available on battering and domestic homicide, and used some of those variables as a guide for what needed to be explained. Additionally, we decided to take a *grounded theory* approach to understanding battering homicides, so we began with what the social scientist can see in the reality of everyday cases. This information was gleaned from the few qualitative case studies on battering and homicide. Then we looked at the theories currently available on this topic and asked why they are problematic—in essence, where do they fail? That provided us with a list of problems to be solved and guidance on new angles that might be taken on the issues. From that point, we began to ask questions about the variety of ways that this phenomena might be examined and understood. This approach allowed us to borrow information from other theories as well as to look for connections to new ideas that might be synthesized into a single explanation. The resulting theory is an integrated product borrowing some variables from the research and some from other theoretical perspectives, and creating new variables that represent a different angle of explanation for the phenomena. We believe this theory provides the best reality-based, social science explanation to date for understanding battering and its escalation to homicide.

Battering is a modern social problem because, historically, battering was not illegal. At the time that self-defense law was evolving, battering was a legally tolerated and accepted activity in society. Women were property rather than full citizens of this country and therefore did not possess the same rights as men. There was a general assumption that men would utilize violence in the home to control their human property, women and children, with the level of restraint and compassion expected of the prudent man, although this moderation often did not prevail. Consequently, most of the laws concerning battering, prior to the 1970s, were created by men for the purpose of regulating the amount of damage that could legally be inflicted without drawing a response from the state (Belknap 2001; Gosselin 2000; Pleck 1983, 1987).

In the 1970s, the women's movement brought to public attention the misuse and abuse of this power and began to demand that women, full citizens since 1920, be given equal protection under the law. This movement precipitated the creation of laws defining battering as a form of simple assault punishable in some states as an ordinance violation and in others as a misdemeanor crime. These developments reflect both some change in our view of women as citizens with rights and a continuation of our unwillingness to see these assaults as a major issue. However, one thing is clear: As men were developing the law of self-defense, they were not thinking about the possibility that such a defense might one day be utilized by women who have killed their abusers to survive.

There has been an enormous amount of scholarship on both the legal and social issues surrounding the defense of battered women who kill their abusers. Most of this scholarship reflects a dissonance between law and social science, particularly with reference to gender issues. The social science literature often criticizes the rigidity of legal approaches for failure to embrace the reality of battered women. However, theoretical understanding of the reality of battering relationships and victim responses seems to lack the development necessary to form a social science framework in which legal change can proceed. The goal of this book is to provide a social interaction theoretical perspective on battering and its escalation that creates a framework for legal change in the handling of these cases within self-defense law.

One problem is that self-defense law reflects a singular and narrow historical standard that arose out of the *barroom brawl* scenario. The law is designed to address a one-time confrontation among men. It assumes two relatively equal combatants with limited knowledge of each other in a single, short-term confrontation where both parties can see a clear beginning and end to the fray. It focuses on a single violent encounter where the combatants, knowing little about each other, evaluate the imminence of the situation and respond reasonably with only the force necessary to protect themselves from death or serious bodily harm in the moment. Unfortunately, battering is not this type of scenario. Battering generally involves two socially and physically unequal combatants with intimate knowledge of each other developed over a long period of time, participating in an ongoing, long-term confrontation where neither party can identify a foreseeable end. The battering cycle is one on-going, long-term confrontation, where violence slowly but surely becomes the primary control method. Consequently, we argue that there are no nonconfrontational periods, only *lulls* of tension building before the violence resumes.

Self-defense law has not been especially successful in the defense of battered women who must claim it as a justification for killing their abusers to survive. This legal defense generally fails because the critical elements of the defense are not met—most often, a factual base for finding that the threat requiring lethal force was *imminent* and a factual base for finding the decision to use deadly force was *reasonable*. Courts often find that either there was no immediate threat of death or serious bodily injury, or that the battered woman's perception of the level of threat in this final violent encounter was unreasonable and concomitantly her response unreasonable. Battered women who have killed their abusers claim that we must examine the previous violent encounters resulting in bodily harm in order to understand their perception of escalating lethality. However, this examination is rarely done in these cases, at least in part because there is no theoretical basis or framework for such an approach. Since the early 1980s, attorneys have attempted to address these problems by supplementing a self-defense defense with a psychological excuse for why a battered woman might act unreasonably and kill her abuser.

To date, the only well-developed social science theoretical framework available to explain why and how battered women kill their abusers that can be used to supplement a self-defense strategy is Dr. Lenore Walker's (1984) theory: *Battered Woman Syndrome*. In this theory, Walker attributes the batterer's control of the victim and the victim's failure to escape from the battering situation to a psychological problem of the victim called *learned helplessness*. As we will discuss in more detail later, this position does not provide a complete, adequate, or logical explanation because it focuses only on the victim and strictly on the psychology of the victim, as if the victim is the causal factor to be understood. It asks the inadequate and archaic question of what is wrong with this victim that causes her to be in this situation. This psychological theory ignores all of the cultural, social, structural, and situational variables that are parts of the battering process and the victim's normal human responses to that process given the social choices available to her. Additionally, this theory ignores the batterer and his contribution to the process both as the initiating participant and as the individual socially, culturally, structurally, and situationally benefiting from maintenance of the battering process.

Another problem in the social science study of battering has been the overwhelming focus on what Websdale (1999) refers to as *abstracted empiricism* that results in ahistorical and microscopic perspectives of the phenomenon. He notes that this concentration on empirical data provides an undiscerning, narrow, and acontextual picture that is less than useful for understanding the real social world, or domestic homicide as a social phenomenon:

Abstracted empiricism is generally ill suited to understanding the complex microprocesses and cultural dynamics of domestic homicide. Using abstracted empiricism, it is difficult to gain access to the interaction between human beings, their respective biographies, and their neighborhoods; it is also difficult to understand the broader social, economic, and political structures that affect and are in turn shaped by those microdynamics. (Websdale, 1999, p. 2)

Empirical studies examining individual characteristics of victims and batterers, while providing some information about similarities and variations among individuals involved in the phenomenon, fall into this problematic category. Battered Woman Syndrome would be another example of this problem because it focuses entirely on the psychology of the battered woman and ignores both her interaction with the batterer over time and the social context in which this interaction takes place. It is unreasonable to suggest that a social phenomenon can be understood outside of the social, cultural, structural, and situational context in which it occurs. Since battering involves interaction between two participants and their social world, any useful theory on battering would need to take into account this three-way interaction process.

To suggest that homicide is an interaction process is not a new idea. Luckenbill (1977) originated the examination of homicide in general as an interaction process. In recent years, the use of a social interaction perspective has flourished in the study of homicide and violence in the field of criminology. Unfortunately, this perspective has never been specifically applied to the examination of battering homicides. Luckenbill (1977) was referring explicitly to the short-term interaction process between two individuals at the time that a killing occurs. However, since the battering relationship is a long-term interaction, we utilize this perspective to explain battering as a series of encounters within a long-term interaction process significantly affected throughout its progression by interaction with social, cultural, and situational variables. Such a perspective requires that we examine the action and reaction process between the two parties regardless of their intentions, and how their responses are conditioned by outside contextual variables. Each participant's interpretation of the other's reaction to his or her actions and their respective evaluations of reaction options given social context should help us understand battering and escalation as a spiralling process of reciprocal exchange.

Recently, battered women who have killed their abusers have begun to speak out, along with their advocates, about the battering victim's homicidal actions as part of a realistic and reasonable survival response rather than a psychological problem (Adams, Jackson, and Lauby 1988; Angel 1996; Blackman 1986; Browne 1987; Downs 1996; Schneider 1980; Stark 1995). This position essentially asks us to think about battering homicides as part of a long-term survival process rather than a psychological aberration or a one-time overreaction based in spite or revenge. Battering victims and their advocates believe that battered women who have killed their abusers do not need a psychological excuse for their actions but rather are justified in proactively, lethally defending themselves in a homicidal process (Adams et al. 1988; Angel 1996; Browne 1987; Copelon 1994; Downs 1996; Stark 1995). This position asks us to think about such behavior from a different perspective that takes into account the complex context in which it occurs.

In response to these ideas, the most recent trend in developing a self-defense defense for battered women who have killed their abusers, in confrontational and nonconfrontational situations, has been to move away from the use of Battered Woman Syndrome to presentation of social framework evidence or contextual evidence (Downs 1996; Maguigan 1991, 1998; Schneider 1996). This movement appears to hold great promise although it is only beginning and social science and legal issues still need to be addressed. One issue concerning full legal acceptance of this approach has to do with the lack of a social science framework within which to develop and clearly present such evidence. The legal system has generally been more willing to embrace new approaches after social science has established a firm theoretical groundwork for such changes. This book represents an effort to alleviate the problem and teach practitioners how to utilize the new approach.

We believe that understanding battering requires the new perspective of viewing battering as an interaction process significantly influenced by social realities. Rather than focusing only on the last violent encounter in a battering relationship, as traditional self-defense law would, this perspective requires that we understand the battering relationship as a long-term homicidal interaction process with a sociologically identifiable pattern to which the realistic, *normal* victim responds *reasonably* to avoid death, often having already endured multiple incidents of great bodily harm. This book details a social interaction theory on battering and escalation that we believe provides the kind of framework necessary to adequately present battering evidence as a homicidal process to supplement a self-defense defense.

OVERVIEW OF THE CHAPTERS

Chapter 2 provides an overview of the literature that led to the development of this new social interaction theory. This chapter is not intended to represent a thorough or complete review of all the literature on battering, only that work relevant to this new perspective. Chapter 3 lays out the new theoretical perspective in detail. It describes the reality of the three-way interaction process beginning with the social, cultural, structural, and physical elements, and then proceeding through their interaction with the two participants in the battering relationship to create escalation toward homicide. Chapter 4 provides an overview of the legal literature and the array of perspectives available on self-defense. This chapter provides the reader with an understanding of how the new theory can be used within both traditional and more modern conceptions of the law. Chapter 5 teaches the reader how to utilize the new social interaction theory as a supplement to a self-defense defense in an actual case. This test case, *People v. Beasley* (1993), is reviewed in detail at the end of Chapter 1, as it was originally tried utilizing a self-defense defense supplemented by Battered Woman Syndrome. Chapter 6 applies the new theoretical perspective to gay and lesbian battering and attempts to enhance our understanding of why that phenomena appears to vary from heterosexual battering in some respects, including its escalation to homicide.

THE TEST CASE AS ORIGINALLY AND TRADITIONALLY TRIED

Traditional Case

In this section we summarize and discuss one case, *People v. Beasley*, in some detail. We focus not only on the facts and the results at trial and on appeal, but we also include the opening statements and closing arguments made by counsel for each side, and the jury instructions that were given. The summary here is based on materials not in the public record, which materials were provided to us by the defendant: the trial transcripts, depositions, hearings on motions, briefs, and the transcript of the sentencing hearing. The appellate opinion is a matter of public record and is referenced as well.

In a later chapter, this case is revisited, and the facts are set out as they would be presented and argued in reliance on the theory introduced in this book, with the purpose of comparing the difference in information traditionally available to the jury and the information that would be available to the jury if our theory were employed.

The *Beasley* case is a most difficult one because it is nonconfrontational, and because the prosecution had evidence to support an argument of motive for murder. The husband was shot while he slept, albeit subsequent to abuse and threats earlier in the evening. Motive, arguably, stemmed from the fact that the defendant was pregnant with another man's child.

The case is good for illustration because it was fully developed at trial with evidence of battering, expert testimony on Battered Woman Syndrome, and testimony by the defendant. The case went to jury on the theory of self-defense, supported by Battered Woman Syndrome.

People v. Beasley, 622 N.E. 1236 (Ill. App. 5 Dist. 1993)

Facts

Sheila Beasley was charged with first-degree murder for shooting her husband. She claimed self-defense. The jury convicted her of second-degree murder, finding that she believed deadly force was necessary to prevent imminent death or serious bodily harm, but that her belief was unreasonable. She was sentenced to eight years imprisonment.

Sheila and Glen began dating when Sheila was 15 years old, a freshman or sophomore in high school, and Glen was 19 or 20. Their relationship was somewhat stormy, but there was no physical violence. Nonetheless, Sheila's parents forbade her from seeing Glen because they were aware of his violent temperament. Glen told Sheila's parents that if they did not allow them to date, he would take Sheila away when she was 18 and they would not see her again. Sheila's parents acquiesced. When Sheila turned 18, she and Glen did run away to another state. They were married eight months later, in April 1983. Glen was then approximately 23. They lived with Glen's sister and her husband at first; when they could not get along, they moved into Glen's mother's apartment where another of Glen's sisters and her husband were also living.

During the course of the marriage Sheila and Glen had three children: Luke (seven years old at the time of the shooting), Amanda (four years old at the time of the shooting), and Nathan (two years old at the time of the shooting). Amanda and Nathan had cystic fibrosis and Amanda was afflicted with leukemia as well.

Sheila testified that there were no beatings before they were married, but Glen had a number of rules she was to follow: She could not cash his check and she had to turn her paycheck over to him; she could write checks to pay bills, but could not write any for cash; she could not leave the house while Glen was at work, and she had to get permission to leave the apartment; she was not allowed to call her parents during the week.

Physical abuse began after Sheila and Glen were married. The record details 19 instances of domestic violence, extending from three weeks after their marriage until the night of the shooting that gave rise to this prosecution:

1. April 1983 [Sheila three months pregnant with Luke]. Event precipitating abuse: Sheila's domestic skills. Glen thought food on the table should be in bowls, rather than in pans, so he picked up a pan of macaroni and hit Sheila in the head with it, knocking her out of her chair and onto the floor.

2. September 1983 [Sheila eight months pregnant with Luke]. Event precipitating abuse: Glen liked to have Ding-Dongs in his lunches, but Sheila forgot to get them for him. He became verbally abusive about it ("You forgot because you were probably busy flirting with the checkout boy," and then, "No, I forgot you're fat and pregnant, nobody would look at you."). He told her she had ten minutes to return to the store and get them. She went to the store but was not able to complete the mission within the allotted time; when she got back, Glen slammed the sack out of her hands and pushed her against the wall and choked her.

3. April 1984. Event precipitating abuse: Sheila criticized a member of Glen's family. Sheila was not working at this time, but Glen would not allow her to leave the house during the day or leave the baby with anyone while she ran errands. Errands were to be run in the evenings after Glen got home from work, and Sheila took Luke with her because Glen would not

baby-sit. On this occasion, she was going for a haircut and asked if she could get a baby-sitter. Glen refused a baby-sitter but said his sister Robin could take care of the baby. While in Robin's care, the baby fell on some concrete stairs. Sheila told Glen what had happened and he beat her for talking negatively about his family. He told her that his family did no wrong and accused her of being an unfit mother.

4. December 1984. Event precipitating abuse: No reason apparent. Glen came home angry and began slapping Sheila in the face for no apparent reason. He slapped her hard enough to knock her down and she fell into Luke, then 15 months old. That knocked Luke into the coffee table and he cut his eye. Glen then beat Sheila for allowing Luke to get hurt.

5. December 25, 1984. Event precipitating abuse: Sheila criticized Glen's family. Sheila fixed Christmas dinner for Glen's family. Glen's sister had offered to bring some food, but she forgot and did not bring any; consequently, dinner was small. Glen was upset at that. After dinner, no one helped Sheila clean up so she had to do it and watch Luke. It took her all day. She mentioned to Glen that she could use some help. Later, he beat her for criticizing his family for not helping.

6. Early 1985. Event precipitating abuse: Sheila put hangers in the closet turned the wrong way.

7. Early 1985. Event precipitating abuse: Sheila left her keys in the outside door lock.

8. July 4, 1985: Event precipitating abuse: Sheila did not socialize with Glen and his friends as he preferred. Sheila's parents and some of Glen's friends were at Glen and Sheila's house to watch fireworks. Sheila asked that Glen's friends not swear or fight in front of her parents; Glen said they were grown men and would do as they pleased. Luke got frightened of the fireworks and Sheila took him indoors. Glen beat her for refusing to socialize with him and his friends.

The couple had moved back to Harrisburg, Illinois, in March 1985 because Glen was unemployed and this would put them closer to Sheila's parents. Sheila testified that Glen's rules and regulations became more stringent after that move, in return for giving in to her requests to move back home. To illustrate, new rules required the toilet paper to be hung in a particular way, shower doors to be cleaned as soon as someone got out of the shower, and everything to be ironed.

Amanda was born in September 1986. When Sheila went into labor, she called Glen who dismissed her by asking, "So, what do you want me to do about it?" and he hung up. She called her mother to take her and Luke to the hospital. After Amanda's birth, Glen came to the hospital and claimed Amanda was not his child because she had dark hair.

During this period, Glen's behavior became more aggressive and violent. His alcohol and drug use seemed to be increasing, as evidenced by six criminal convictions for driving under the influence (DUI), disorderly conduct and battery, driving on a suspended license, attempted sexual assault, and sexual assault.

Instances of abuse between July 1985 and 1988 are described in the testimony, but they are not detailed as separate incidents nor are they identified by date. The defendant testified that she withstood numerous beatings while she was pregnant with Amanda, sometimes as often as once a week. She was also abused during her pregnancy with Nathan, as confirmed by her employer at the time. Sheila worked at Baby World for approximately a year, beginning in the summer of 1987. Her employer at Baby World testified that she observed bruises on Sheila's arms beginning about two months after Sheila started working. Beyond that, she testified that on one occasion, when Sheila was approximately five months pregnant with Nathan, Sheila could barely work due to cramps. Sheila showed a bruise on her stomach that the employer described as the size of a softball. She said Sheila did not complain but, when asked about it, explained that Glen had kicked and punched her repeatedly in the stomach because he did not want her to be pregnant.

9. April 1988. Event precipitating abuse: Sheila was not attentive enough. Luke was three years old. Amanda was about a year old and had just been diagnosed with cystic fibrosis. Sheila was seven months pregnant with Nathan. Glen had been partying with friends and he was drunk. He came home to drop off Luke, then left again for more partying. He totaled Sheila's car and got a citation for DUI. After he made bond, he came home and beat Sheila because she did not ask how he was.

Nathan was born in June 1988 and was diagnosed immediately with cystic fibrosis. Glen rejected Nathan. He was attentive to the other two children and would hold Amanda when she had her breathing treatments, but if Nathan tried to crawl into his lap he would get up and walk away.

Sometime in late 1988, Sheila contacted an attorney to explore the possibility of divorce. Glen found out and threatened to kill her. He raped her and forced her, undressed, outdoors into the cold.

10. December 1988. Event precipitating abuse: Sheila was talking with another man in a bar. Glen and Sheila were at a bar with Julie and Merle Cozart. Merle had asked Sheila to dance, and that had not pleased Glen. When Glen went to the restroom, another man approached Sheila and asked where Glen was. Glen came out of the restroom and saw them talking. He ran over, grabbed Sheila by the hair, and pulled her away. He then chased the other man outside to fight. Sheila drove Glen home because he

was too intoxicated to drive. On the way home, he grabbed the steering wheel and stomped on the gas pedal. After they got home, he knocked Sheila to the floor and kicked her in the sides.

11. February 1989. Event precipitating abuse: Glen discovered Sheila had contacted an attorney to file for divorce. While she was out of the house on an errand for Glen, someone from the attorney's office called to change the appointment. The caller left a message with Glen since Sheila was not there. When Sheila returned home, Glen beat her and threatened to kill her, the children, and her parents if she ever tried to get a divorce. He told her she was never leaving him.

12. January or February 1989. Event precipitating abuse: No reason apparent. Glen and Sheila had been to a bar and they had not experienced any problems while there. When they got home, he hit her immediately. When she asked why he had done that, he said, "You know what's wrong," and instructed her to go to bed. She went to Amanda's bedroom (which is where Sheila normally slept). Glen told her to get into his bedroom and to take her clothes off. She begged him not to make her do that, but he pushed her onto the bed and put his shotgun next to her on the bed. He forced her to have intercourse and to perform oral sex. Then he told her to get up and put on her pants and bra; she complied. As she was picking up her clothes, he forced her out of the trailer, with only her pants and bra, and told her to get out before he did something he would regret. Sheila went outdoors in the snow wearing just her underwear. She hid in the neighbor's bush where she could not be seen and waited for approximately 30 minutes until she could no longer bear the cold. She looked in the bedroom window and determined that Glen was sleeping, so she reentered the trailer and slept on the couch in the living room.

Sheila testified that, by this time, Glen had stopped apologizing for the beatings after they occurred. She attributed this to the fact that his drug and alcohol use precluded his even remembering the violence. If the violence was evidenced by broken furniture or bruises, he would sometimes say he was sorry. At other times, he would not believe the harm had been a product of his behavior.

13. January 1990. Event precipitating abuse: A man talked with Sheila at the bar in the bowling alley. Glen and Sheila were at a bowling alley/bar with Julie and Merle Cozart. Glen was on drugs and angry at his bowling performance. Julie and Sheila went to the bar section of the establishment to escape Glen's acting out. While they were at the bar, a man came up to Sheila and asked her to dance. Before she could answer, Glen picked up a table and threw it, spilling drinks on other patrons. He dragged Sheila outdoors. When they got home, Glen punched Sheila and knocked her back-

ward over a chair. Her tailbone was broken. He grabbed her by the arm to hit her again and she screamed in pain; he dropped her back on the floor. Sheila was in bed with this injury for approximately 10 days. She told her mother she had fallen on the ice.

Although Sheila was still not admitting to her family that she was the target of serious abuse, her friends knew. Julie and Merle Cozart had been witnesses at the bar, as had strangers. By this time, Glen's violence was becoming more public. Glen was less careful about confining it to the home, and he was inflicting more obvious injuries.

14. January 1990. Event precipitating abuse: Sheila criticized Glen. Glen had dressed Luke in mismatched clothes for school and Sheila told the boy to change. Glen backhanded her across the face and his fingernail caught her in the eye, scratching it and causing a black eye. Sheila testified that the black eye was hard to hide and other people saw it, but she continued to hide the truth from them. She told her mother that Luke had hit her in his sleep accidentally and she gave no explanation to anyone else.

Sheila said that Glen's beatings had usually been confined to her chest, sides, arms and legs; but now he was causing bruises to appear on more obvious sites. She said she had gotten better at hiding them with the use of makeup and long-sleeved clothing.

In February 1990, Amanda was diagnosed with leukemia. She was hospitalized in Memphis for extended periods, during which Sheila and the other two children stayed in Memphis with her.

Between February and August 1990 the record reflects numerous incidents of domestic violence that are not detailed by date or precipitating event. Beyond that, Glen wrecked several cars that Sheila's parents had provided for transporting the children to medical appointments in Memphis and Evansville. On one such occasion, Glen had accompanied Sheila and the children to Memphis for Amanda's cancer treatment. While Sheila was at the hospital, Glen took Luke and went drinking. He totaled the car and threatened to kill Sheila and the children if she did not leave the hospital and come to the motel to lie to the police so that he would not get another citation for DUI. She complied and lied to the police, reporting the car as having been stolen from the motel where they were staying. The police officer confirmed that the car was reported stolen and was found wrecked. He further confirmed that Glen had refused to provide information to the police, and that he appeared to be of little help to Sheila in handling three children.

15. August 1990. Event precipitating abuse: Sheila flushed Glen's drugs. It was around midnight when Sheila got up to put dishes away, to avoid a beating she feared if Glen found dishes in the sink when he got

home. She found drugs in the kitchen cabinet, accessible to the children, and she flushed them. Glen came home, after having been out partying with friends. He looked for the drugs and finally asked Sheila what she had done with his stash. She told him she had flushed it. He became angry and beat her. He took her jewelry and said he would sell it to pay for the drugs she had destroyed.

This is the first time the record reflects that Sheila stood up to Glen in an assertive manner. But Glen then increased the violence to the point that Sheila locked herself in the bathroom with the telephone and called the police. When the police came, Glen admitted that this incident stemmed from theft of his drugs. The police told them to work it out on their own. When the police started to leave, Glen attacked Sheila, prompting the police to arrest him.

That night, while Glen was in jail, Amanda became seriously ill and Sheila took her to the hospital. While they were at the hospital, Glen was released from jail. He was home by the time Sheila returned.

In September 1990, Glen was arrested for battery (not against Sheila, against another woman). According to information in the presentence investigation, it was his seventh arrest for crimes against the person since 1981.

16. October 1990. Event precipitating abuse: Glen claimed Sheila did not want people to know they were together. Glen and Sheila had gone to a bar with Julie and Merle Cozart. While they were dancing, Sheila complained of feeling hot and told Glen she needed some air. Glen became angry and screamed that she just did not want anyone to know they were together. People stopped dancing and stared at them. Glen then began yelling at the people for staring. He and Sheila left, and when they got home, Glen beat Sheila and raped her. He then passed out on the couch.

17. November 1990. Event precipitating abuse: No reason apparent. Glen had gone hunting and he intentionally poached a deer. He ran from the game warden and went home. When he got home, he beat Sheila until she agreed to lie to the game warden for him.

This incident was only three weeks after the previous one. The beatings were coming at closer intervals. The next one came only two weeks later.

18. December 1990. Event precipitating abuse: Glen was angry because Sheila was not at home. Glen was looking for Sheila and enlisted Sheila's mother to join in the search. Sheila was with Kevin Rice, the man with whom she was having an affair. Julie Cozart alerted Sheila that Glen was hunting for her, so Sheila went to her mother's home to pick up the children, and she called Glen from there. Glen told her to come home and not to bring the children with her. Sheila understood this to mean that he was

going to do something to her that he did not want the children to see. She complied. He beat her that evening multiple times. At one point, her mother came over to bring the children home and she saw the abuse: Sheila was on the floor and Glen was throwing the coffee table at her just as her mother walked in. Sheila's mother stopped the incident and told them to work out their problems. Her mother then left the children and went home. After she departed, the beating resumed. Later that evening, as Sheila was putting Nathan to bed, Glen grabbed her by the neck and beat her head against the window frame. Nathan screamed and Glen tried to hit him as well, yelling that he should shut up or he would be next.

Defendant testified that, at this point, she had begun withdrawing from the relationship, finding it exhausting to manage the stress at home and to deal with the needs of the three children. She recognized that the stakes were much higher now because Glen was not only threatening to kill her and the children, but he was also physically acting out against Nathan.

At approximately 8:00 A.M. on January 17, the defendant and a friend left the house to take Amanda to the hospital for her weekly leukemia treatments. Glen was still sleeping when they left, and when they returned at approximately 4:00 P.M. he had left for work. That evening, Sheila was at home with Luke. The other two children were staying overnight with her parents. Glen called Sheila from work at 6:00 P.M. and 9:00 P.M., as he always did. At 6:00, he asked her to call his father and give him a message; at 9:00 he called to make sure she had done as he had instructed at 6:00. There was no indication in either of these telephone conversations that Glen was upset or mad at the defendant.

19. January 18, 1991. The night of the shooting. Event precipitating abuse: Glen discovered Sheila's affair and her pregnancy. Glen came home from work at approximately 1:30 A.M. Sheila and Luke were in the house; the other two children were staying with Sheila's parents for the night. Glen was drunk. He awakened Sheila, dragged her by the hair into the living room, and talked about killing her. He blamed her for the children being ill, and told her that he hated her because she was spoiled and he hated her parents for spoiling her. He forced her into a chair and said that if she closed her eyes, she would never open them again.

Glen told Sheila he was going to take Luke to his uncle's house so Luke would not see what he was going to do to her. He then pulled her by the hair out of the chair and into the bathroom, where he pushed her to her knees and forced her head into the toilet bowl. He asked her if she liked it and then said, "Have you had enough, bitch?" The defendant testified that she answered, "Yes."

Glen said he was going to take her somewhere else to finish her off. He released her and went into the kitchen where he undressed. He told her to sit in the chair and think about what he was going to do to her. Glen then returned to the living room, lay on the couch, told Sheila he was tired of the torture she had put him through for eight years, and fell asleep.

Sheila went into the bedroom and looked to see if Glen's handgun was still in its place above the dresser. She testified that she became more worried when she discovered it was not there.

At approximately 3:30–4:00 A.M., Sheila took the telephone into the closet and called Kevin Rice. She told Rice that Glen was going to kill her and she needed a gun to protect herself. Rice agreed to give her his gun if she promised not to fire it. She told him to hide the gun behind the house, beside the dog pen. A few minutes later, she went outdoors and retrieved the gun. She left the gun in the bag in which she found it, returned to the house, and put the gun in the closet. Then she went to bed.

Later that night/early morning, Glen awakened, returned to the bedroom, and said, "How can you go to bed when you know you ain't going to wake up?" He began threatening Sheila again and complaining that she had caused the children's illnesses. Sheila testified that he knelt beside the bed and stroked her nose with his finger, saying "dead bitch" over and over. Defendant testified that she begged him not to hurt her.

Glen ordered Sheila into a chair in the living room and warned her not to close her eyes. He returned to the couch to sleep. She watched him for a while to be sure he was asleep. She then returned to the bedroom where she got into the closet and called Kevin Rice again. She asked him to tell her how to use the gun.

Rice tried to talk her out of using the gun, but he told her how to use it. Sheila cocked the gun and returned it to the bag in the closet. She then returned to the living room and to the chair where Glen had told her to stay.

She continued to worry. As her worry increased, she retrieved the gun, still cocked, from the closet and put it under her chair. She heard a car outside and when she got up to look out the window, Glen awakened. He asked her what she was doing and she told him. He told her to return to the chair and to think about living in a casket; she said she was not going to think about that. He replied that he was going to kill her and her parents and bury them all together.

Glen then jumped up and grabbed her chair. He and Sheila argued about his drinking, but eventually he returned to the couch. She asked him why he wanted to kill her. He said it was because she and his father were driving him crazy and because David Riley had seen her at the Gateway Bar.

Glen told Sheila to go back to bed. She went into the kitchen to get a drink of water, and he began talking about the right to a last drink and a smoke.

While Sheila was in the kitchen, she saw a picture Glen had set on the counter, of a baby in a casket. She asked him about it and he said he got it the day before because the little girl in it looked like Amanda. She told him Amanda was going to be all right, but he said, "No, Amanda's not going to be okay and neither are you." Then he threw the blanket from the couch at her and said, "I have something for you." "What?" "A bullet through the heart."

Sheila begged Glen to release her and Luke. She told Glen she would pay for the lawyer and for a divorce and he would be rid of her. Glen replied that she was not going to get off that easily and that he was not going to be a weekend father like others. He said he was not going to leave and let her have everything.

Glen then jumped up and tilted her chair back and said he would kill her and make it look like a suicide. When the chair was tilted up, he saw the gun under it. He asked her what it was, and she said she did not know. He slapped her and called her a lying bitch.

Glen asked what she intended to do with the gun and Sheila told him she had it for protection. He said, "Beasleys don't die easy." He then picked up the gun, forced it into her mouth, and said "bang." He said next time he would fire it in her mouth. Then he put the gun down and went to the bathroom.

Glen called Sheila into the bathroom, where he again grabbed her, forced her to the floor, and pushed her face into the toilet bowl where he had just urinated. He screamed at her and told her to "lick it." He then pulled her to her feet. He pulled a used sanitary napkin from the trash and wiped it on her face. Then he dragged her by the hair back into the living room.

The defendant broke loose from Glen and ran for the front door. He caught her by the nightgown, pulled her back, and pushed her into the chair. When he released her, Sheila grabbed the gun and ran for the door again. He told her she would have to shoot him and Luke would hear it. At that, Sheila sat down in the doorway and cried.

It was starting to get light. Glen ordered Sheila over to the couch. She tried to touch him, but he made her stop. She returned to the chair. He turned out the light and lay back down and shouted to her to go to bed.

Sheila testified that at this point she did not know where the gun was. She went to bed as ordered. A few minutes later, Glen came into the bedroom and demanded to know why she was shaking. She said she was scared.

He said, "I ain't done half to you what my dad done to me," and then left the bedroom.

Glen returned to the bedroom with the gun, laid it on the floor next to her bed, and said, "Here's your protection." Then he returned to the living room.

The defendant testified that she suddenly realized that Julie Cozart was coming to pick her up at 6:00 A.M., ostensibly to go shopping but really to go for Sheila's appointment for an abortion.

Sheila was afraid Glen would kill Julie when she arrived, so she got up and looked through the keyhole to see if Glen was asleep. She could not see, so she cracked the door slightly. Glen immediately said, "What are you doing?" Sheila told him it was hot in the bedroom and she needed some air, so he told her she could open the door. Then he asked her what she wanted. She told him that she wanted things to be okay between them. Glen told her things were okay.

Sheila went into the living room and sat down. Glen told her things were okay because she was going to get what she deserved. He said he had been hearing things. He told her David Riley had told him that Riley had seen Sheila at the Gateway Bar. She denied that and began crying; he said he liked to see her cry. He then covered himself again, went to sleep, and began snoring.

At about 6:45 A.M., Sheila went to one of the bedrooms, called Julie Cozart, and told her not to come over. Then she returned to the living room chair and cried.

The defendant testified that she may have returned to the bedroom and retrieved the gun and put it on the floor. She sat and watched Glen for a while, then went to Luke's room to check on him. She called Lia English, who had been scheduled to take Luke to school, and told her they had overslept and she would take Luke to school later herself. She returned to the living room chair. Later she picked up the gun.

Evidence of what happened next is inconsistent. In the original police report, Sheila is reported to have said that she knelt next to Glen, knowing that he really would kill her and her parents, and she kissed him and said she was sorry, then stood up and shot him. At trial, Sheila testified that when Glen moved and started to wake up she shot him before he could start the abuse again. She denied ever having told the police that she had kissed him before she shot. She testified that after she shot him, she dropped the gun and ran into Luke's room, got Luke up and dressed for school, then took the gun, returned it to the bag, and left with Luke. When Sheila left the house, she left the front door open a ways so it would look like someone else had come in and shot Glen.

She took Luke to school and then went to Julie and Merle Cozart's house, where she told them what she had done. She said Julie and Merle did not believe her, but she said she and Julie needed to go shopping so she would have an alibi. On their way, they saw some water along the road and threw the gun in the water to dispose of it.

Sheila testified that when she and Julie got back and Sheila returned to her house, she was still uncertain whether Glen was alive; but when she saw him lying in blood she ran out the door and, at that moment, realized she had killed her husband. She ran to a neighbor's home for help and the neighbor called the ambulance. Ambulance attendants determined that Glen was dead.

Police officers who investigated found the defendant to be very upset. She eventually told them that she had gone shopping and had returned home to find the main door partially open and the inside front door all the way open. The interview was terminated because the defendant was getting sick to her stomach. Officers testified that when the interview resumed, Sheila never told them that she and her husband had been having marital problems until after she confessed to having killed him.

Sheila's friend showed the police where the gun was. After they confronted Sheila with that discovery, she initially denied any knowledge of it, but then told them that Glen had been beating her and was going to kill her and her family.

Turning to the other evidence at trial, we organize it here broadly by witnesses.

Expert Witnesses

A *forensic pathologist* testified that Glen died from a gunshot to the head, and that he may have been alive but unconscious for two to five minutes after the shooting.

A *physician* hired by the state testified that he had examined Sheila approximately six days after the shooting, at the request of the prosecution and at the request of the defense. His examination revealed an injury consistent with Sheila's report of a broken tailbone. He observed scratches on her arms, one of which resembled a puncture wound, and tenderness of the scalp. He testified that those observations were consistent with the history of abuse Sheila had reported to him.

A *psychologist* was called by the defense to address the issue of Battered Woman Syndrome, the theory relied upon by the defense to justify the defendant's action was one of self-defense.

Dr. Althoff, the psychologist, testified that he had treated approximately 48 abused women, had treated one woman "whose criminal defense was

Battered Woman Syndrome," and had evaluated two individuals whose criminal behavior had been related to self-defense. Beyond that, he had evaluated approximately a dozen women with recent histories of spousal abuse, who had been admitted to private psychiatric facilities. He testified that he was familiar with the research on Battered Woman Syndrome.

With respect to Battered Woman Syndrome, Dr. Althoff explained that it is "a collection of characteristics and effects of abuse upon women." He testified to the frequency of spousal battering, quoting one study estimating that marital violence occurs in 60% of marriages, more often than alcohol abuse. He testified to statistics gathered by the local woman's center, demonstrating that there had been 1,270 instances of domestic violence in the Illinois counties served by that center in the last fiscal year.

Dr. Althoff testified that socialization influences domestic violence and that socialization essentially condoning domestic violence was reflected in our laws until just a few years ago (e.g., the rule of thumb law allowing a husband to beat a wife with a stick as long as it was no larger than the width of a man's thumb).

Dr. Althoff specifically discussed Dr. Lenore Walker's work and the fact that abuse may come in the form of physical, sexual, or psychological abuse. He explained the cycle of violence and said that psychologists do not consider a woman to be a battered woman until the cycle of violence has occurred at least two times. He specifically referenced and explained Walker's research and detailed for the jury the tension building phase, the acute battering phase, and the contrition phase; he characterized the last phase as one "of profound relief for both individuals."

Learned helplessness, according to Dr. Althoff, is one of the characteristics of Battered Woman Syndrome. He acknowledged that this concept is a difficult one to understand, especially for men. He offered an analogy of an employee who knows he will eventually lose his job, an analogy designed to illustrate a feeling of helplessness but having no association with violence, the marital relationship, or self-defense.

The other characteristics of women who suffer from Battered Woman Syndrome, according to Dr. Althoff, are having witnessed or experienced battering in their family of origin, stereotypical sexual socialization, and having suffered chronic illness and health problems.

Besides discussing Battered Woman Syndrome, Dr. Althoff testified to the general effects of battering on women, specifically post-traumatic stress disorder, lowered self-esteem, development of self-destructive coping mechanisms, and denial of abuse.

Finally, Dr. Althoff discussed Walker's study of battered women who have killed their batterers, characterizing this work as not scientifically rigorous because there was no control group, but nonetheless illustrating commonalities among women who kill their spouses: They had experienced physical and psychological abuse and often sexual abuse as well; they were often more severely abused than women who did not kill; they tended to be older and less educated, and they had fewer resources for coping (e.g., no job skills). Often, they were threatened with weapons or retaliation if they left; they felt socially isolated; "more death threats . . . occurred to this group"; the batterer abused alcohol and his alcohol abuse was progressive; the batterer degraded the wife while she had a weapon in her hand and, often, he ordered her to kill him as another form of intimidation; the batterer was jealous and possessive; the woman knew the batterer was capable of killing because he owned a firearm or had a history of violence; there was an increased loss of control and an increased level of violence preceding the incident; the woman felt less essential to the batterer prior to the incident than before; in most cases, the woman's intent was not to kill, but to stop the violence; the predominant emotion prior to the killing was fear, not anger; the incident did not occur during the actual battering, but sometime afterward.

Dr. Althoff testified that he had examined Sheila Beasley. His examination consisted of interviewing Sheila twice and conducting interviews with her parents and friends of the family. He administered the Minnesota Multiphasic Personality Inventory (MMPI) (an objective test of personality), the Rorschach inkblot test (a projective test of personality), the Shipley Institute of Living Scale (an examination of intellectual function), the Thematic Apperception Test (another projective test of personality), and the Multimodal Life History Questionnaire (not explained). Dr. Althoff testified that, without these tests, a psychological decision about Battered Woman Syndrome would be highly suspect. He reviewed all of the discovery information provided him by defense counsel and the sheriff's department, including police reports and reports of witnesses. He testified that he had examined the defendant on several occasions subsequent to the shooting and had interviewed her family and friends. Based on those interviews and the defendant's personality tests, he concluded that Sheila Beasley suffered from Battered Woman Syndrome on January 18, 1991.

That conclusion that Sheila Beasley suffered from Battered Woman Syndrome was based, in part, on Dr. Althoff's gathering and analysis of historical information, including the fact that Glen Beasley had one DUI offense, one case of disorderly conduct, and "questionable other arrests"; the police had come to the Beasley residence once on a domestic call; Glen's father had been arrested on several occasions for domestic violence; Glen abused alcohol and was verbally combative toward Sheila and tried to control her actions. Dr. Althoff's investigation did not demonstrate a "clear consensus as to abuse" because Sheila did not tell others about the abuse. The witness found that to be consistent with other women who suffer from Battered Woman Syndrome. He found evidence of psychological and physical abuse and instances of forced sex. He found evidence of "a cycle of violence in terms of tension building, battery incident occurring and then loving contrition or the bond that heals the relationship between the batterer and their victim." With respect to Sheila's socialization, Dr. Althoff noted:

she had a pretty traditional upbringing in terms of little girls do this and little boys do this when they grow up to be adults in terms of marriage partners and other aspects of their lives. One of the things she stated was [sic] that was noteworthy is that, as I believe as an adolescent one of her aspirations for the future is "I always wanted to marry and have kids and live happy [sic] ever after." Now, that's important in that that is a kind of traditional way of viewing the world and kind of naive and sugarcoated, in that that's the way it ought to be. The way of Ozzie and Harriet. ... [S]he had a very traditional view of how one behaves in a marriage. Once you're married, stay married.

On the basis of the history and testing, Dr. Althoff concluded that Sheila did not have any mental illness, although there was evidence of a post-traumatic stress disorder. He found "evidence of psychological torture and of learned helplessness." He concluded that her MMPI profile was consistent with scores shown for 106 documented battered women; in short, she suffered from Battered Woman Syndrome. Dr. Althoff concluded his discussion of Sheila Beasley with this description of his diagnosis:

The diagnosis that I arrived at, these are called three different axis. [sic] It is a way of describing or ordering one's diagnosis. The first axis, I viewed her as having an adjustment disorder with mixed emotional features. That means that there has been some identifiable stress in the person's life, and that they are responding to it with mixed emotional feelings in terms of depression and anxiety. I also made a diagnosis of a post-traumatic stress disorder, and also, the diagnosis of what is called other specific found circumstances, which simply indicates that there was something striking in her family, which was a history of abuse and also the children being significantly ill. The second diagnosis on the second axis, one of the things that that does is describes a person's personality. There were some personality traits that were somewhat mal-adapted and they can be described as dependent and histrionic, which basically means that she tended to defer, apply [sic] to others, in situations. She tended to do others' bidding. There was also evidence of her tending to tough it out when emotional crisis [sic] are there and perservere [sic]. And also, in cases tending to over-generalize.

On cross-examination, the prosecutor challenged Battered Woman Syndrome because it does not appear in the most recent version of the *Diagnostic and Statistical Manual*, the manual generally regarded as the most authoritative on types of mental illness. Dr. Althoff explained that Battered Woman Syndrome does not appear there because, if it did, it may lead to the mislabeling of women suffering from Battered Woman Syndrome as being mentally ill. Nonetheless, he admitted that the defendant suffered from post-traumatic stress disorder and he suggested that Battered Woman Syndrome is a subtype of post-traumatic stress disorder. On redirect examination, the matter was revisited and Dr. Althoff stated clearly, although without elaboration, that Battered Woman Syndrome is not considered a mental illness.

Lay Witnesses

Defendant's testimony about abuse was corroborated by her mother, the coroner, the coroner's daughter who was one of Sheila's friends, her employer at Baby World, and two former friends (Julie and Merle Cozart). It was further corroborated by the psychologist who testified to what Sheila had reported to him.

Two witnesses testified to Glen's propensity for violence. One witness testified to Glen's violence toward others, specifically toward her. The witness testified that she was 17 years old in the summer of 1986 when Glen Beasley, naked, assaulted her. She escaped and reported the incident to the police. Thereafter, Glen and members of Glen's family threatened to kill her and members of her family if she pressed criminal charges. She dropped the charges. She further testified that she had observed bruises on Sheila during the summer of 1990, specifically that she had observed a black eye and fingerprint marks up and down Sheila's arms. She described Sheila's face as swollen and blue.

A second witness testified to witnessing a fight in which Glen Beasley and his uncle, who was armed with a gun, attacked a man and continued the attack even after police arrived to break it up.

Jury Instructions

First- and second-degree murder. The judge instructed the jury on first-degree murder because that was the charge brought by the prosecutor:

A person commits the offense of first-degree murder when she kills an individual without lawful justification if, in performing the acts which caused the death,
 (1) she intends to kill or do great bodily harm to that individual or another; or
 (2) she knows that such acts will cause death of that individual or another; or

(3) she knows that such acts create a strong probability of death or great bodily harm to that individual or another.

Mitigating factor for second-degree murder. The court further instructed the jurors that if they found each element of first-degree murder, they should proceed to determine if any mitigating factor was present to reduce the offense to second-degree murder. It is clear from this instruction that the mitigating factor the jury was instructed to consider was a self-defense that was unreasonably founded. That is, if the jury found that the defendant actually believed that she was justified in using deadly force, but that belief was unreasonable, the jury could find that she had committed second-degree murder. The judge explained:

The defendant has the burden of proving by a preponderance of the evidence that a mitigating factor is present so that she is guilty of the lesser offense of second-degree murder instead of first-degree murder. By this I mean that you must be persuaded, considering all the evidence in the case, that it is more probably true than not true that the following mitigating factor was present: that the defendant, at the time she performed the acts which caused the death of Luther Glen Beasley, believed the circumstances to be such that they justified the deadly force she used, but her belief that such circumstances existed was unreasonable.

Reasonableness. In light of the instruction on mitigation and the instruction that follows on self-defense, the most important finding in this case would be the reasonableness of the defendant's conclusion that she needed to defend herself with deadly force. In determining whether her belief was "reasonable," the jury was instructed to use an objective standard:

The phrases "reasonable belief" or "reasonably believes" mean that the person concerned, acting as a reasonable person, believes that the described facts exist.

Self-Defense. The defense relied upon self-defense and, in that regard, the jury was instructed:

A person is justified in the use of force when and to the extent that she reasonably believes that such conduct is necessary to defend herself against the imminent use of unlawful force.

However, a person is justified in the use of force which is intended or likely to cause death or great bodily harm only if she reasonably believes that such force is necessary to prevent imminent death or great bodily harm to herself or another.

Battering. There was a good deal of evidence in the case about the violence experienced in the marriage and, specifically, about battering. The only instruction given with respect to the impact of battering was this: "A physical beating qualifies as conduct which could cause great bodily harm."

Each lawyer had an opportunity to give an opening statement to the jury. The opening statement is designed to give the jurors a glimpse of what the case is about and to alert them to the important issues that each side will be emphasizing.

Prosecutor's Opening Statement

The prosecutor did not mention battering or the violent relationship between Glen and Sheila Beasley; he simply told the jury that the defendant did not report any marital discord to the investigating officers. He focused on inconsistent statements given by the defendant to investigating officers, drawing attention away from Battered Woman Syndrome and self-defense, and toward the facts clearly demonstrating that Sheila Beasley had shot her husband while he slept.

Defense Counsel's Opening Statement

Counsel for the defendant discussed battering as a widespread social problem, alerted the jury to the different kinds of abuse, and told them that the defendant would be shown to be a battered woman. He went on to describe critical elements of Walker's theory, specifically the cycle of violence and learned helplessness. He told them that the psychologist would testify that Sheila was a battered woman who suffered from Battered Woman Syndrome, and that the psychologist would further testify that she truly believed she had to kill her husband or he would kill her on January 18, 1991. Counsel described at length 19 battering incidents they would be told about during the course of the trial. Finally, he talked with them about unsuccessful efforts Sheila had made to leave Glen and unsuccessful efforts she had made to get help before the violence escalated to the point it did on the night of the shooting.

At the end of the trial, each attorney has a chance to give a final argument. It is the last chance to persuade the jurors and to help them put the facts in context in the way that each side wishes the facts to be interpreted. For purposes of summary here, we focus on the arguments made with respect to battering and with respect to important elements in self-defense.

Prosecutor's Closing Argument

Battering. The prosecutor characterized the defendant's reliance on Battered Woman Syndrome as an "excuse for executing Luther Glen Beasley." He minimized the difference between Glen's behavior on the night of the shooting and on any other night because the defendant did not offer any reason for what might have fired him up. But in that regard, the prosecutor clearly relied upon her pregnancy and her need to hide it from Glen as a motive for murder.

The prosecutor characterized Battered Woman Syndrome as just "a theory to explain human behavior . . . it is not the truth, that's just terminology used within the psychology world." He emphasized that Battered Woman Syndrome is not a mental illness that is documented in the manual most often relied upon for diagnosing and treating mental illness, and that more research is required.

When he discussed learned helplessness and the fact that the defendant did not leave her abusive husband before or during the night of their final confrontation, the prosecutor reminded the jury that Sheila's husband was sleeping when she went outdoors to get the gun left for her. He explained the import of that:

Now the learned helplessness theory in the Battered Woman Syndrome, [Dr. Althoff] explained that you become capactive [sic] [captive], that you can't get away, but somebody as in her situation and got outside, there had been no complaints, no threats towards Luke. As a matter of fact, the testimony has been that Luke and his dad were pretty close. So that learned helplessness, that busted that theory right there. When she went outside, she could have went [sic] on past the dog house and went somewhere else. Her hands weren't tied.

Self-Defense: Imminent Harm. The imminence argument was standard for a nonconfrontational case: "Now her husband is sleeping there, how could a sleeping man put a spouse in such an imminent situation, after you came back to the house, after you made the call for the gun?"

Self-Defense: Reasonableness. No argument was made with respect to the reasonableness of defendant's belief that lethal force was necessary for her protection.

Defense Counsel's Closing Argument

Battering. The history of battering during the course of the marriage and Glen's reputation for violence generally were emphasized by counsel. He did not enumerate again each of the incidents of domestic violence, but focused on the testimony of the defendant and others that illustrated Glen's capacity for violence. In the context of the marriage, he emphasized that Glen's violence had escalated and Glen had shown increasing loss of control, a pattern that the expert psychologist testified was common in cases in which battered women kill their husbands. Countering the prosecutor's argument about why Sheila did not leave, her lawyer argued:

A lot of talk in this case, why didn't she just leave. She was outside the house, why didn't she just leave. When she got on the telephone, why didn't she call the police. [The prosecutor] asked [the defense psychologist] didn't she have the right to leave. Of course, she had the right to leave. . . . She also had the right to stay there that night as she did hoping that things were going to calm down as they had in times in the past. Hoping Glen was going to go to sleep and that would be the end of it, that he wouldn't get back up and there wouldn't be any more assaults or battery. She had the right to tough it out just like [the psychologist] described her personality is. . . . There is no legal requirement for her to call the police, to go outside the house to leave, none. . . .

[The psychologist] explained why battered women do not leave their husbands. They feel psychologically entrapped. They're entrapped in the cycle of violence. They feel helpless. It doesn't matter what they do, they continue to be battered.

In the event the jurors may not have believed Sheila's testimony of the abuse, counsel reminded them of the confirmation of battering that came from testimony of co-workers, Sheila's mother, and a physician who had x-rayed Sheila in 1990 and found evidence of a bone chip consistent with her claim of a broken tailbone.

Defense counsel also discussed the facts that Sheila had tried to get help, but that help had not been forthcoming. Sheila's mother had asked her pastor to talk with Glen and Sheila because she thought maybe Glen had a drinking problem; the pastor told the couple to try to stay together. On the one occasion when police officers were called, they made Glen leave but then released him. After his release, Glen called Sheila's mother and told her to tell Sheila to take him back or else he would burn the truck, quit his job, and thus remove any health insurance for the children.

Self-Defense: Imminent Harm. Counsel discussed the fact that the violence had increased over the span of the relationship. Beyond that, he discussed the fact it had increased on the night of the shooting in a manner that was different from other times. The general pattern was that Glen would abuse Sheila, then go to sleep. But this night he went to sleep and then he got up—about three or four times. Each time Glen got up, he would abuse Sheila again. In that regard, counsel reminded jurors of Sheila's testimony that, although Glen had fallen asleep on the couch before she shot him, he appeared to be awakening. The argument was this:

[W]as it reasonable for her to believe that she was in imminent danger after the night she went through—the repeated death threats, the abuse that?s put on her, how imminent does it have to get? He tells her, I am going to lay down here and give you a few minutes to think about dying and when I get up I am going to kill you. Is she supposed to let him get up at that point in time? What chance would she have had if he would have got [sic] up? . . . Could she stand up to him really? . . . It was as imminent as it could possibly get and Sheila have a chance.

Self-Defense: Reasonableness. Defense counsel urged the jury to consider the physical characteristics of Glen in contrast to the much smaller Sheila; the fact that she suffered from Battered Woman Syndrome; and her knowledge of her husband and his propensity for violence. He vividly reminded them that Glen not only threatened numerous times to kill Sheila that night, but he also stuck the gun she had claimed for protection in her mouth. That gun had already been cocked. It was a gun, cocked and ready to fire, that he stuck in her mouth and said "bang." Counsel argued it was reasonable for Sheila to believe she needed to use deadly force for her own protection given the general history of abuse, the abuse that night and the ways in which it was more sustained and more violent than other nights. This situation was compounded by the fact that Glen had his own gun which Sheila was unable to locate, and then he had the gun she had secured for her own protection. Given these facts, counsel argued, it was reasonable for Sheila to conclude that deadly force was necessary for her defense.

The jury returned a verdict for second-degree murder, apparently finding that Sheila had intentionally shot Glen but had unreasonably believed that deadly force was necessary to protect herself.

Sentencing

The trial court sentenced Sheila Beasley to eight years imprisonment, followed by a two-year period of mandatory supervisory release. Additionally, she was required by law to pay the costs of the prosecution. At the sentencing hearing, the trial judge did not discuss the issue of whether Sheila Beasley reasonably perceived the necessity to use deadly force on the night she shot her husband. The judge did, however, summarize the evidence as he saw it. He made these comments with respect to the issues of domestic violence that had been the focus of this trial:

From a factual standpoint, I feel that in this case you were an abused woman; however, to what extent or degree we'll probably never know. There was very little testimony regarding injuries sustained by you as [a] result of abuse. And indeed, many of your closest friends and your relatives did not observe any type of abuse in the past eight years. The majority of testimony of abuse came from you, yourself, and Dr. Althoff [the psychologist called as an expert witness by the defense]. And one significant point is that Dr. Althoff obtained his results as a result of directly interviewing you. He testified that you were, in fact, a victim of Battered Woman Syndrome. I can't understand why in this case, the State, although it had the opportunity, did not have you examined by one of its own experts. This may or may not have rebutted Dr. Althoff's testimony. Unfortunately, again, we will never know. The testimony in this case further revealed that you had an affair with one Kevin Rice. As a result of that affair, you became pregnant. That you arranged for an abortion on January 18, 1991. That on the evening of January 17, 1991, the victim came home and according to you he was drunk and abusive, at one point putting a revolver in your mouth as well as committing other abusive acts towards you. Again, whether the victim was drunk or not is an issue that could have been but was not raised. [The prosecutor], again, had the opportunity to introduce the blood samples drawn from the victim at the funeral home but did not. I feel that this could have layed [sic] to rest that argument once and for all. The results of these tests for some reason or another which the Court can't consider at this point, were not admitted into evidence. The testimony further shows that you called Kevin Rice; that you arranged for him to deliver a gun to your residence; you went outside, you retrieved the gun; you even called him at a later time to inquire as to how to use this weapon. Again, I have questions as raised by [defense counsel] as to why Kevin Rice was never charged in this case. That is not the Court's function. I don't charge people. I simply raise the issue for consideration. According to Kevin Rice, you said that you were going to kill your husband. A point that you deny. In fact, you shot your husband contrary to what you maintain and apparently made a statement to the police in which you say you shot him while he was asleep. This was not a confrontational situation. Whether there was an argument or abusive treatment immediately prior to this shooting. Thereafter, you took the gun and went to Julie Cozart's house and left with her, took the gun, and went off to establish an alibi. Only after being confronted by the police at a later time, did you admit this offense, and the jury did find you guilty of second-degree murder. Dr. Althoff did, in fact, testify and later wrote a letter contained in the presentence investigation that your predominant emotion throughout all of this was fear. I don't doubt this. However, I question whether you were fearful of abuse merely because he was an abuser or whether you were afraid he would discover your affair with Rice and your subsequent pregnancy. He already knew of the Townsend affair. Quite likely, Sheila Beasley, I feel that you really believed he might kill you if he discovered the subsequent affair. It is to be noted that the shooting did, in fact, take place in the early morning hour of the very day that you had arranged for an abortion. . . . I am reminded of the fact that the shooting took place not in a confrontational setting but at a time when this Court feels the victim was, in fact, asleep. Why couldn't you merely have retreated out of the house and gone, perhaps, even to the Anna Bixby Center at that time for shelter and protection. This Court alone will average four to five orders of protection per week on behalf of abused women. There is no one in the courtroom more protective than this Court of abused women. I have had many women who have sustained great injuries. I've seen women in my Court who couldn't even open their eyes because their husband had beat them so bad. I've seen them with broken legs. I've seen them maimed to all degrees; yet, despite their injuries and despite the length of the abuse, they did not mortally wound their abusers. Indeed, Barbara Wingo, from the Anna

Bixby Center testified Friday that out of the 1200 clients last year, this is the only case involving a fatal shooting. Also, I note that—I've received many letters on your behalf. Many of them victims of domestic violence. People that have been abused, and I note that there is not one of these ladies who mortally wounded their spouses. I guess I get back to the question of questioning your motive in this case, Sheila Beasley. I do feel that you acted out of fear that your husband would subsequently discover your affair and your subsequent pregnancy. This, I believe, to be the primary reason for the shooting. . . . However, in deference to the fact that you were the victim of abuse again, to what extent we will never know, I will not impose the maximum sentence in this case.

On appeal, the defendant argued that the second-degree murder conviction should be reversed because her belief that she needed to use deadly force was reasonable. The appellate court rejected that contention, declaring that "the jury could have concluded from the evidence presented that the defendant did not act in self-defense" (*People v. Beasley* 1993, p. 1243).

REFERENCES

Adams, D., J. Jackson, and M. Lauby (1988). Family violence research: Aid or obstacle to the battered women's movement. *Response, 11*, 14–16.

Angel, M. (1996). Criminal law and women: Giving the abused woman who kills "a jury of her peers" who appreciate trifles. *American Criminal Law Review, 33*(3), 229–348.

Belknap, J. (2001). *The invisible woman: Gender, crime, and justice* (2nd ed.). Belmont, CA: Wadsworth.

Blackman, J. (1986). Potential uses for expert testimony: Ideas toward the representation of battered women who kill. *Women's Rights Law Reporter, 9*(3–4), 227–238.

Browne, A. (1987). *When battered women kill.* New York: Free Press.

Copelon, R. (1994). Intimate terror: Understanding domestic violence as torture. In R.J. Cook (Ed.), *Human rights for women: National and international perspectives* (pp. 116–152). Philadelphia: University of Pennsylvania Press.

Downs, D.A. (1996). *More than victims.* Chicago: University of Chicago Press.

Gosselin, D.K. (2000). *Heavy hands: An introduction to the crimes of domestic violence.* Upper Saddle River, NJ: Prentice Hall.

Liska, A.E., M.D. Krohn, and S.F. Messner (1989). Strategies and requisites for theoretical integration in the study of crime and deviance. In A.E. Liska, M.D. Krohn, and S.F. Messner (Eds.), *Theoretical integration in the study of deviance and crime: Problems and prospects* (pp. 1–19). Albany, NY: State University of New York Press.

Luckenbill, D.F. (1977). Criminal homicide as a situated transaction. *Social Problems, 25*, 176–186.

Maguigan, H. (1998). It's time to move beyond battered woman syndrome. Review of *More than victims: Battered women, the syndrome society, and the law*, by Donald Alexander Downs, *Criminal Justice Ethics, 17(1) (winter/spring)*, 50–57.

———. (1991). Battered women and self-defense: Myths and misconceptions in current reform proposals. *University of Pennsylvania Law Review, 140 (December)*, 379–487.

Pleck, E. (1987). *Domestic tyranny: The making of social policy against family violence from colonial times to present*. New York: Oxford University Press.

———. (1983). Feminist responses to "crimes against women," 1868–1896. *Signs: Journal of Women in Culture and Society, 8(3)*, 451–470.

Schneider, E. (1996). Resistance to equality. *University of Pittsburgh Law Review, 57(3)*, 477–525.

———. (1980). Equal rights to trial for women: Sex bias in the law of self-defense. *Harvard Civil Liberties-Civil Rights Law Review, 15(3)*, 623–646.

Stark, E. (1995). Re-presenting woman battering: From battered woman's syndrome to coercive control. *Albany Law Review, 58*, 973–1026.

Walker, L. (1984). *The battered woman syndrome*. New York: Springer.

Websdale, N. (1999). *Understanding domestic homicide*. Boston, MA: Northeastern University Press.

Case Cited:

People v. Beasley, 622 N.E. 1236 (Ill. App. 5 Dist. 1993).

Chapter 2

A Review of the Relevant Literature

A BRIEF OVERVIEW OF HISTORY:
SOCIAL AND LEGAL ISSUES

Historically, battering has been shrouded in *privacy* as a legally acceptable form of social control within the family. Since churches originally possessed the power to define, demand, and sanction social control, many religious traditions, including Judeo-Christian tradition, support the submission of all family members to the control of the male head of household. These traditions also prescribe the responsibility of that male head of household for maintaining control and discipline by whatever means necessary, even through corporal punishment (Belknap 1992; Davidson 1977; Dobash and Dobash 1979; Gordon 1989; Gosselin 2000; Pleck 1983, 1987). Consequently, battering became a socially and legally acceptable form of social control.

Under Roman Civil Law, men had full property ownership of and control over their wives, children, and slaves. Ownership rights included the ability to buy, sell, punish, or impose a death sentence upon their property. Consequently, any harm committed against a wife was a crime against the male owner. During this era, women and children had no legal or human rights because they were simply property, and therefore, had no access to the courts to appeal excessive punishment and certainly no voice to claim the male head of household had committed a crime against himself or his own property. He had every legal and cultural right to do whatever he chose to his own property (Gosselin 2000; Masters 1964).

According to Gosselin (2000), this legal philosophy continued through the Christian Era. It established patriarchy as including the ownership of women and children and the right to control and punish his property as a man deemed appropriate. Some scholars even note the specificity of the Christian Bible concerning the subordination of women to men and the need for men to use corporal punishment for control (Davis 1971; Davidson 1977; Gosselin 2000; Masters 1964). Other scholars note that during medieval times, men were required by the church to maintain complete and absolute control of their wives and children and that failure to do so would result in social chaos and their own punishment (Dutton 1998; Masters 1964; Pushkareva 1997). The church did, however, warn men to be careful not to beat their property about the ears and head because this could cause deafness or blindness which would decrease the value of their property (Masters 1964).

Before the late 19th century, women and children also had no access to assistance or government to contest their abuse. While divorce was available to men, it was not available to women. In some areas, men were simply advised to make their former wife a servant in their home or to kill her before marrying someone else (Lefkowitz and Fant 1992; Pagelow 1984; Pushkareva 1997). Divorce for women, for any reason including severe cruelty, would not become an issue until the late 19th century when the first wave of the women's movement would challenge existing laws with little success (Pleck 1983; Harper 1898).

Gosselin (2000) notes that the French Civil Code of the late 1700s specifically declared women to be legal minors their entire lives, and thus the property of a father or a husband. These laws also specified the responsibility of the male owner for corporal punishment of a wife, including the use of punching, kicking the body, and permanent disfigurement (especially breaking her nose) so that the injuries were observable by others to increase her shame (Dobash and Dobash 1978; Gosselin 2000; Pagelow 1984).

In 1768, Sir William Blackstone codified the British Common Law. In this work, he specified that man and woman become one entity by marriage and the woman's legal existence ceases (Dobash and Dobash 1979; Gosselin 2000; Pagelow 1984). While Blackstone never attempted to criminalize battering, he did create the first effort to regulate the severity of allowable battering. He codified the "rule of thumb" stating that a husband had the legal right and responsibility to control and punish his wife. However, this punishment was to be done with a stick no bigger than the husband's thumb (Dutton 1998; Gosselin 2000; Pagelow 1984; Ulrich 1991). This codification of common law was the version that formed the foundation for law in the United States. There were isolated efforts in the United States to regulate battering even more, to declare its immorality, and even a Massachusetts civil law that allowed a severely battered woman a temporary separation (not divorce) from her husband. However, the "rule of thumb" remained the social and legal policy on battering in the United States until well into the 1800s (Dobash and Dobash 1979; Gosselin 2000; Pagelow 1984; Pleck 1983).

Battering received little attention as a social issue or problem until the late 19th century when the first wave of the women's rights movement questioned the validity of such complete control by husbands and fathers, corporal punishment as a tool of that control, and the significance of alcohol in promoting or escalating such violence against women and children (Dubois 1978; Gage 1891; Harper 1898; Pleck 1983, 1987).

During the 19th century, some legal actions were taken to address the most extreme forms of battering. However, since battering was socially and legally acceptable, most of these new laws were simply intended to regulate the level of violence used and the severity of injury allowed. Examples of such laws ranged from the common law rule of thumb to the more modern *certain rule* and *stitch rule*. The certain rule of the mid-1800s indicated that no outside interference would occur in wife battering unless the husband created a permanent injury to the wife. The stitch rule of the early 1900s cautioned men not to cause injuries requiring stitches because police could be called to intercede in such situations. These rules were intended to advise men of the level of injury allowed before outside sources would intervene (Belknap 1992; Gosselin 2000; Hart 1992). However, most scholars note that even where social and/or legal restrictions on the severity of battering existed, these laws were rarely enforced (Belknap 1992; Dobash and Dobash 1979; Gosselin 2000; Hart 1992; Pleck 1987). Battering of wives and children simply was not considered a major issue (Belknap 1992; Davidson 1977; Dobash and Dobash 1979; Pagelow 1984; Pleck 1989). Consequently, law concerning battering developed from a foundation of acceptability and regulation rather than one of social disapproval and criminalization. This foundation has drastically influenced the development of both modern laws that criminalize battering and social resources for battered women in need of protection (Jasinski 1996; Kaufman-Kantor, Jasinski, and Aldarondo 1994; Ogle and Garner 2000; Roberts 1996).

During the late 1800s, the issue of battering was taken up by feminists in the first wave of the women's movement (Harper 1898; Pleck 1983). Pleck

(1983) indicates that feminists subscribed to two different schools of thought regarding the cause of and solution to battering. First, conservatives like Lucy Stone joined forces with the temperance movement to argue that alcohol use caused battering and child abuse, thereby slowly destroying the institution of marriage which they felt was the necessary foundation of society (Pleck 1983). Their ultimate solution was temperance. More liberal feminists like Susan B. Anthony and Elizabeth Cady Stanton felt that men would never address battering or other violence against women and children because such behavior supported maintenance of male power and privilege. These feminists worked for women to obtain suffrage, full citizenship, representation in government, property rights, and divorce rights so that women would be able to force legal change and enforcement of new laws (Harper 1898; Pleck 1983). However, even with this massive push by feminists in the late 1800s, there was little social pressure for substantial change in social and cultural expectations about marital roles and behavior. Consequently, there were no legal changes or sanctions forthcoming to stop battering even after women received suffrage in 1920. States simply refused to acknowledge the right of women, as citizens, to equal protection under the law (Belknap 1992; Davidson 1977; Gordon 1989; Pleck 1983).

By the end of World War I, battering was firmly entrenched behind closed doors and protected by references to privacy and the sanctity of the family unit. Most scholars indicate that this situation persisted unabated for the next 50 years (Belknap 1992; Davidson 1977; Dobash and Dobash 1979; Gordon 1989; Gosselin 2000; Pleck 1983, 1987).

During the second wave of the women's rights movement (1960s and 1970s), activists begin to push for the reduction in barriers that prevented women from exercising their human and civil rights in American society. One of those barriers involved the government-sanctioned power of men to exercise coercive control of all family members. As a result of this effort, laws began to emerge that moderately criminalized battering. For example, police began to respond to domestic disputes and attempted to diffuse these situations, and some governments made battering an ordinance violation or a misdemeanor crime so that fines could be levied (Gosselin 2000; Ogle and Garner 2000). This slow, roundabout progression toward criminalization reflects our historical views of battering as acceptable, necessary, and benign, and our unwillingness to interfere with male control in the privacy of the home. This may well explain why most of our social efforts to address battering, assist victims, and prevent the injuries and deaths associated with battering have primarily been done in the form of women's social helping agencies rather than state law and law enforcement agencies.

Roberts (1996) notes that one of the earliest social efforts of this kind was the establishment of a women's and children's protective agency in Chicago in 1885. This agency was intended to provide shelter and other assistance for physical and sexual abuse victims (Pleck 1987; Roberts 1996). These types of agencies continued to appear in major U.S. cities through the 1920s. However, most of them began to close or disappear by 1940 because women had suffrage and police departments were developing their women's bureaus, which, though intended to assist female crime victims, did not provide the needed social or legal assistance (Pleck 1987; Roberts 1996).

The women's bureaus in police departments did not last long, in part because of the changing roles of women in police work following World War II. Women were beginning to move into more traditionally male roles in police departments. The women's bureaus, the work sites of most women in policing prior to the war, were no longer needed to confine women's work roles. These agencies all but disappeared by the 1950s, along with the social calm or bliss of the 1950s and the concomitant police-social work movement (Roberts 1996). Agency assistance for battering victims was rare until the second wave of the women's rights movement took up the issue again in the 1970s.

By the late 1970s, a shelter and crisis hot line system had been developed. That same system remains in place today, an indication that we have made little additional progress toward prevention of domestic violence. The only exceptions to the lack of progress are minor criminal justice system changes utilizing more restraining or protection orders and mandatory arrest practices. Although these practices might at first seem significant, the reality is that they have not shown a particularly consequential impact on domestic violence rates and they clearly represent an after-the-fact or post-domestic violence approach rather than efforts to eradicate violence and assist victims. There is a history of failure or refusal to address battering as a serious problem worthy of the direct and proactive attention of the criminal justice system rather than depending on social helping agencies to provide minimal safety (Ogle and Garner 2000; Martin 1976; Pleck 1987; Roberts 1996; Zimring 1989). We have not yet figured out a way to combine our social and legal system resources to successfully, proactively prevent domestic violence and assist victims in safely ending the violence in their lives.

BATTERING

As a result of this history, the study of battering as a social and legal "problem" is a relatively recent phenomenon, likely associated with changes in the structural and social status of women and our society's changing views on the use of violence. The following is a brief review of the literature on battering relevant to development of our new theory.

Most of the research in the past 30 years on battering has, in general, been divided into three major categories. The first involves individual/biological approaches that focus on substance abuse and psychological traits such as the self-esteem of batterers. This is clearly a psychopathological approach to understanding both the batterer and the effects of battering on the victim. The second category involves sociocultural theories that focus on the influence of social, structural, and family processes involving male domination, gender socialization, and power relations. This is the theoretical position generally put forth by feminist researchers. The third approach is a social-psychological perspective used primarily by family violence researchers. This approach focuses on social learning experiences of both parties, stress, and violence in the family of origin. Researchers in this area have worked diligently toward the identification of causal variables.

Individual/Biological Perspectives

Individual perspectives focus almost entirely on the biological and psychological traits of the batterer and victim (Hamberger and Hastings 1986). Such theories posit that factors within the individual cause battering behavior. Some of this research branches off into very specific types of psychological maladies, such as attention deficit and head injury disorders (Elliott 1988; Warnken, Rosenbaum, Fletcher, Hoge, and Adelman 1994), or things like antisocial personality (Holtzworth-Munroe and Stuart 1994). These theories generally do not utilize many social variables, and their use in the other areas of theory development has been extremely limited. However, some researchers in the family violence tradition are now utilizing some of this research in an effort to understand the batterer and create more effective treatment programming (Dutton 1994; Gondolf 1988; Holtzworth-Munroe and Stuart 1994).

Socio-Cultural Perspectives

These theories focus primarily on social factors concerning class, sex, and income as these are related to power relations in society and the family. Feminists in particular focus on the influence of a male- and white-dominated society and the impact of strictly gendered socialization on the use of power (Bograd 1988; Pagelow 1984; Smith 1990). Consequently, these perspectives attempt to combine the significance of social and structural variables to explain the behavior of both batterers and victims. However, these macro-level theories often fail to address the micro-level variations that occur in battering relationships.

Family Violence Perspectives

These theories take a social learning approach to explaining battering. They stress the significance of factors such as exposure to or being a victim of violence in the family of origin, substance abuse, marital distress, and violence-prone personality types (O'Leary 1988; Straus, Gelles, and Steinmetz 1980). Some of these researchers include additional social variables such as low income and educational levels, violence toward others, and sexual aggression (Aldarondo and Sugarman 1996; Hotaling and Sugarman 1986; Kaufman-Kantor and Straus 1989; Straus and Gelles 1990).

It is from this research that we will attempt to develop a basic picture of battering in general. This research estimates that somewhere between 2 and 4 million women are battered by an intimate partner each year (Bachman and Saltzman 1994; Bureau of Justice Statistics 1993; Stanko 1988; Straus and Gelles 1990). While some researchers report almost equal domestic violence participation by men and women (Gelles and Straus 1988), many experts feel that this is a misevaluation of the data and reflects our failure to clearly delineate the difference between proactive violence by men and reactive or self-defensive violence most often seen from women (Dobash, Dobash, Wilson, and Daly 1992; Stanko 1988). These researchers contend that about 95% of proactive domestic violence is committed by men (Bachman and Saltzman 1994; Browne 1987; Roberts 1996; Stanko 1988). Gelles and Straus (1988) reported that the survey research (National Family Violence Survey) indicated that women are more likely to be victims of violence by their male partners at home than anywhere else or by anyone else. They noted that 39% of these attacks involve very aggressive and serious violence (e.g., punched with a fist, kicked, bitten, or assaulted with a weapon).

Each year, about 1.5 million of these cases require medical treatment. Over half of those require a visit to, or overnight stay at, a hospital (Dobash, Dobash, and Cavanagh 1984; Kurz and Stark 1988; Stanko 1988; Straus and Gelles 1986). Bachman and Saltzman (1994) note that injuries, especially serious injuries, to women were two times more likely if the attacker was an intimate. They also note that while only about 3% of male murder victims are killed by a female intimate, about 50% of female murder victims are killed by a male intimate.

The following is a brief review of some of the correlates of domestic violence identified by the individual and social perspectives. Many researchers have identified low self-esteem in both batterer and victim. This low self-esteem isolates the victim to ensure her focus is all on the batterer. The low self-esteem batterer, since he fears abandonment, loss of partner or her full attention, uses violence to control or create a crisis that places her attention back on him (Hendricks and McKean 1995). Prince and Arias (1994) found that self-esteem plays one of two roles in batterers: (1) Men with high self-esteem but poor self control used violence to feel in control; and (2) Men with low self-esteem and feelings of powerlessness resorted to violence in frustration. The female victim, since she has been socialized into dependence and passivity feels trapped physically and views the failure as hers for not adequately performing her roles as peacemaker and comforter (Hendricks and McKean 1995). Family of origin is also believed to be a key factor. Individuals who experience or who are victims of violence in their family of origin are thought to be more likely to participate in domestic violence themselves as a way of solving their relationship problems and meeting personal needs for power and control. Female victims may be more likely to be victims of domestic violence again later in life because of their experience with violence in the family as a common way of solving problems (Hendricks and McKean 1995).

Much of the research in this area indicates that maritally violent men are poor communicators with low impulse control, poor social skills, emotional dependence, insecurity, and a lack of empathy (Gondolf 1988; Holtzworth-Monroe 1992; Holtzworth-Monroe and Stuart 1994). Other researchers report that stress and marital distress are often precursors of domestic violence (Hendricks and McKean 1995; Hotaling and Sugarman 1986), as are very traditional and stereotypical sex role beliefs and machoism (Browning and Dutton 1986; Dutton 1988; Frieze and Browne 1989; Gondolf 1988; Hendricks and McKean 1995; Kahn 1984; Prince and Arias 1994). In fact, Hotaling and Sugarman (1986) found eight factors associated with being a batterer:

1. sexual aggression;
2. violence toward children;
3. witnessing parental violence as a child or a teen;
4. working-class occupational status;
5. excessive alcohol use;
6. low income;
7. low assertiveness;
8. low educational level.

But they note only one characteristic associated with being a battering victim: witnessing violence in the family as a child or an adolescent. Other researchers have added aggressive personality style, stress, marital dissatisfaction, and machoism to this list (Browning and Dutton 1986; Dutton 1988; Frieze and Browne 1989; Gondolf 1988; Kahn 1984; O'Leary 1988; Straus and Gelles 1990).

In more recent years, there has been significant disagreement between the family violence researchers and sociocultural researchers over the differences in the two types of data they collect and the very different pictures of battering those data provide. Family violence research relies primarily on national survey samples and the use of results from the Conflict Tactics Scale (CTS). This data tends to show frequent use of minor violence by both males and females in large numbers of families. This violence may or may not adhere to the battering cycle identified by Walker (1979), and the interpretation of this family violence research has posited a focus on violence generated by an isolated and particularly stressful situation (Jasinski and Williams 1998; Johnson 1995). This type of battering process could be affected by desistance for some unknown reason early on in these relationships, or it simply could be that some intervention occurs before the battering cycle becomes established. It is also possible that some of these relationships may follow the battering cycle, but its repetition is more difficult to identify because the cycle is elongated, making fewer revolutions over a longer time period.

Some family violence scholars have noted that this data may be missing some of the most serious battering cases. Such couples are unlikely to respond to the survey. This is especially true for couples in which the in victims fear a response might result in repercussions from an angry batterer who would interpret the survey as threatening (Fagan 1989; Feld and Straus 1989; Johnson 1995). Additionally, there have been serious questions about the value of the information obtained using the CTS because it fails to distinguish between aggression initiated by a controller and defensive violence by victims. The family violence research has also led to other studies indicating assumptions about high levels of self-administered desistance of violence in these families when the particular stressful situation ends (Fagan 1989; Feld and Straus 1989; Johnson 1995).

While some desistance undoubtably exists in battering relationships, there is no clear evidence that desistance is necessarily permanent. It is always possible that temporary desistance may exist or appear to exist because of the victim's success at extreme compliance for periods of time to stave off the next occurrence of violence. Temporary desistance might represent an elongated version of the battering cycle, at least until the cycle begins to escalate. The research is still unclear as to whether this type of battering during situational stress can escalate to a more regular cycle of battering over time, like that identified by Walker (1979).

Websdale (1999), in his study of intimate partner homicide, notes a variety of problems with the current concentration on abstracted empiricism seen in family violence research. He believes this approach using micro-level individual characteristics is ill suited to understanding the complex macro processes and dynamics of intimate partner homicide. He argues that these studies miss the dynamics of interaction between people and the broader workings of power seen in the social, economic, cultural, and political macro-level structures that shape the homicidal process. He calls for a significantly expanded macro-level theory of battering that would allow an examination of the whole picture. We agree with Websdale's (1999) position on this issue.

Since no one has yet identified a set of characteristics that can readily define batterers or victims as individuals, it seems clear that the dynamics of battering are far more complex than just the characteristics of the two individuals involved. Certainly, the individual batterer may choose aggressive responses because he is socialized to do so or lacks the communication or anger control skills to act otherwise, but once he begins the interaction, the process involves two parties and his original intentions may not still exist or govern the process by its end. The intended outcome is affected by far broader social, structural, cultural, and situational factors which fall beyond his individual characteristics.

On the other hand, feminist and some sociocultural researchers have relied more heavily on case studies taken from among battering and domestic homicide cases seen in the courts, hospitals, and shelters. These case studies indicate a closer adherence to Walker's cycle of battering (1979), more frequent and intense violence, little dependence on any particular stressful situation, little self-administered desistance, and even the more frequent escalation to homicide. In these case studies, researchers rely less on survey and evaluation tools like the CTS, because they have access to the full step-by-step story from victims, batterers, and other observers (Adams, Jackson, and Lauby 1988; Browne 1987; Downs 1996; Ewing 1987; Goetting 1988; Jones 1980; Stark 1995; Walker 1984, 1989).

Although this research does not provide a broad picture of the prevalence or extent of family violence in society, it does allow a more specific focus on intimate partner violence, particularly where this violence leads to serious injuries, fear, and even homicide. The case study approach expands the examination beyond micro-level predictors to include the social, economic, cultural, and political workings of power that shape the homicidal process as noted by Websdale (1999). This research provides a richer and more detailed reconstruction of how battering happens, its structural supports, its social meaning, and the influence battering has on victims, offenders, and their relationships.

Johnson (1995) examined this argument and the differences between the research methods and results. He concluded that these researchers are likely studying two different phenomena. Johnson (1995) divided battering into two types: The first type, common couple violence, involves minor violence and reciprocity of assaults between partners. This type is likely to occur less frequently and only under certain extremely stressful conditions. In the second type, patriarchal terrorism, female partners are systematically terrorized by a male partner. This type of battering would involve more serious and frequent violence against the victim and a greater need for physical self-defensive action by the victim. Patriarchal terrorism more closely resembles situations that are likely to lead to homicide as described by Browne (1987). In this respect, this qualitative social data on battering provides a better foundation for our theoretical development purposes in this book. However, we do not necessarily agree with Johnson (1995) that these are two entirely separate phenomena. We would argue that there is no clear evidence to indicate that such a delineation exists in reality and/or that common couple violence does not escalate over time to lethal levels. Certainly a victim could be killed in any battering incident. For example, blows to the torso or head could easily cause fatal internal organ injuries regardless of the batterer's initial intentions.

Additionally, we would argue that there is little evidence to suggest that common couple violence is anything less than an elongated version of the battering cycle with a longer time line for escalation rather than a one-time occurrence followed by permanent desistance. Walker's (1979) Cycle of Battering Theory does not posit a specific time constraint on any of the phases of the cycle. In fact, Walker notes that the time within phases and the time between phases can and does vary from relationship to relationship. Such variation would be expected by most social scientists in examining any long-term social phenomenon and does not mean that the cycle does not exist. We will argue here that variation is a result of social, cultural, and structural issues, the victim's response, the batterer's reaction to the victim's response, and other factors that affect the interaction. Consequently, in this book, we do not assume some major difference between common couple violence and patriarchal terrorism, although we rely more on the data from these sociocultural case studies because it is more adept.

SOCIAL SCIENCE RESEARCH ON WOMEN WHO KILL

Social science research reveals a great deal about women and homicide. The first, and most obvious point, is that women do not kill very often. In any given year, women commit only about 10% of homicides and the large majority of those involve women trying to survive battering relationships (Browne 1987; Dobash, Dobash, Wilson, and Daly 1992; Hart 1996, 1991; FBI 1993, 1998). Consequently, the homicides by women display more consistency in their characteristics and circumstances than those committed by men (Browne 1987; Ewing 1987; Goetting 1988; Jones 1980; Jurik and Winn 1990; Ogle, Maier-Katkin, and Bernard 1995; Wolfgang 1958). The homicide victims of women are usually intimates, the majority of whom are abusive partners (Browne 1987; Browne and Williams 1989; Dobash et al. 1992; Ewing 1987; Goetting 1988; Jones 1980; Jurik and Winn 1990; Ogle et al. 1995; Wolfgang 1958). Killings by women most frequently occur in the home (Goetting 1988; Ogle et al. 1995; Totman 1978; Wolfgang 1958). They involve very little planning, explosive sudden aggression, a lone killer (without co-conspirators), and homicide victim provocation (Browne 1987; Ewing 1987; Goetting 1988; Jones 1980; Ogle et al. 1995; Roberts 1996; Wolfgang 1958).

Female killers tend to be more socially conforming than the average woman, holding very traditional sex role and lifestyle expectations (Blackman 1988; Browne 1987; Bunch, Foley, and Urbina 1983; Ewing 1987; Goetting 1988; Jones 1980; Ogle et al. 1995; Widom 1979). Not only are female killers generally provoked, but they report insurmountable life pressures, depression, despair, and desperation at the time of the offense (Browne 1987; Bunch et al. 1983; Ewing 1987; Goetting 1988; Jones 1980; Piven and Cloward 1979; Totman 1978; Widom 1979). Additionally, even though the number of homicides are higher among lower-class women and women of color, the patterns noted above do not vary much with class and race (Browne 1987; Dawson and Langan 1994; Ewing 1987; Goetting 1988; Jones 1980; Ogle et al. 1995).

Ogle et al. (1995) provide a theoretical perspective on why these patterns do not vary with race and class. They note that the oppression suffered by all women is simply increased for lower-class women and women of color, as is the lack of adequate coping resources to manage the problems leading to homicidal actions. These patterns provide a rich picture of the complex context in which women who kill generally do it. The patterns highlight the significance of social, cultural, structural, and situational variables in the female homicide phenomenon.

BATTERING HOMICIDE

Much of the information on the demographics and prevalence of intimate partner homicide comes from the quantitative survey research by family violence researchers and uniform crime reports collected by police agencies. While homicide is arguably the most accurately reported and solved crime, there are still some problems with statistics on intimate partner homicides. One problem is that some intimate partner homicides are recorded without reference to the battering relationship that existed between the parties. Consequently, they are not considered to be battering cases that resulted in a killing. This means the statistics on battering-related homicides are almost always underestimated. A second problem concerns the nature or progression of battering. Sometimes the victim is killed by the batterer fairly early in the relationship, before the full development of a pattern of battering is evident. This kind of case may not be officially recognized as a battering homicide. A third problem is that in some cases the batterer is so successful at hiding the battering from outside sources that the true nature of the relationship is only known to the victim and the batterer. Consequently, after the killing, no battering information is reported. A fourth problem is general uneasiness in our society about recognizing battering. We are generally reluctant to acknowledge such behavior unless absolutely forced by the evidence to accept it. This means that investigators, lawyers, families, and friends are likely to not bring it up unless it is undeniable.

In general, the research on partner homicides indicates that these cases may have declined in the past 25 years, from a high of about 3,000 in 1976 to about 2,000 in 1996 (Bureau of Justice Statistics 1998; Browne and Williams 1989; Dawson and Langan 1994; Websdale 1999). Most scholars agree that the majority of intimate partner homicides are committed by men and that the large majority of these homicides involve male partners battering their female partners (Currens 1991; Dobash et al. 1992; Hart 1996, 1991; Marzuk, Tardiff, and Hirsch 1992; Rosenbaum 1990; Stanko 1988). Stack (1997), in the largest domestic homicide study to date, found that men are more likely to kill their victims and then kill themselves, as if on principle, while women are more likely to kill to survive. Younger people are more likely to be both perpetrators and victims of intimate partner homicides and the frequency of these homicides increases as the age differential between the partners increases (Daly and Wilson 1988; Websdale 1999).

According to Uniform Crime Report statistics, African Americans appear to have an eight-times-higher rate of intimate partner homicides than whites (Block and Christakos 1995; Mercy and Saltzman 1989; Websdale 1999). However, it should be noted that some scholars believe that this difference is a result of socioeconomic status rather than race or ethnicity (Centerwall 1984; Stark and Flitcraft 1996). Centerwall (1984) notes that when we control for socioeconomic status in these studies, the differences between racial and ethnic groups disappear. Davis (1976) indicates that if racial difference really mattered, we should see much higher rates of intimate partner homicide in Africa than in other areas; and this is not the case. Other researchers have noted that socioeconomic status is also connected to power, access to fewer personal and social assistance resources, and less vigilance by law enforcers (Ogle and Jacobs 1998; Ogle et al. 1995; Stark 1993).

This analysis of the empirical data supports the position that this data misses social, economic, cultural, and structural variables that influence partner homicide. The research indicates that women are at a much higher risk of being killed in an intimate partner homicide than are men, although the risk may be closer to equal among blacks (Bureau of Justice Statistics 1998). These statistics also indicate that the overall decrease in intimate partner homicides from 1976 to 1996 is mainly due to a decrease in the number of women killing their abusive partners, rather than a decrease in male batterers killing their victims (Browne and Williams 1989; Bureau of Justice Statistics 1998; Dawson and Langan 1994). Studies generally support Wolfgang's (1958) results indicating that male intimate partner homicide victims were far more likely than female victims to have precipitated their own deaths with provocation. For example, Barnard, Vera, Vera, and Newman (1982) indicate that the majority of female killers in their study reported they were being battered by their male victims. The majority of male killers said that their killings were precipitated by their female victims threatening to leave them or making demands that they felt were beyond the socially assigned sex role for females.

Most scholars agree that domestic violence progressively increases the level of "entrapment" of victims, and this may very well be the most significant risk factor for intimate partner homicide (Blackman 1988; Browne 1987; Coker 1992; Copelon 1994; Ewing 1987; Hart 1996, 1991; Kellermann, Rivara, Rushforth, Banton, Reay, Franciso, Locci, Prodzinski, Hackman, and Somes 1993; Ogle and Jacobs 1998; Stanko 1988; Stark and Flitcraft 1996). These findings would again indicate that the statistics seen in survey data tend to miss the very important social, economic, cultural, and structural variables that influence the interactions in violent relationships and the potential escalation to homicide.

The sociocultural research does indicate some relatively consistent characteristics in battering cases that escalate to homicide. Many scholars have found that violence toward the battering victim and homicides increase when the victim tries to leave or shortly after the victim has left (Allen 1983; Barnard et al. 1982; Browne 1987; Easteal 1993; Hart 1991; Mahoney 1991; Wilson and Daly 1993). Other studies indicate an increase in homicides when the batterer has made threats to kill the victim or himself (Bureau of Justice Statistics 1998; Dobash and Dobash 1979; Hart 1988). Browne (1987) looked at the Detroit and Kansas City domestic violence enforcement studies and found that in the battering homicides, 85% to 90% of the cases involved at least one call to police during the two years prior to the homicide. In 54% of the cases, the police had been summoned five or more times for domestic violence in that residence. Browne (1987) found that all of the women in her partner homicide study reported having contacted the police for protection at least five times before killing their abusers. She also notes the contribution of failed attempts to utilize outside assistance to escalating the danger in these relationships. Others have echoed this situation as a symptom of entrapment (Blackman 1988; Coker 1992; Copelon 1994; Downs 1996; Easteal and Easteal 1992; Elk and Johnson 1989; Ewing 1987; Felder and Victor 1996; Hart 1996, 1991; Ogle and Jacobs 1998; Sherman and Schmidt 1993; Stanko 1988; Stark 1995).

Stark and Flitcraft (1996) have noted that health, justice, and social service responses to battering often end up reinforcing the victim's entrapment, and therefore, increase the chances of a homicide (Easteal and Easteal 1992; Felder and Victor 1996; Klein 1996; Kurz and Stark 1988; Ogle and Jacobs 1998). Other research has found that male perpetrators of intimate partner violence and homicide are much more likely than their female victims or counterparts to have a prior criminal record and often a record for assaultive behavior outside the home (Block and Christakos 1995; Bureau of Justice Statistics 1998; Fagan, Stewart, and Hansen 1983; Felder and Victor 1996; Klein 1993). The research overwhelmingly supports the argument that over half of batterers report the use of alcohol, drugs, or both, at the time when they committed the homicide (Block and Christakos 1995; Easteal 1993; Felder and Victor 1996; Kaufman-Kantor and Straus 1989; Websdale 1999). Still other research points to the existence of substance use, depression, obsessive possessiveness, and jealousy as major factors in the escalation of battering to homicide (Barnard et al. 1982; Daly and Wilson 1988; Easteal 1993; Kaufman-Kantor and Straus 1989).

Lester (1992) and Buteau, Lesage, and Kiely (1993) note the significance of depression among batterers and the influence depression may have on the batterers' adherence to protection orders. Keilitz, Hannaford, and Efkeman

(1998) found that the large majority of women receiving protection orders indicated benefits from that effort, including reduced abuse and threats. However, other researchers have found that almost 30% of their sample were victims of extreme violence by their abusers while a protection order was in force (Buzawa and Buzawa 1996; Harrell and Smith 1996, 1998; Klein 1996; Websdale 1999). These scholars all note significant failure of protection orders and the need to move toward social policy that supports the use of protection orders as only one part of a more comprehensive strategy to prevent domestic violence and homicides. Other scholars have noted the failure of a variety of social helping agencies to end the violence, including the medical community (Easteal and Easteal 1992; Felder and Victor 1996). Many of these scholars have noted that this failure of resources not only may magnify the victim's feelings of entrapment, but may also escalate the risk for increased violence following the failed effort at assistance.

Aldarondo and Straus (1994) found ten risk factors for marital homicide:

1. High frequency of violence;
2. Dependency;
3. Physical injuries;
4. Violent behavior outside the home;
5. Rape of partner;
6. Physical violence in family of origin;
7. Possession or use of weapons;
8. Threats to hit and/or kill partner;
9. Having killed or abused pets;
10. Controlling and psychological maltreatment.

Browne (1987) found a similar list of factors when she compared her sample of battered women who killed their abusers to Walker's sample of battered women who had not killed. She notes seven major differences:

1. The increased frequency of abuse;
2. Frequent intoxication and drug abuse;
3. Higher level of seriousness to injuries;
4. Increased seriousness of sexual abuse;
5. High levels of isolation for the victim;
6. The existence of threats to kill;
7. The victim's failed attempts to leave or to utilize outside assistance, leaving her with feelings of hopelessness.

These characteristics all match very closely to the "Type I" batterer outlined in typologies by other researchers (Dutton 1988; Gondolf 1988; Gottman, Jacobson, Rushe, Shortt, Babcock, Taillade, and Waltz 1995). Kaufman-Kantor and Jasinski (1998) note that these are the typologies more likely to be seen in homicide cases. Again, this does not mean that none of these cases began initially as common couple violence. It only suggests that these terroristic types of battering are at a point to allow us to more readily see and study their conformity to Walker's cycle of battering than other types.

While these antecedents to intimate partner homicide give us information about demographics and prevalence, they tend to provide snapshots of problems including social, economic, cultural, and structural issues, but little in terms of a theoretical perspective on how all of these antecedents come together in battering relationships that result in homicides. Our goal in this book will be to utilize these quantitative and qualitative data to develop such a theoretical perspective.

EXISTING THEORIES ON WOMEN WHO KILL

To date, there are only three theories specifically intended to explain female commission of homicide. The first is an integrated social science theory developed in 1995 by Ogle, Maier-Katkin, and Bernard that purports to explain female homicide in all its contexts. We review this theory here because we do rely on some of their theoretical ideas in the development of our new perspective. The second is a theory of postpartum depression or psychosis intended to explain why women kill their children. We will touch on this theory here, but it is less useful to our discussion because it focuses only on women's psychopathology and has little relevance for understanding battered women who kill. The third theory is commonly called Battered Woman Syndrome. This theory was developed in 1984 by Walker and is intended to provide an explanation for why battered women remain in these relationships and the psychological pathology created by such a relationship.

The First Theory: Homicidal Behavior Among Women

The *Homicidal Behavior Among Women Theory* (Ogle et al. 1995) was not created as a supplement for a legal defense; it is a social science effort to simply explain homicide by women in any setting. The theory posits that the social, cultural, and structural conditions of modern society generate more strain for women than they do for men. When people suffer from strain, they experience negative feelings and must use their coping resources to either manage or end the situation. This higher level of strain is even more problematic for women because they also face this strain with fewer coping resources than are available to men. Because they do not have as many coping resources, women tend to internalize the negative feelings as guilt or hurt and to utilize their resources to manage those negative feelings rather than to externalize their anger toward a target. This results in a situation very similar to overcontrol, which creates low overall rates of violence by women punctuated by occasional instances of extreme violence when their overcontrol is overwhelmed by situational *peaks* of stress. Ogle et al. note that the conditions found in pre- and postpartum environments and abusive relationships often produce these peaks of stress because these environments and relationships involve loss of personal space and autonomy, perceived lower social position, some types of discrimination, and significant isolation. When the peaks of stress are combined with fewer coping resources (which women have fewer of and batterers continuously try to block), it can overwhelm the stressed-out individual's overcontrol and result in homicide as a coping option.

While this theory makes a significant contribution to our understanding of the social, cultural, situational, and structural (macro-level) processes that may impact homicide by women, it makes no attempt to specifically explain how this might occur in the battering relationship. We might ask how these variables interact in the relationship and play themselves out in a way that leads battered women to the conclusion that they have no other option but to utilize lethal self-defense. We will utilize some of the concepts, variables, and ideas of this theory as we attempt to develop a new social interaction theory on battering relationships that escalate to homicide by women. Specifically, we will borrow the ideas concerning blockage of coping mechanisms for women, the socialization of women against experiencing or expressing anger and aggression, and the roles of isolation, density, discrimination, and perceived lowered social status in battering relationships.

The Second Theory: Postpartum Depression or Psychosis

The second theory on women and homicide is intended to be a supplement to an insanity defense for women who kill their children at birth or in postpartum periods. This is often referred to as *postpartum depression or psychosis theory*. This theory argues that most women suffer some level of depression following childbirth as a result of hormonal or chemical changes naturally occurring in the body during pregnancy or following birth. In most women, the depression is a mild form called *the baby blues*. However, many scholars argue that in some women a more severe form of this psychological malady develops and can create psychosis in which the woman is so out of touch with reality that she may harm or kill her child without realizing what she is doing. This theory is commonly used in England, the United States, and throughout Europe to supplement an insanity defense for such women. Ogle et al. (1995) argue that this theory is too narrow because it focuses only on women who kill their children. Additionally, just like the history of criminological theory on women, this theory focuses on individual causes and primarily psychological causes. This focus reflects our history of stereotypes about women and a belief that femininity makes crime impossible, thus any woman committing a crime must be *crazy* to go so far outside her social role. This misconception may prevent our evolution of theory on women by ignoring social, structural, cultural, and situational factors that criminologists today believe affect the behavior of both men and women.

The Third Theory: Battered Woman Syndrome

The third theory out there, and the only one presently available to explain why battered women kill as a supplement to a self-defense defense, is *Battered Woman Syndrome*. This theory, developed by Lenore Walker in 1984, complements her theory of the cycle of battering developed in 1979.

The cycle of battering theory (see Figure 1 for a depiction of the battering cycle) posits that battering involves an identifiable pattern. Walker (1979) indicates that this pattern has three phases:

1. tension building, in which the batterer seeks to create tension through intimidation, degradation, and threats in order to build a case for his next episode of violence and during this time the victim is attempting to forestall the next battering incident (usually by hyper-compliance or seeking assistance);

2. acute battering incident, in which the batterer becomes violently abusive toward the victim in order to make his point, regain complete control of both the relationship and the victim, and prevent the victim from trying to leave;

3. contrition, in which the batterer, early in the relationship, makes gestures of apology, promises desistance, asks for forgiveness, and seeks reconciliation in order to keep the victim from fleeing.

Walker finds that the battering relationships in her studies went through these phases repeatedly. However, she does note that the cycle seems to change over time such that the contrition phase becomes minute or disappears, while the tension building phase becomes longer and the acute battering incidents become more frequent and intense (Walker 1979). Even if the batterer still sees the relationship as involving contri-

Figure 1
The Battering Cycle

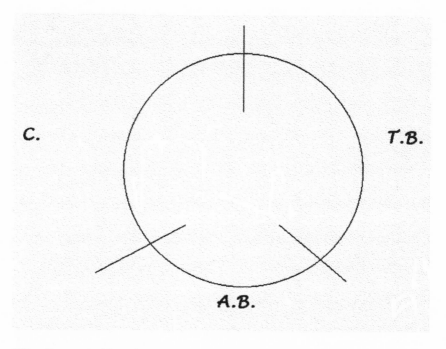

T.B. = Tension Building Phase; A.B. = Acute Battering Phase; C. = Contrition Phase
Illustration created by Whitney L. Shockley and Christian A. Nolasco.

tion, the victim will have given up on contrition and promises of desistance becaue of the continued violence.

Walker never specifically explains why changes in the cycle occur, although she implies that the variation is related to the interaction in each individual relationship. She notes that the cycle rarely ceases without intervention. We will attempt in this book to explain why and how the cycle changes over time. We will argue that once contrition disappears or the victim no longer believes it due to continued violence, the cycle simply vacillates from tension building to acute violence and back to tension building. From this perspective, there would be no nonconfrontational periods in the relationship for the victim. For her, the relationship becomes a cycle of constant tension building with its climax in the next round of violence. This may be why most studies on battered women who kill have reported that these women felt they were eventually in a daily desperate survival mode awaiting the arrival of the next incident and hoping it would not be their last (Barnard et al. 1982; Browne 1987; Ewing 1987; Jones 1980).

Walker's theoretical perspectives have been widely accepted in both social science and the courts. In the Battered Woman Syndrome theory, Walker attributes the control of the battering victim to a psychological problem of the victim called *learned helplessness*. The essence of this explanation is that over time in the battering relationship, the battered woman learns that no matter what she does, she cannot change the situation. Eventually, the victim gives up trying to change her situation and accepts her fate.

Battered Woman Syndrome theory has been used to supplement an insanity defense by claiming that the psychological problem inherent in learned helplessness renders the victim unable to distinguish right from wrong, thereby resulting in the choice to act unreasonably. This supplement to self-defense is problematic because battered women generally appear emotionally distraught but not mentally ill or insane. They are generally aware of what they have done ("it had to be me or him"), and they generally also view their actions, while necessary, as morally and legally wrong.

More often, Battered Woman Syndrome is used as a supplement to self-defense. In this instance, the theory claims that the victim will have made efforts over time to try to prevent the battering by pleasing the batterer, obtaining assistance, or leaving, only to be sought out again by the batterer. It indicates that the psychological problem suffered as a result of the ongoing battering causes the victim to become completely passive, believing nothing she does will change things, staying in the relationship waiting for the batterer to change or kill her. This theory may explain the response of some battered women. It has certainly been widely accepted in the courts, but it has not been particularly successful. The literature contains a variety of criticisms by social science and legal scholars, and we will review the most significant of these here.

First, Battered Woman Syndrome concentrates the explanation on some assumed psychological pathology of the victim, which leaves the victim's perspective, decisions, and actions open to questions of reasonableness in a court of law (Adams et al. 1988; Downs 1996; Ewing 1987; Gillespie 1989; Roberts 1996; Schneider 1980; Stubbs, and Tolmie 1992; Stark 1995). This is a form of blaming the victim for her victimization. It seeks to explain the victim's failure to end the violence or leave successfully as the problematic behavior to be explained rather than asking the question of why the batterer batters and how we address that problem.

Second, Battered Woman Syndrome does not explain how a woman suffering from learned helplessness (resigned to dying, hopeless, sure that nothing she does will have any influence on the outcome) suddenly becomes proactive and defends herself lethally (Adams et al. 1988; Downs 1996; Ewing 1987; Gillespie 1989; Roberts 1996; Schneider 1980; Sheehy, Stubbs, and Tolmie 1992; Stark 1995). In other words, if she has psychologically given up, how do we understand the sudden change to self-determination involving proactive lethal force?

Third, learned helplessness creates a psychological and behavioral stereotype of the battering victim that can then be turned around and used against her in court if she does not exactly fit the typology of a battered woman suffering from this psychological problem. When this happens, the battered woman is often not allowed to present certain testimony on the battering because she is believed not to be a battered woman. In other words, if psychologists, through interviews and testing, cannot make a diagnosis of learned helplessness, then the woman does not fit the typology of a battered woman and cannot use that as a supplement to self-defense (Adams et al. 1988; Downs 1996; Ewing 1987; Gillespie 1989; Roberts 1996; Schneider 1980; Sheehy et al. 1992; Stark 1995).

Beyond these criticisms, a fourth issue is significant to the argument made in this book. Battered Woman Syndrome focuses only on psychology and only on the victim, as if the victim is the causal factor to be understood. This psychological theory ignores all of the cultural, social, structural, and situational factors that are parts of the battering process and the victim's responses to that process. Additionally, this theory ignores the batterer and his contribution to the process both as the initiating participant and as the individual socially, culturally, structurally, and situationally benefiting from maintenance of the battering process. As Adams et al. (1988) have noted, while the terms used are more subtle, the focus even among researchers is on woman abuse as a psychological and pathological phenomenon, a theme that continues to imply that battering victims need therapy rather than justice. In essence, Battered Woman Syndrome as a theoretical approach stands outside reality, ignoring all of the social, cultural, structural, and situational variables and patterns that have been identified in the social science research on battering and women who kill.

In recent years, battered women who kill, and their advocates, have begun to call for a better understanding of battering victims' actions as part of a realistic and reasonable survival process rather than a psychological problem (Adams et al. 1988; Angel 1996; Blackman 1988; Browne 1987; Downs 1996; Schneider 1980; Stark 1995). This position asks us to think about battered women who kill their abusers from a different perspective, one that likely does not yet exist.

bell hooks (1984) says that when we have studied something extensively and are still unable to understand it, it is time to change. She calls for scholars to give up our tired old perspectives, useless old categories, and to look at the issue from a new angle to identify what we have missed before. It is our position in this book that understanding battering and its escalation requires a new perspective involving battering as a social interaction process heavily influenced by the weight of social reality.

INTERACTION THEORY

In recent years, the study of violence has migrated toward an interaction perspective. This approach emphasizes variables that create the motivation which leads to violent behavior through a series of sequential interactions between the parties involved. This theoretical position argues that while the parties involved begin with a set of cultural or social expectations about behavior making some responses predictable, situations also involve behavior where the parties respond to the specific actions of each other and change continuously depending on the other's response (Birkbeck and LaFree 1993; Heimer and Matsueda 1994; Katz 1988; Luckenbill 1977). This back-and-forth exchange to each other's reactions and the situational context produce unique interactional sequences that may vary significantly from those originally intended by the participants. In other words, the interaction process in an exchange is just as important as understanding the two parties involved in the exchange and their initial intentions (Birkbeck and LaFree 1993; Heimer and Matsueda 1994; Katz 1988; Luckenbill 1977). Consequently, to understand a particular outcome, we would have to reconstruct the interaction process between the two parties. We would have to learn how each party interpreted the other's responses and reacted to them over time, in order to see the developmental stages in the interaction as the participants saw them and adjusted to those dynamics.

Katz (1988) notes that interaction process theory is particularly well suited to explaining individualized deviance such as lethal assault occurring in interpersonal encounters, as opposed to other forms of organized deviance. From this perspective, the tools for understanding any violent incident, including battering, would lie in reconstruction of the history of the ongoing interaction.

Most theorists would use this interaction perspective to analyze the last violent encounter in a battering relationship that results in a death (Katz 1988; Luckenbill 1977; Birkbeck and LaFree 1993). However, it could also be used to understand the entire battering relationship as an ongoing, long-term interaction for two reasons.

First, most battered women indicate that their actions in the final violent incident are predicated on their long-term knowledge about the batterer's behavior and the predictability of previous incidents (Barnard et al. 1982; Browne 1987; Ewing 1987; Jones 1980; Walker 1979). This would seem to indicate that judging their decisions would require an understanding about previous incidents in the relationship. Second, it might well be a misconception to assume that battering relationships return to some semblance of normality following each violent battering incident. Walker (1979) notes that over time the battering cycle changes such that the contrition phase disappears or becomes only a tool of the batterer to create unpredictability for the victim, and the cycle then consists primarily of tension building, acute battering, and an immediate return to further tension building. Although Walker does not specify why this occurs, she notes its existence as have other scholars examining this phenomenon (Browne 1987; Ewing 1987; Ogle and Jacobs 1998). Ewing (1987) specifically puts forth the idea that battering should be understood as an ongoing confrontation rather than a series of single and isolated incidents of violence. Browne (1987) notes the importance of analyzing the escalation of battering to homicide by understanding the battered woman's view of changes in the violence during successive cycles that create the belief that the level of harm and potential lethality is escalating. While none of these researchers have relied on interaction process theory in their analyses, it does seem like a reasonable way to proceed in our efforts to better understand battering and domestic homicides.

In this book, we utilize Walker's (1979) cycle of battering theory as the macro-level or outer shell of an interaction process. We use a social interaction approach to examine the micro-level action-and-reaction process that takes place between the two parties in the battering relationship. The combination of these two perspectives yields a new integrated theory of battering escalation that helps to explain the subtle changes in the cycle and how those changes may lead to homicide.

CONCLUSION

This chapter has reviewed all of the literature necessary to compose a new social interaction perspective on battering. The literature on individual characteristics of batterers and victims is admittedly sparse because our argument contends that these factors are not nearly as important to understanding the battering relationship and victim survival as the ongoing interaction process between the two parties. For example, while we agree that the excessive use of alcohol, a previous brain injury, or growing up in a family practicing violence may have some effect on the individual participant's behavior, these things cannot explain how battering becomes the primary characteristic of a relationship, or how and why escalation occurs. Relationships involve two people, not one, and those two people are in an ongoing interaction that takes on a life of its own, rarely restricted solely to the desires or intentions of one party. Consequently, we focus on the long-term interaction process between the two participants and the social, structural, cultural, and situational variables that contribute to the maintenance and escalation of that process. We believe that this perspective will better explain the survival actions of victims in these relationships and provide a supplement for a self-defense defense for battered women who kill.

This chapter argues that our society suffers from a misguided reliance on social helping resources rather than direct law enforcement to assist and protect battered women. These social resources are often failure-prone because they are not equipped to fully accomplish this task, and ultimately may do more to support the maintenance of battering than to end it. This problem is, at least in part, the result of our history of legality and cultural toleration and acceptance of battering as a reasonable and supported method of male domination and control in the family. As battering became a major focus of women's rights groups, its social support as a private matter waned, although significant time would pass before our society would create legislation criminalizing it. When such laws were enacted, the social willingness, infrastructure, policy, and procedural prerequisites to enforce these laws were nonexistent. Consequently, victims met with a criminal justice system unwilling and unable to assist and protect. This situation has not drastically improved in the past 20 years.

As a result of this history of legality, the study of battering as a "social problem" is a recent phenomenon. The research on battering has focused on three primary approaches: individual/biological causes; psychological/social (family violence research); and sociocultural. The research on individual causes has been very narrow and less than useful for understanding battering relationships, although it may hold promise along with social variables for development of more effective treatment for batterers. Family violence research has provided a host of potential social and psychological causes, as well as prevalence rates and useful information on types or degrees of violence. However, this research has yet to manage any cohesive theoretical explanation that utilizes those variables. Currently, some researchers believe that the reliance of family violence researchers on vague national survey data and the always controversial CTS may reduce the value of their work for understanding macro-level social, structural, and cultural factors necessary to explain battering as a sociological phenomenon. Sociocultural research has focused more on case studies of battered women located through the hospitals, shelters, and court system. This research provides a much broader and richer picture of battering as a social issue. This data is more likely to catch the cases that result in serious injuries and homicides, often missed in the surveys. These cases present the factors identified by domestic homicide researchers as significant (Bernard et al. 1982; Browne 1987; Ewing 1987; Jones 1980; Walker 1989; Websdale 1999), and more closely resemble those identified by Johnson (1995) as patriarchal terrorism. Therefore, these cases are the focus of our theoretical development in this book.

To develop this new theory, we utilize Walker's (1979) cycle of battering theory as the macro-level framework in which to place the interaction process. We understand and accept that this pattern may vary in relationships. Walker (1979) even notes the existence of some variation in the pattern and changes in the phases of the cycle over time. One variation in particular involves the contrition phase. It seems that in some battering relationships contrition disappears completely when the victim doesn't believe it anymore or the batterer no longer needs it because violence has now become the primary method of preventing the victim from leaving. However, in other relationships, contrition changes as a tool of the batterer. It can be used to create further tension (especially if the victim knows it is intended as a lie), and it can create instability and reduced predictability for the victim. Occasionally, it may still exist because the escalation in the relationship happens so quickly (if the batterer so chooses) that contrition appears to exist even at the point when the batterer actually kills his victim or the victim realizes the level of lethality and acts to kill the batterer in order to survive. So, while we accept some variability in the cycle of battering, we believe it currently provides the best known framework for developing a social interaction perspective on battering.

In recent years, interaction process theory has come into common usage in criminology, particularly as a method of examining interpersonal violence. This theory involves the analysis of ongoing actions and reactions between the two parties of an interaction. It proposes that as the participants act and react to each others' responses, the interplay takes on a life of its own which may be far different than the original intentions or goals of either party. This variation is created by the "context" of the interaction which involves social, cultural, situational, and structural variables. Although Luckenbill (1977) proposed this method for analyzing a single incident between participants, there is little evidence to suggest that it could not be used to examine a long-term or "mega" interaction involving multiple incidents in a process. We believe that battering represents a long-term interaction where neither party sees a predictable end to the interaction and must respond to each succeeding incident based upon knowledge developed in previous incidents during this interaction. Interaction process theory and borrowed bits and pieces from the Ogle et al. (1995) theory of homicidal behavior among women form the internal or micro-level explanation of battering and battering escalation to homicide in this new theory. Ogle et al. (1995) discuss the significance of socialization of women against the use of aggression, the higher stress level of women, the lower number of coping resources possessed by women, how stress causes high chronic arousal and negative affect, and the response of normal persons to negative affect (use of coping resources to manage or end the negative feelings and strain they create). We utilize these ideas in our new theory to explain the context of the battering interaction, how it progresses, and how it escalates to lethal levels. In this respect, if battering can be seen as a long-term interaction involving multiple incidents with escalating levels of violence, it can be understood as a homicidal process requiring the victim to learn from each incident in the interaction and utilize that knowledge to survive as the interaction progresses. This allows us to argue that battered women who kill must be able to present a self-defense explanation that includes this context of the long-term interaction process rather than a single snapshot of the final incident resulting in homicide.

REFERENCES

Adams, D., J. Jackson, and M. Lauby (1988). Family violence research: Aid or obstacle to the battered women's movement. *Response, 11*, 14–16.

Aldarondo, E., and M.A. Straus (1994). Screening for physical violence in couple therapy: Methodological, practical, and ethical considerations. *Family Process, 33*, 425–439.

Aldarondo, E., and D.B. Sugarman (1996). Risk marker analysis of the cessation and persistence of wife assault. *Journal of Consulting and Clinical Psychology, 64(5)*, 1010–1019.

Allen, N.H. (1983). Homicide followed by suicide: Los Angeles, 1970–1979. *Suicide and Life Threatening Behavior, 13(3)*, 155–165.

Angel, M. (1996). Criminal law and women: Giving the abused woman who kills "a jury of her peers" who appreciate trifles. *American Criminal Law Review, 33(3)*, 229–348.

Bachman, R. and L.E. Saltzman (1994). *Violence against women: A national crime victimization survey report* (NIJ 154348). Washington, DC: U.S. Department of Justice.

Barnard, G.W., H. Vera, M.I. Vera, and G. Newman (1982). Till death do us part: A study of spouse murder. *Bulletin of the AAPL, 10(4)*, 271–280.

Belknap, J. (1992). Perceptions of women battering. In Imogene L. Moyer (Ed.), *The changing roles of women in the criminal justice system* (2nd ed., pp. 181–201). Prospect Heights, IL: Waveland Press.

Birkbeck, C., and G.L. LaFree (1993). The situational analysis of crime and deviance. *Annual Review of Sociology,19*, 113–137.

Blackman, J. (1988). Exploring the impacts of poverty on battered women who kill their abusers. A paper presented at the American Psychological Association meeting in Atlanta, Georgia.

Block, C.R., and A. Christakos (1995). Intimate partner homicide in Chicago over 29 years. *Crime and Delinquency, 41*, 496–526.

Bograd, M. (1988). Feminist perspectives on wife abuse: An introduction. In K. Yllo and M. Bograd (Eds.), *Feminist perspectives on wife abuse* (pp. 11–28). Newbury Park, CA: Sage.

Browne, A. (1987). *When battered women kill.* New York: The Free Press.

Browne, A., and K.R. Williams (1989). Exploring the effect of resource availability and the likelihood of female perpetrated homicides. *Law & Society Review, 23(1)*, 75–94.

Browning, J., and D. Dutton (1986). Assessment of wife assault with the conflict tactics scale: Using couple data to quantify the differential reporting effect. *Journal of Marriage and the Family, 48(2)*, 375–379.

Bunch, B.J., L.A. Foley, and S.P. Urbina (1983). The psychology of violent female offenders: A sex-role perspective. *The Prison Journal, 63*, 66–79.

Bureau of Justice Statistics (1998). *Violence by intimates: Analysis of data on crimes by current or former spouses, boyfriends, and girlfriends* (NCJ 167237). Washington, DC: U.S. Department of Justice.

———. (1993). *Family violence: Interventions for the justice system.* Washington, DC: U.S. Department of Justice.

Buteau, J., A. Lesage, and M. Kiely (1993). Homicide followed by suicide: A Quebec case series, 1988–1990. *Canadian Journal of Psychiatry, 38*, 552–556.

Buzawa, E.S., and C.G. Buzawa (1996). *Domestic violence: The criminal justice response* (2nd ed.). Thousand Oaks, CA: Sage.

Centerwall, B.S. (1984). Race, socioeconomic status, and domestic homicide, Atlanta, 1971–1972. *American Journal of Public Health, 74*, 813–815.

Coker, D.K. (1992). Heat of passion and wife killing: Men who batter/men who kill. *Review of Law and Women's Studies, 2*, 71–89.

Copelon, R. (1994). Recognizing the egregious in the everyday: Domestic violence as torture. *Columbia Human Rights Law Review, 25(2)*, 291–367.

Currens, S. (1991). Homicide followed by suicide—Kentucky, 1985–1990. CDC *Morbidity and Mortality Weekly Report, 40(38)*, 652–659.

Daly, M., and M. Wilson (1988). *Homicide.* Hawthorne, NY: Aldine de Gruyter.

Davidson, T. (1977). Wife beating: A recurring phenomenon throughout history. In Maria Roy (Ed.), *Battered women: A psychological study of domestic violence* (pp. 19–57). New York: Van Nostrand Reinhold.

Davis, E.G. (1971). *The First Sex*. New York: Penguin Books.

Davis, J.A. (1976). Blacks, crime, and American culture. *Annals of the American Academy of Political and Social Science, 423*, 89–98.

Davis, R.C., and B. Smith (1995). Domestic violence reforms: Empty promises or fulfilled expectations? *Crime and Delinquency, 41(4)*, 541–553.

Dawson, J., and P. Langan (1994). *Murder in families. (NCJ 143498). Washington, DC: U.S. Department of Justice.*

Dobash, R.E., and R.P. Dobash (1979). *Violence against wives: A case against the patriarchy*. New York: The Free Press.

———. (1978). Wives: The "appropriate" victims of marital violence. *Victimology: An International Journal, 2(3–4)*, 426–442.

Dobash, R.E., R.P. Dobash, and K. Cavanagh (1984). The contact between battered women and social and medical agencies. In J. Pahl (Ed.), *Private Violence and Public Policy* (pp. 142–165). Boston: Routledge and Kegan Paul.

Dobash, R.E., R.P., Dobash, M. Wilson, and M. Daly (1992). The myth of sexual symmetry in marital violence. *Social Problems, 39(1)*, 71–91.

Downs, D.A. (1996). *More than victims*. Chicago: University of Chicago Press.

Dubois, E. (1978). *Feminism and suffrage: The emergence of an independent women's movement in America, 1848–1869*. Ithaca, NY: Cornell University Press.

Dutton, D.G.(1998). *The abusive personality*. New York: Guilford.

Dutton, D.G. (1998). *The domestic assault of women: Psychological and criminal justice perspectives* (3rd ed.).Vancouver, British Columbia: UBC Press.

———. (1994). The origin and structure of the abusive personality. *Journal of Personality Disorders, 8(3)*, 181–191.

———. (1988). Profiling of wife assaulters: Preliminary evidence for a trimodal analysis. *Violence and Victims, 3(1)*, 5–29.

Easteal, P.W. (1993). *Killing the beloved: Homicide between adult sexual intimates*. Canberra: Australian Institute of Criminology.

Easteal, P.W., and S. Easteal (1992). Attitudes and practices of doctors toward spousal assault victims: An australian study. *Violence and Victims, 7(3)*, 217–228.

Elk, R., and C.W. Johnson (1989). Police arrest in domestic violence. *Response to the victimization of women and children, 12(4)*, 7–13.

Elliott, F.A. (1988). Neurological factors. In V.B. Van Hasselt, R.L. Morrison, A.S. Bellack, and M. Hersen (Eds.), *Handbook of family violence* (pp. 359–382). New York: Plenum.

Ewing, P. (1987). *Battered women who kill: Psychological self-defense as legal justification*. Lexington, MA: D.C. Heath.

Fagan, J. (1989). Cessation of family violence: Deterrence and dissuasion. In L. Ohlin and Michael Tonry (Eds.), *Family violence: An annual review of research*, vol. 11 (pp. 377–425). Chicago: University of Chicago Press.

Fagan, J.A., D.K. Stewart, and K.V. Hansen (1983). Violent men or violent husbands? Background factors and situational correlates. In D. Finkelhor, R.J. Gelles, G.T. Hotaling, and M.A. Straus (Eds.), *The dark side of families* (pp. 49–68). Beverly Hills, CA: Sage.

Federal Bureau of Investigation (1998). Uniform crime reports: Crime in the U.S. 1997. Washington D.C.: Federal Bureau of Investigation.

———. (1993). Uniform crime reports: Crime in the U.S. 1992. Washington D.C.: Federal Bureau of Investigation.

Feld, S.L. and M.A. Straus (1989). Escalation and desistance from wife assault in marriage. *Criminology, 27(1)*, 141–161.

Felder, R., and B. Victor (1996). *Getting away with murder: Weapons for the war against domestic violence*. New York: Simon & Schuster.

Frieze, I.H., and A. Browne (1989). Violence in marriage. In L. Ohlin and M. Tonry (Eds.), *Family violence: An annual review of research*, vol. 11 (pp. 163–218). Chicago: University of Chicago Press.

Gage, M.J. (1891). *Woman, church, and state* (Reprinted 1981). Watertown, MA: Persephone Press.

Gelles, R., and M. Straus (1988). *Intimate violence*. New York: Simon & Schuster.

Gillespie, C. (1989). *Justifiable homicide: Battered women, self-defense, and the law*. Columbus, OH: Ohio State University Press.

Goetting, A. (1988). Patterns of homicide among women. *Journal of Interpersonal Violence, 3*, 3–20.

Gondolf, E.W. (1988). Who are those guys? Toward a behavioral typology of batterers. *Violence and Victims, 3(3)*, 187–203.

Gordon, L. (1989). *Heroes of their own lives: The politics and history of family violence*. New York: Penguin Books.

Gosselin, D.K. (2000). *Heavy hands: An introduction to the crimes of domestic violence*. Upper Saddle River, NJ: Prentice Hall.

Gottman, J.M., N.S. Jacobson, R.H. Rushe, J.W. Shortt, J. Babcock, J.J. Taillade, and J. Waltz (1995). The relationship between heart rate reactivity, emotionally aggressive behavior, and general violence in batterers. *Journal of Family Psychology, 9(3)*, 227–248.

Hamberger, L.K., and J.E. Hastings (1986). Personality correlate of men who abuse their partners: A cross-validation study. *Journal of Family Violence, 1(4)*, 323–341.

Harper, I.H. (1898). *The life and work of Susan B. Anthony*, vol. 1. Indianapolis, IN: Hollenbeck Publishers.

Harrell, A., and B.E. Smith (1998). Effects of restraining orders on domestic violence victims. *Legal interventions in family violence: Research findings and policy implications* (NCJ 171666). Washington, DC: U.S Department of Justice.

———. (1996). Effects of restraining orders on domestic violence victims. In E.S. Buzawa and C.G. Buzawa (Eds.), *Do arrests and restraining orders work?* (pp. 214–242). Thousand Oaks, CA: Sage.

Hart, B. (1996). Battered women and the criminal justice system. In E.S. Buzawa and C.G. Buzawa (Eds.), *Do arrests and restraining orders work?* (pp. 98–114). Thousand Oaks, CA: Sage.

———. (1992). *State codes on domestic violence: Analysis, commentary, and recommendations.* Reno, NV: National Council of Juvenile and Family Court Judges.

———. (1991). *Testimony on the family violence prevention and services act.* Reauthorizing Hearing, July 1991.

———. (1988). Beyond the duty to warn: A therapist's duty to protect battered women and children. In K. Yllo and M. Bograd (Eds.), *Feminist perspectives on wife abuse* (pp. 234–48). Newbury Park, CA: Sage.

Heimer, K., and R.L. Matsueda (1994). Role-taking, role commitment, and delinquency: A theory of differential social control. *American Sociological Review, 59*, 365–390.

Hendricks, J.E., and J.B. McKean (1995). *Crisis intervention: Contemporary issues for on-site interveners* (2nd ed.). Springfield, IL: Charles C. Thomas.

Holtzworth-Monroe, A. (1992). Social skill deficits in maritally violent men: Interpreting the data using a social information processing model. *Clinical Psychology Review, 12*, 605–617.

Holtzworth-Munroe, A., and G.L. Stuart (1994). Typologies of male batterers: Three subtypes and the differences among them. *Psychological Bulletin, 116(3)*, 476–497.

hooks, b. (1984). *Feminist theory: From margin to center.* Boston: South End Press.

Hotaling, G.T., and D.B. Sugarman (1986). An analysis of risk markers in husband to wife violence: The current state of knowledge. *Violence and Victims, 1(2)*, 101–124.

Jasinski, J.L. (1996). *Structural inequalities, family and cultural factors, and spousal violence among Anglo and Hispanic Americans.* Unpublished doctoral dissertation. Durham: University of New Hampshire, Durham.

Jasinski, J.L., and L.M. Williams (1998). *Partner violence: A comprehensive review of 20 years of research.* Thousand Oaks, CA: Sage.

Johnson, M.P. (1995). Patriarchal terrorism and common couple violence: Two forms of violence against women. *Journal of Marriage and the Family, 57(May 1995)*, 283–294.

Jones, A. (1980). *Women who kill.* New York: Holt, Rinehart, and Winston.

Jurik, N.C., and R. Winn (1990). Gender and homicide: A comparison of men and women who kill. *Violence and Victims, 5(4)*, 227–242.

Kahn, A.S. (1984). The power war: Male response to power loss under equality. *Psychology of Women Quarterly, 6*, 234–247.

Katz, J. (1988). *Seductions of crime: Moral and sensual attractions in doing evil.* New York: Basic Books.

Kaufman-Kantor, G., and J. Jasinski (1998). Dynamics and risk factors in partner violence. In J.L. Jasinski and L.M. Williams (Eds.), *Partner violence: A comprehensive review of 20 years of research* (pp. 1–43). Thousand Oaks, CA: Sage.

Kaufman-Kantor, G., and J. Jasinski, and E. Aldarondo (1994). Sociocultural status and incidence of marital violence in Hispanic families. *Violence and Victims, 9(3),* 207–222.

Kaufman-Kantor, G., and M.A. Straus (1989). Substance abuse as a precipitant of wife abuse victimization. *American Journal of Drug and Alcohol Abuse, 15,* 173–189.

Keilitz, S., P. Hannaford, and H.S. Efkeman (1998). The effectiveness of civil protection orders. In *Legal interventions in family violence: Research findings and policy implications* (pp. 47–49, NCJ 171666). Washington, DC: U.S. Department of Justice.

Kellermann, A., F. Rivara, N. Rushforth, J. Banton, D. Reay, J. Franciso, A. Locci, J. Prodzinski, B. Hackman, and G. Somes (1993). Gun ownership as a risk factor for homicide in the home. *New England Journal of Medicine, 329(15),* 1084–1091.

Klein, A.R. (1996). Re-abuse in a population of court-restrained male batterers: Why restraining orders don't work. In E.S. Buzawa and C.G. Buzawa (Eds.), *Do arrests and restraining orders work?* (pp. 192–213). Thousand Oaks, CA: Sage.

———. (1993). Spousal/partner assault: A protocol for the sentencing and supervision of offenders. In *Domestic violence: The challenge for law enforcement.* Quincy, MA: Commonwealth of Massachusetts.

Kurz, D., and E. Stark (1988). Not-so-benign neglect: The medical response to battering. In K. Yllo and M. Bograd (Eds.), *Feminist perspectives on wife abuse* (pp. 249–266). Newbury Park, CA: Sage.

Lefkowitz, M.R., and M.B. Fant (1992). *Women's life in Greece and Rome: A source book in translation.* www.uky.edu/ArtsSciences/Classics/wlgr/wlgr-copyright.html.1998.

Lester, D. (1992). *Why people kill themselves.* Springfield, IL: Charles C. Thomas.

Luckenbill, D.F. (1977). Criminal homicide as a situated transaction. *Social Problems, 25,* 176–186.

Mahoney, M. (1991). Legal images of battered women: Redefining the issue of separation. *Michigan Law Review, 90(1),* 1–94.

Martin, D. (1976). *Battered wives.* New York: Praeger.

Marzuk, P.M., K. Tardiff, and C.S. Hirsch (1992). The epidemiology of murder-suicide. *Journal of the American Medical Association, 267(23),* 3179–3183.

Masters, R.E.L. (1964). Misogyny and sexual conflict. In Robert E. L. Masters and Eduard Lea (Eds.), *The anti-sex: The belief in the natural inferiority of women: Studies in male frustration and sexual conflict* (pp. 3–52). New York: Julian Press.

Mercy, J.A., and L.E. Saltzman (1989). Fatal violence among spouses in the United States, 1976–1985. *American Journal of Public Health*, 79(5), 595–599.

Ogle, R.S., and A. Garner (2000). Managing scarce criminal justice and social resources: Adjusting the role of resolution resources in the era of illegality in domestic partner abuse. A paper presented at the American Society of Criminology annual meeting, November 2000.

Ogle, R.S., and S. Jacobs (1998). Battered women who kill: A sociological perspective on the battering process and the use of self-defense. A paper presented at the annual Law and Society Conference in St. Louis, MO., June 1998.

Ogle, R.S., D. Maier-Katkin, and T.J. Bernard (1995). A theory of homicidal behavior among women. *Criminology*, 33(2), 173–193.

O'Leary, K.D. (1988). Physical aggression between spouses: A social learning theory perspective. In V.B. Van Hasselt, R.L. Morrison, A.S. Bellack, and M. Hersen (Eds.), *Handbook of family violence* (pp. 31–56). New York: Plenum.

Pagelow, M.D. (1984). *Family violence*. New York: Praeger Publishers.

Piven, F.F., and R.A. Cloward (1979). Hidden protests: The channeling of female innovation and resistance. *Signs: Journal of Women in Culture and Society*, 4, 461–487.

Pleck, E. (1989). Criminal approaches to family violence, 1640–1980. *Family Violence*, 11, 19–57.

———. (1987). *Domestic tyranny: The making of social policy against family violence from colonial times to present*. New York: Oxford University Press.

———. (1983). Feminist responses to "crimes against women," 1868–1896. *Signs: Journal of Women in Culture and Society*, 8(3), 451–470.

Prince, J.E., and I. Arias (1994). The role of perceived control and the desirability of control among abusive and nonabusive husbands. *American Journal of Family Therapy*, 22(2), 126–134.

Pushkareva, N. (1997). In Eve Levin (Ed./Trans.), *Women in Russian history: From the tenth to the twentieth century*. Arnonk, NY: M. E. Sharpe.

Roberts, A.R. (Ed., 1996). *Helping battered women: New perspectives and remedies*. New York: Oxford University Press.

Rosenbaum, M. (1990). The role of depression in couples involved in murder-suicide and homicide. *American Journal of Psychiatry*, 147(8), 1036–1039.

Schneider, E. (1980). Equal rights to trial for women: Sex bias in the law of self-defense. *Harvard Civil Liberties-Civil Rights Law Review*, 15(3), 623–646.

Sheehy, E., J. Stubbs, and J. Tolmie (1992). Defending battered women on trial: The battered woman syndrome and its limitations. *Criminal Law Review*, 16(6), 369–394.

Sherman, L., and J. Schmidt (1993). Does arrest deter domestic violence? *American Behavioral Scientist*, 36(5), 601–609.

Smith, M.D. (1990). Sociodemographic risk factors in wife abuse: Results from a survey of Toronto women. *Canadian Journal of Sociology*, 15(1), 39–58.

Stack, S. (1997). Homicide followed by suicide: An analysis of Chicago data. *Criminology*, 35(3), 435–453.

Stanko, E.A. (1988). Fear of crime and the myth of the safe home. In K. Yllo and M. Bograd (Eds.), *Feminist perspectives on wife abuse* (pp. 75–88). Newbury Park, CA: Sage.

Stark, E. (1995). Re-presenting woman battering: From battered woman's syndrome to coercive control. *Albany Law Review*, 58, 973–1026.

———. (1993). Mandatory arrest of batterers. *American Behavioral Scientist*, 36(5), 651–680.

Stark, E., and A. Flitcraft (1996). *Women at risk: Domestic violence and women's health*. London: Sage.

Straus, Murray A., and Richard J. Gelles (1990). *Physical violence in American families: Risk factors and adaptations to violence in 8,145 families*. New Brunswick, NJ: Transaction Books Books.

Straus, M.A., and R.J. Gelles (Eds.) (1990). *Physical Violence in American Families*. New Brunswick, NJ: Transaction Books.

Straus, M.A., and R.J. Gelles (1986). Societal change and change in family violence from 1975 to 1985 as revealed by two national surveys. *Journal of Marriage and the Family*, 48 (3), 465–479.

Straus, M.A., R.J. Gelles, and S.K. Steinmetz (1980). *Behind closed doors: Violence in the American family*. Garden City, NY: Anchor Press/Doubleday.

Totman, J. (1978). *The murderess: A psychological study of criminal homicide*. San Francisco: R and E Research Associates.

Ulrich, L.T. (1991). *Good wives: Image and reality in the lives of women in northern New England, 1650–1750*. New York: Vintage Books.

Walker, L. (1989). *Terrifying love: Why battered women kill and how society responds*. New York: Harper & Row.

———. (1984). *The battered woman syndrome*. New York: Springer.

———. (1979). *The battered woman*. New York: Harper & Row.

Warnken, W.J., A. Rosenbaum, K.E. Fletcher, S.K. Hoge, and S.A. Adelman (1994). Head injured males: A population at risk for relationship aggression. *Violence and Victims*, 9(2), 153–166.

Websdale, N. (1999). *Understanding Domestic Homicide*. Boston: Northeastern University Press.

Widom, C.S. (1979). Female Offenders: Three assumptions about self-esteem, sex role identity, and feminism. *Criminal Justice and Behavior*, 6, 365–382.

Wilson, M., and M. Daly (1993). Spousal homicide risk and estrangement. *Violence and Victims*, 8(1), 3–16.

Wolfgang, M.E. (1958). *Patterns of criminal homicide*. Philadelphia, PA: University of Pennsylvania Press.

Zimring, F.E. (1989). Toward a jurisprudence of family violence. In L. Ohlin and M. Tonry (Eds.), *Family violence: An annual review of research*, vol. II (pp. 547–569). Chicago: University of Chicago Press.

Chapter 3

Battering as a Slow Homicidal Process: A Social Interaction Perspective

INTRODUCTION

When a battering relationship results in a homicide, attention is naturally focused on the final murderous encounter, but that final act is the last, not the only, homicidal encounter in a battering relationship. This chapter is designed to explain a new social interaction perspective for understanding the battering relationship as a long-term, ongoing homicidal process that is very likely to end in the death of one of the parties.

We propose that to understand the battering relationship and its escalation to homicide, we must examine the entire history and context of the relationship. Focusing only on a final homicidal encounter disadvantages the victim because it ignores the batterer's initiation of the acute violence and his escalation of the violence in order to maintain complete control of both the relationship and the victim. Thus, it unfairly portrays the context of the battering victim's survival efforts. To more fairly and completely explore that context, we seek to understand the cultural, social, structural, and situational forces, as well as the interaction process, that assist the batterer in maintaining the battering relationship and result in the escalation to homicide.

As noted in the previous chapter, we borrow concepts from three established theoretical perspectives to develop this new social interaction theory on battering. First, while accepting the potential variability in Walker's

(1979) Cycle of Battering Theory, we utilize this cyclical pattern as the macro-level framework in which to set or explain the interaction process of the battering relationship. We assume the initial existence of all three phases of this battering cycle in one form or another: (1) tension building phase; (2) acute battering phase; and (3) contrition phase. We also accept Walker's (1979, 1984) contention that the cycle is repetitive and that the phases change over time as the cycle is repeated. However, we respectfully disregard Walker's (1984) theory of Battered Woman Syndrome which attributes the actions of battered women to the psychological malady of learned helplessness.

We utilize interaction process theory to explain the internal, micro-level interplay between the parties of the battering relationship. This interaction between batterer and victim is examined as a long-term interaction containing multiple incidents over time. We use some of the concepts from the Ogle, Maier-Katkin, and Bernard (1995) Homicidal Behavior Among Women Theory to explain the context in which the interaction occurs. This context consists of the social, cultural, situational, and structural variables that affect the interaction sequences and provide the support necessary to maintain the battering interaction as well as to create the basis for escalation by the batterer.

We believe that understanding battering requires a new perspective viewing battering as an interaction process heavily influenced by social realities. The new perspective requires that we understand the battering relationship as a homicidal process rather than focusing only on the isolated final violent encounter, as self-defense has been interpreted traditionally. It requires that we define battering relationships as long-term interactions with a sociologically identifiable pattern to which the realistic, *normal* victim responds reasonably to avoid death or great bodily harm.

THE THEORY

In this section we develop a theoretical framework which supports this approach to understanding the battering relationship by providing the social context and interaction process that make it a slow homicidal process. First, we examine from a realistic perspective cultural, social, and structural issues that are significant to the existence, maintenance, and success of battering in our society. Second, we develop a new social science theory for viewing the battering cycle in its entirety as a homicidal process, including the cultural, social, and structural supports.

The battering process can be viewed as homicidal once it reaches the point when contrition disappears or changes to a form of control, and threats and violence become the primary method of control in the relationship. This framework is significantly different than the traditional self-defense approach which focuses exclusively on the last violent encounter. Battering is a process, and any single act or confrontation within the process cannot be adequately understood outside of the context of the entire process. Our position is that the entire repetitive cycle of battering can itself be understood as a homicidal process and the battering victim's actions as a reasonable response to that long-term, ongoing homicidal process.

There seems to be a misconception that battering relationships return to some semblance of *normalcy* between violent incidents. In other words, we assume that Walker's (1979) cycle of battering does not change throughout a battering relationship, that all three phases continue to exist essentially in the same pattern as when they started. Even Walker noted changes in the cycle over time, particularly the reduction and/or disappearance of the contrition phase. At the very least, this presumed return to normalcy does not necessarily exist for victims (Browne 1987; Ewing 1987; Downs 1996; Stark 1995). Once contrition disappears or changes to just another control mechanism for the batterer, and threats or violence become the primary form of control, then periods between beatings simply involve a return to tension building. These periods represent *lulls* in the potentially homicidal encounters rather than a return to normalcy. These lulls in the violence are filled with tension building created by the batterer through the use of threats, degradation, intimidation, and other abusive acts intended to relieve stress for the batterer and provide justification for the next period of extreme violence. In this process, ongoing potentially homicidal violence becomes the *primary* characteristic of the relationship rather than just *one* characteristic of the relationship.

Within this framework, the victim, in order to cope with this stress and danger, utilizes coping resources (i.e., personal resources and social resources) to protect herself and end the violence. The batterer will perceive these actions as a *loss of control* and will likely respond by increasing the frequency and intensity of the violence in order to *make his point* and regain control. If resources accessed by the victim fail to protect the victim completely and end the violence, then the batterer's power has increased and the victim's coping options have decreased such that she might reasonably perceive herself as living in an ongoing lethal encounter. If battering is understood as a homicidal process, battered women who kill should be able to present contextual evidence that explains the entire confrontational interaction providing a firm foundation for self-defensive action.

Battering Issues in Realistic Social Perspective

In order to examine the battering relationship as a social process, we have to understand some of the social, cultural, and structural elements that make this ongoing confrontation different than that traditionally recognized in self-defense law. In this section, we examine three issues inherent to the battering relationship which have an impact on the existence, maintenance, and process of the interaction: (1) the role of socialization differences; (2) the strength differential; and (3) the role of social helping resources that, if failure-prone, may unintentionally do more to maintain the battering interaction than they do to end it.

Socialization Differences

The first element of the battering relationship that has an influence on the ongoing interaction process is the role of socialization differences. Women are only rarely violent in our society because they are socialized not to be aggressive (Bernardez-Bonesatti 1978; Broidy and Agnew 1997; Campbell 1993; Dornfeld and Kruttschnitt 1992; Frost and Averill 1982; Kopper and Epperson 1991; Lerner 1980; Mirowsky and Ross 1995; Ogle et al. 1995). This is supported by the majority of homicide studies which indicate that killings by women are consistently more likely to involve provocation and instrumental action than those by men (Browne 1987; Goetting 1988; Jones 1980; Ewing 1987; Mann 1996; Wolfgang 1958). Women are, however, socialized to fear the aggression of men who are strangers and to tolerate the aggression of men they know because a certain amount of aggression is both accepted and expected from men in our society (Arnold 1995; Bottcher 1995; Broidy and Agnew 1997; Browne 1987; Campbell 1993; Dobash and Dobash 1978, 1979; Downs 1996; Frost and Averill 1982; Mahoney 1991; Messerschmidt 1993; Morris 1987; Naffine 1987; Schechter 1982; Sommers and Baskin 1993; Stanko 1988; Steffensmeier and Allan 1995; Walker 1979). Many studies indicate that women killers tend to be very traditional in their sex role and lifestyle expectations (Browne 1987; Bunch, Foley, and Urbina 1983; Daly 1992; Cernkovich and Giordano 1979; Piven and Cloward 1979; Totman 1978; Widom 1979). This is why we generally see battered women first attempt to appease the batterer by doing everything exactly as he wants it. Only later do we see some women attempt to actually physically defend themselves against the batterer's assaults. Additionally, women tend to be socialized into relational responsibility; women are taught that relationships, a happy home, and a nurturing family environment are primarily their responsibility.

The success of relationships is an important part of self-esteem for women (Bernardez-Bonesatti 1978; Beutel and Marini 1995; Broidy and Agnew 1997; Cernkovich and Giordano 1979; Chesney-Lind and Sheldon 1992; Conger, Lorenz, Elder, Simons, and Ge 1993; Gilligan 1982; Gilligan, Lyons, and Hanmer 1989; Jordon 1995; Lerner 1980; E. Miller 1986; J. Miller 1986; Morris 1987; Thoits 1982). This finding is consistent with the cultural/social message that women are responsible for the success or failure of relationships (i.e., "stand by your man") and the idea that because relationships always involve two people, women are at least half responsible for the battering (i.e., "it takes two to tango", "her nagging provoked him"). Consequently, women are unlikely to attempt proactive self-defense (as opposed to protective reactive self-defense) until they have tried to manage the problem by appeasing the batterer, verbally reasoning or diffusing the situation, reactive self-defense, and at least some social coping options. Research overwhelmingly supports the position that most battered women who kill have attempted the use of multiple social helping resources before they resort to proactive self-defense (Browne 1987; Browne and Williams 1989; Ewing 1987; Felder and Victor 1996; Stark 1995).

The Physical Size and Strength Differential

The second element of the battering relationship which has an influence on the interaction is the physical strength differential between men and women. Women, in general, are not as physically strong as men are, which is likely related to their smaller stature and lower muscle mass. Additionally, women are not socialized into the use of aggression in our society, so they have little experience and practice in its use (Bernardez-Bonesatti 1978; Broidy and Agnew 1997; Campbell 1993; Chesney-Lind and Sheldon 1992; Egerton 1988; Frost and Averill 1982; Gilligan 1982; Kopper and Epperson 1991; Lerner 1980; Ogle et al. 1995; Piven and Cloward 1979). Women tend to be more verbal and concerned with relational aspects of interaction (Bernardez-Bonesatti 1978; Broidy and Agnew 1997; Campbell 1993; Egerton 1988; Gilligan 1982; Kopper and Epperson 1991; Lerner 1980). Consequently, battered women are more likely to use their verbal communication skills to diffuse the situation and appease the batterer before they ever attempt to physically defend themselves (Bernardez-Bonesatti 1978; Broidy and Agnew 1997; Campbell 1993; Gilligan 1982; Klein 1973; Ogle et al. 1995; Stark, Spirito, Williams, and Guevremont 1989; Thoits 1982; Turner, Wheaton, and Lloyd 1995; Wethington, McLeod, and Kessler 1987). Once women try physical self-defense, they generally have firsthand experience of the strength differential and the batterer's willingness to use it to his advantage. Worse yet, they often experience an increased level of violence and injury for their efforts (Browne 1987; Copelon 1994; Dobash and Dobash 1978, 1979; Downs 1996; Ewing 1987; Gillespie 1989; Stark 1995). At this point, they have learned a valuable survival lesson about the physical strength differential; they simply do not possess the skills or the physical strength to utilize such a coping method to end the violence.

In the end, the victim has learned that if she has to participate in another one-on-one physical fight with the batterer to save herself and end the battering, she will have to utilize a weapon in order to have any reasonable chance of survival. This is a reasonable assessment of her situation, and it is unreasonable to expect a person to wait for her attacker to be ready before she acts in her own defense (Downs 1996; Ewing 1987).

Misconceptions about Social Resources

In order to understand the battering relationship, we must recognize that social coping resources may do as much to foster the battering/homicidal process as they do to eliminate it. There are two common misconceptions concerning social helping resources: (1) the misconception that social resources for battered women are plentiful and successful, and (2) the misconception that society provides ready, easy access to these resources and encourages or supports their use.

Social resources or coping mechanisms for battered women are neither particularly plentiful nor successful (Hart 1991; Schechter 1982; Senate Judiciary Committee 1992). The Senate Judiciary Committee noted in its 1992 report that there are about 1,200 known shelters in the United States serving thousands of women and children each year, although we know that between 2 and 4 million women face battering each year (Hart 1991; Schechter 1982; Senate Judiciary Committee 1992). The Senate report also notes that there are three times as many animal shelters in this country as there are battered women shelters, indicating the lower priority level given to battered women in our society (1992). Battered women's shelters are rarely adequately funded, and many of them barely survive on sporadic grants and donations (Felder and Victor 1996; Hart 1991; Schechter 1982). Generally the shelters cannot provide much more than temporary assistance (Blackman 1988; Giles-Sims 1985; Kahn 1984; Kaufman-Kantor, and Jasinski 1998). These programs often have lengthy waiting lists, especially for women with multiple children, and lack the resources to address the more diverse needs of minorities (Felder and Victor 1996; Giles-Sims 1985; Gondolf, Fisher, and McFerron 1991; Hart 1991; Rasche 1988; Schechter 1982).

When victims leave abusers, they require more than just immediate safety, although this is the first concern. They have to develop a long-term plan for remaining safe and keeping their children safe. Victims often lack work skills or a work history as a result of the battering process, and therefore they need job training, financial assistance, and time to adequately support themselves and children. The lack of income-earning skills and opportunities is hard enough to overcome with a family and a support network, but this task becomes almost insurmountable when faced alone and in hiding (Blackman 1988; Felder and Victor 1996; Giles-Sims 1985; Kahn 1984). Leaving or obtaining assistance becomes even more difficult when we consider that, according to the research in this area, over half (50% to 75%) of the women who are killed by their batterers are killed when they try to leave or have just left the battering relationship (Davis and Smith 1995; Dutton 1998; Kahn 1984; Mahoney 1991). That assistance and time are often not readily available further inhibits or blocks successful use of this coping option and, in essence, unintentionally supports the maintenance of the battering process by the batterer.

Contacting the police for arrest of the batterer may create some temporary safety. However, many women find themselves facing the batterer again after he has become even angrier because of the arrest (Browne 1987; Copelon 1994; Downs 1996; Felder and Victor 1996; Stark 1995). The only recourse in this situation is a protection order which only works if enforced and, if violated, only involves a misdemeanor charge in most jurisdictions. This is of little help to a victim facing a life-and-death situation (Browne 1987; Downs 1996; Ewing 1987; Felder and Victor 1996; Gillespie 1989; Kahn 1984; Klein 1996; Mahoney 1991; Stark 1995). Additionally, some jurisdictions do mutual arrests so that the victim, in order to get help, must accept an arrest record which can later be used against her if she has to defend herself in a homicide case, or if she ends up in a custody battle for her children (Browne 1987; Felder and Victor 1996; Klein 1996; Mahoney 1991; Stark 1995). The system often appears to be "programmed to fail the victim" (Felder and Victor 1996, p. 44).

The second misconception is that society provides ready access and support for the use of social resources. Batterers are aware that there may be social and criminal justice consequences to battering. Thus, it is an essential part of the successful batterer's efforts to prevent obvious evidence of battering outside the privacy of the home (Browne 1987; Cardarelli 1996; Kahn 1984; Ptacek 1988; Sonkin, Martin, and Walker 1985; Stark 1995).

Society in general unintentionally but tacitly supports these efforts by the batterer (Downs 1996; Felder and Victor 1996; Grossman 1985; Novello 1992; Stark 1995). Neighbors, out of fear of retaliation or privacy violation, do not always call the police when they hear a disturbance. Families still sometimes encourage women to return to the relationship and do what is necessary to work it out and avoid the failure and shame that public knowledge of the battering might bring (Downs 1996; Ewing 1987; Felder and Victor 1996; Grossman 1985; Novello 1992). Clergy and counselors, failing to comprehend the danger involved, still sometimes minimize battering and encourage reconciliation for the sanctity of the family (Downs 1996; Felder and Victor 1996; Grossman 1985; Novello 1992). Even though the surgeon general of the United States and Congress have declared battering to be the number one health risk for women, medical personnel continue to avoid dealing with it by not pursuing unrealistic injury explanations, and not questioning the victim in a safe environment away from the batterer (Browne 1987; Copelon 1994; Felder and Victor 1996; Sheehy, Stubbs, and Tolmie 1992). Batterers are then able to monitor the information exchanged between the victim and the doctor and ensure that the victim's treatments are done at a variety of facilities where the medical history is unknown and falsified causes will more readily be accepted. In fact, medical organizations and personnel currently refuse to support standardized and/or mandatory reporting and recording procedures for battering cases, because there are no adequate social referral resources to follow up on such efforts which makes doing so a waste of the doctor's time (Felder and Victor 1996; Kurz and Stark 1988). Certainly, a few contacts with social or criminal justice resources that fail to help should be enough to convince any intelligent and reasonable victim that she really is isolated and on her own.

Beyond these issues are even more disturbing problems that unintentionally support non-reporting or avoidance of social resources by victims. Insurance companies reserve the right to cancel health and life insurance on women and children living in battering situations because of the high risk of injury or death (Kansas Insurance Department 1995). Unlike the criminal justice system and society in general, the insurance industry recognizes and adjusts for this highly lethal setting. Battering, if it is reported, can be used by social service agencies as the basis for terminating custody of children even if the victim is struggling to end the battering (Downs 1996; Felder and Victor 1996; Mahoney 1991). It is important to note that efforts to utilize inadequate resources in the past are likely to have resulted in increased violence, control regained by the batterer, and a lesson for the victim on the batterer's power and her isolation. These things all provide further stress for the victim and assist the batterer in his efforts to block coping options. Given the existence of these kinds of problems with resource adequacy and utilization, and the fact that the criminal justice system often requires substantial documentation of the battering before the victim can really get relief (Browne 1987; Campbell 1992; Elk and Johnson 1989; Ewing 1987; Stark 1995; The Police Foundation 1977), there seems to be significant reason for victims to feel all alone and resigned themselves to self-help. Consequently, when victims finally do defend themselves, the law provides the "final beating" by requiring *substantial evidence* of battering which the batterer has fought hard to prevent all along, with society's unintentional support.

The Battering Cycle as a Slow Homicidal Process

Historically, our efforts to understand battering have rested on two misconceptions. First, there is the misconception that battering is an infrequent phenomenon in our society. We now know that this is incorrect. Much of the battering research indicates that, at the very least, one out of every four women will experience battering in her lifetime (Bureau of Justice Statistics 1993, 1998). Battering is common in our society, and this knowledge lends credence to the feminist argument that battering is less about psychological pathology of a few people and more about sexual inequity and a society whose relationship model is based on male domination and female subordination.

Second, there is the misconception that battering is primarily about abuse and control, not killing, even though killing may occur occasionally. This assumption is untenable because the reality is that battering does result in many killings each year. About 500 to 600 batterers are killed each year by their victims and between 2,000 and 4,000 battering victims are killed each year by their abusers (FBI 1993). In other words, battering is often a homicidal process regardless of the batterer's initial intentions. More disturbing yet, in the cases where batterers kill victims, about 50% to 75% involve what experts call *separation attacks* (Bachman 1994; Browne 1987; Copelon 1994; Felder and Victor 1996; Gillespie 1989; Kahn 1984; Klein 1996; Mahoney 1991), when the victim is trying to leave or has just left the batterer. Another large proportion of killings occurs at the climax of a battering incident or when the victim attempts to utilize other social resources to end the battering (Bachman 1994; Browne 1987; Copelon 1994; Downs 1996; Felder and Victor 1996; Kahn 1984; Klein 1996; Mahoney 1991). In essence, the victim's chances of being killed increase significantly each time she attempts to do what we socially expect and require her to do to end the battering: leave or utilize social resources that often fail to accommodate the lethality of her situation. In light of these realities, we offer a different approach to understanding the imminence of threat, lethality, and reasonableness of battering victim response in these relationships.

In a typical self-defense scenario, we are accustomed to thinking of homicide as a single incident resulting in death. This single incident generally involves two physically equal combatants, with relatively superficial knowledge of each other, in a short-term confrontation in which both parties see a foreseeable end. This is because laws were created by men to serve the interests of men. Sometimes referred to as the *barroom brawl* scenario, self-defense law was intended to give men the right to protect themselves lethally if necessary in a fight. Battering, however, is a long-term, ongoing confrontation between parties who are not physical equals, wherein the parties have intimate knowledge of each other, and with no foreseeable end to the interaction. In fact, battering has most often been described as a repetitive cycle punctuated by intermittent periods of extreme violence (Angel 1996; Browne 1987; Browning and Dutton 1986; Blackman 1986; Douglas 1991; Downs 1996; Ewing 1987; Finkel 1991; Frieze and Browne 1989; Stark 1995; Steinmetz 1977; Walker 1979). However, in the battering cycle, what occurs between these intermittent periods of violence does not represent a return to so-called *normalcy* but rather the beginning of tension development, degradation, and other abuse leading to the next incident of extreme violence (Browne 1987; Browning and Dutton 1986; Campbell 1992; Douglas 1991; Downs 1996; Ewing 1987; Frieze and Browne 1989; Kahn 1984; Prince and Arias 1994). To deny the existence of this ongoing violent interaction process in battering relationships is to ignore the social reality in which battering victims function and make decisions.

This contextual or *social framework* is essential to understanding the battering relationship as an ongoing homicidal interaction (where, after contrition disappears or changes, violence is not just *one* characteristic of the relationship as an interaction but rather is the *primary* characteristic of the relationship). Violence becomes the defining characteristic in the relationship because it is the basis for all interactions and the foundation upon which the two participants respond to each other. This perspective would allow a more realistic examination of the battering victim's perception of danger and imminence, as well as the victim's chosen response to this knowledge.

Walker (1979) identifies a battering cycle consisting of three phases: tension building, acute violence, and contrition. Tension building involves the steady creation of degradation, intimidation, anxiety, and arousal through the use of threats, sexual abuse, minor violence, and verbal abuse. The second phase is the acute battering incident in which the batterer escalates the level of violence to one of extreme physical danger in order to punctuate the seriousness of the threats to the victim and enhance fear and compliance. The third phase is called contrition because the batterer, not having complete control yet, must use references to trust, love, caring, and commitment as methods to squelch the victim's inclination to leave. Walker (1979) notes that this appears to be a repetitive cycle and an escalating process, where contrition eventually disappears or changes and the victim is left to cope with tension building and acute violence. In essence, Walker may have been describing a homicidal process even though she never identifies it as such.

Walker (1979) never explains why the contrition phase disappears from the cycle, only that it progressively decreases and may even cease to exist and that the cycle appears to be self-perpetuating in that this interaction process is unlikely to end without intervention. It becomes the interaction style or process of that relationship. We believe that our theory explains why contrition disappears or at least changes into a tool of control to create unpredictability for the victim, and how violence becomes the *primary* characteristic or interaction style in the battering relationship. In essence, our theory establishes how we can explain and understand battering as an interaction process similar to that utilized in sociology and criminal justice today (e.g., see Katz 1988; Luckenbill 1977; Birkbeck and LaFree 1993; discussed in Chapter 2).

Battering can be viewed initially (in its earliest stages) as a type of discrimination, where the intention of the batterer is to exert power and control over the target to the extent that retaliation and escape are not viable options (Ogle et al. 1995). The batterer does this through the use of threats, intimidation, violence, and the blockage of the victim's goal-directed activities and coping resources or options (Ogle et al. 1995). However, battering is different than discrimination in its later stages, because after contrition disappears or changes, and violence becomes the primary method of controlling the victim, the situation is constantly potentially homicidal. As noted in Chapter 2, sociology and criminal justice researchers have moved toward an interaction analysis of violence in general (Katz 1988; Luckenbill 1977; Birkbeck and LaFree 1993). Such an examination lends itself comfortably to the concept and progression of battering, at least to understanding the type of battering that Johnson (1995) has called patriarchal terrorism. He believes that patriarchal terrorism is the type of battering most likely to fit Walker's (1979) battering cycle and the type represented in cases that end up in courts, hospitals, and crisis centers. These are the cases we are most concerned with, because they are not dependent on a single stressful situation but rather persist based on a cultural/social acceptance and practice of male privilege. Consequently, these are the cases more likely *not* to end when a particularly stressful situation ends, but rather to be ongoing throughout the relationship and more likely to escalate over time, creating a consistently homicidal interaction in which the victim must cope to survive. To really understand this progression, we must examine it as a complete, ongoing interaction in its entirety, as we would any social interaction between individuals.

Putting It All Together in a Theoretical Framework

Battering creates negative affect (i.e., fear, anger, etc.) for the victim and high chronic arousal for both parties which is periodically relieved for the batterer through the use of violence against the victim. But, never relieved for the victim, it simply continues to build (Allport 1954; Browne 1987; Browning and Dutton 1986; Campbell 1992; Douglas 1991; Downs 1996; Ewing 1987; Frieze and Browne 1989; Kahn 1984; Ogle et al. 1995; Stark 1995). Consequently, the victim exists in a constant high state of arousal and negative affect, walking on eggshells as she witnesses the tension building and violence, and fearing homicidal progression.

When *normal* people face negative affect and chronic arousal, they utilize their coping mechanisms to end it or manage it (Agnew 1992; Ogle et al. 1995). Since women are socialized against the use of aggression and into the maintenance of relationships, they are likely to begin by trying to manage the situation by using their personal coping mechanisms to appease the batterer, keep him calm, and ease their fear and injuries. For example, the victim may attempt to do everything the batterer wishes, not do anything to "rock the boat," and not consult anyone outside of family or clergy for support or reassurance. Finally, as things progress and this approach does not work to stop the violence, she may even try to reactively, physically defend herself (e.g., she is likely thinking that the batterer loves her and will not go so far as to actually seriously injure her or that the violence has already escalated to the point that she must find a way to periodically protect herself). When she tries to physically defend herself, the batterer will interpret this as defiance and a direct threat to his power and control. He will now see that contrition (i.e., love, concern, promises of no further violence, etc.) is not working to restore his power and control because the victim does not seem to believe it anymore and is now seeking her own defense or assistance for defense. In reaction, it would be natural for the batterer—since his goal is complete and absolute control—to interpret her actions as defiance or resistance. The batterer would then naturally respond to reduce or discontinue the use of contrition, increase the threats and abuse of tension building, and increase the frequency and intensity of violence to *make his point* and regain control. Additionally, the batterer will likely act during tension building to block the victim's personal coping resources so that they are not a threat to him again (i.e., forbid calls to family, friends, or clergy; require the victim to sell her vehicle so her mobility is reduced; or require the victim to quit her job so a coping source is eliminated; etc.).

After the victim finds her personal coping resources either blocked by the batterer or exhausted, and realizes she cannot successfully physically defend herself, she will have made a reasonable conclusion that she cannot *manage* the violence and will need outside social resources to help her *end* the violence. Studies do indicate that most battered women have attempted to utilize a variety of social coping resources to end the violence before they resort to proactive self-help (Browne 1987; Coker 1992; Downs 1996; Ewing 1987; Felder and Victor 1996; Ptacek 1988; Roberts 1996; Sonkin et al. 1985; Walker 1989). Additionally, some studies indicate that killings by battered women decrease when social resources actually accommodate the lethality of these situations and successfully end the violence (Browne and Williams 1989).

When the victim attempts to utilize outside social resources, she takes a greater risk because the risk becomes greater for the batterer. The batterer will perceive these efforts by the victim as an even greater threat to his power and control. Social resources are a greater threat to the batterer because they include the potential for public exposure of the battering, which may have social and criminal justice system consequences. This often results in escalation of the level of violence by the batterer as he responds to reduce the threat of being caught. This is particularly dangerous if the chosen social resources fail to fully accommodate the lethality of the victim's situation and fail to completely end the violence. Again, the batterer will see these survival efforts by the victim as his *loss of control and power*, or even as her retaliation or escape attempts, which he seeks to make too costly. He will respond by attempting to block the use of those outside coping resources and regain control by upping the ante which involves increasing the victim's punishment for the effort. This response is likely to involve the complete end of the contrition phase if it still exists at all, a decrease in the length of the tension building phase, an increase in the frequency and intensity of violence, and efforts to completely block the victim's use of any social resource (i.e., threatening to kill pets, children, or others if she contacts the police or shelter again; refusing to allow her medical treatment unless he is present; restrict her contact with the children unless he is present; cutting off access to money and important papers that would be needed to leave and reestablish her life; etc.).

The contrition phase will have disappeared from the cycle or will simply be used by the batterer as a source of tension and unpredictability for the victim, as noted by Walker (1979). Because the victim no longer believes the contrition, it is not useful to the batterer to prevent the victim from leaving, and abuse and violence will now be the primary methods utilized. At this point, the relationship consists of shorter periods of threats, abuse, and degradation (tension building) punctuated by more frequent and intense violence (acute battering) in order to regain and maintain complete power and control. This situation is constantly potentially homicidal. At this point, there are no *nonconfrontational* periods in the relationship; it is one ongoing homicidal confrontation (See Figure 2). The victim is constantly experiencing high levels of negative affect (i.e., fear, anger, etc.) and high chronic arousal which the batterer seeks to maintain because it serves his purposes (e.g., the next beating could be right around the corner if she is not completely compliant and only he can change that). It would be reasonable for the victim to perceive herself in constant danger of death or serious bodily injury with fewer and fewer coping options available to her.

With each passing progression of the cycle, the chance of desistance by the batterer becomes less likely because success in regaining and maintaining power and control is self-reinforcing (Fagan 1989; Renzetti 1992). The

Figure 2
The Homicidal Escalation of the Battering Cycle

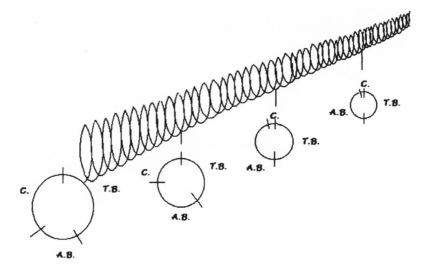

T.B. = Tension Building Phase; A.B. = Acute Battering Phase; C. = Contrition Phase
Illustration created by Whitney L. Shockley and Christian A. Nolasco.

cost to the batterer for losing control or allowing public discovery becomes greater because the level of violence he is now using is greater, increasing the action that can be taken against him. Even in their (1990) study on desistance, Feld and Straus note that their high percentage of voluntary desistance may be caused by the fact that some cases refused to participate in the second phase of the study which examined desistance. Those were likely cases where the violence was more frequent and intense, making desistance less likely.

This problem in the data is further noted by Fagan (1989), Johnson (1995), Giles-Sims (1985), Adams, Jackson, and Lauby (1988), and others who have examined this problem. It may also be, as noted by Johnson (1995), that these cases examined by family violence researchers in national survey samples may involve a type of common couple violence which is limited primarily to stressful situations, where the battering partner's goal is control of the situation rather than complete control of the other partner and the relationship. But in the sociocultural research, which relies on court, hospital, and shelter samples, the frequency and intensity of violence are much higher, the violence is not related to a particular stressful situation, and desistance is almost nonexistent. These are the cases that Johnson (1995) refers to as patriarchal terrorism rather than common couple violence. However, we must keep in mind that there is no research indicating a clear distinction between these two groups or refuting the argument that common couple violence left unchecked might eventually escalate into patriarchal terrorism.

From the victim's perspective, the lethality of the situation continues to increase with each cycle. Her chances for successfully ending the violence look remote, especially if she has attempted the use of social resources as coping mechanisms and witnessed their failure and the aftermath. She is seeing the batterer's increasing power and control (seeming invulnerability) as the social resources fail to end the violence and he regains control.

This is not to say that the victim does not experience trauma as a result of this interaction process. However, it is not unreasonable to expect that trauma and reasonableness can coexist for the battering victim (Downs 1996; Maguigan 1998). It would be perfectly reasonable for the victim to view this progression as lethal. The victim will perceive a change in the cycle where contrition has disappeared or changed (because she no longer believes it, therefore it is no longer useful to the batterer), the tension building phase has become shorter, and acute battering violence is more frequent and intense as the batterer struggles to maintain power and control in response to the victim's coping efforts. This is a consistently lethal progression where the failure of coping efforts (whether blocked by the batterer or simply socially inadequate) would likely lead a reasonable victim to perceive herself to be in an ongoing "kill or be killed" interaction where she will have to resort to proactive self-defense in order to survive. However, having witnessed the physical strength differential firsthand, she should also be aware that a weapon will be necessary to actually protect herself and ensure an end to the violence.

CONCLUSION

This theory presents an interaction perspective of the battering relationship which includes the influence of social, cultural, structural, and situational variables in the interaction process. We seek to understand how patriarchal terrorism battering relationships operate and how they escalate into homicidal interaction. One aspect of this is to accept the current thinking. Then we can understand battering as patriarchal terrorism which is intended to net the batterer complete control of the female partner and the relationship, rather than isolated aggression over a particular stressful situation seen in common couple violence.

The second issue involves the need to study and understand battering relationships as ongoing, long-term interactions. This is to say that a homicide occurring in such a long-term interaction process cannot be understood as an isolated violent incident. It must be examined as only one part of an extensive interaction involving multiple incidents, any of which could have ended in homicide of one of the parties, particularly of the victim as the climax of a battering incident. This perspective then requires that we examine battering relationships that end in homicide with particular attention to the context of this ongoing interaction and how that process changes over time creating escalation, isolation of the victim, and the need for lethal self-defense.

This new theoretical framework posits that battering is *initially* a form of discrimination where the batterer seeks to control the victim and make retaliation or escape too costly. However, over time this effort moves from moderate control, using threats and minor violence and then contrition, to a need for complete and absolute control of the relationship and the victim. Such complete control is unlikely to be accomplished with threats, intimidation, and contrition when the victim no longer believes in those. At that point, the battering cycle changes from three phases to two phases; tension building becomes shorter and acute violence more frequent and intense. The victim will recognize this change and begin to utilize her personal coping resources to end the increasing violence. The batterer will interpret these efforts by the victim as a *loss of complete control* and will again increase the violence to *make his point* and regain control. We should also see efforts by the batterer to block coping resources of the victim so that they cannot threaten his control again.

Eventually, the victim will realize she needs outside assistance in order to end the violence and protect herself. She will then contact social helping resources (e.g., police, shelter, crisis center, counselor, doctor, etc.) to obtain assistance for ending the violence. This involvement of outside resources increases the risk for the victim because it increases the risk to the batterer. The chances of being identified and sanctioned for the battering have increased. If those social helping resources fail to completely and successfully end the violence, the victim faces increased violence and isolation. The batterer will interpret these efforts by the victim as an even greater risk to his complete control, prompting an even more aggressive response to shut off access to those social helping resources and to regain control of the victim and the relationship. This represents an escalation process where the victim becomes increasingly isolated in the escalating violence and the batterer more powerful each time an effort is made to end the battering and fails.

This perspective represents an interaction process whereby the victim's efforts to obtain assistance to end the violence result in an escalation of the violence by the batterer and efforts to block coping mechanisms so that they do not threaten his control again. In this escalation process, there are no *nonconfrontational periods* for the victim. There is no return to normal relations; threats, intimidation, and violence become the primary method of control and the primary characteristic of interaction in the relationship. The victim lives in constant fear with high negative affect, high arousal, simply waiting for the next explosion of violence. The victim would reasonably come to view her situation as constantly lethal. Consequently, the choice of lethal self-defense anywhere in this cycle could be interpreted as legally justified.

REFERENCES

Adams, D., J. Jackson, and M. Lauby (1988). Family violence research: Aid or obstacle to the battered women's movement. *Response*, *11*, 14–16.

Agnew, R. (1992). Foundation for a general strain theory of crime and delinquency. *Criminology 30*, 47–87.

Allport, G.W. (1954). *The nature of prejudice*. Reading, MA: Addison-Wesley.

Angel, M. (1996). Criminal law and women: Giving the abused woman who kills "a jury of her peers" who appreciate trifles. *American Criminal Law Review*, *33(3)*, 229–348.

Arnold, Regina A. (1995). Process of victimization and criminalization of black women. In B.R. Price and N.J. Sokoloff (Eds.), *The criminal justice system and women: Offenders, victims, and workers*, 2nd ed. (pp. 136–146). New York: McGraw-Hill.

Bachman, R. (1994). Bureau of Justice, *Violence against women report*. Washington, D.C.: Bureau of Justice Statistics.

Bernardez-Bonesatti, T. (1978). Women and anger: Conflicts with aggression in contemporary women. *Journal of American Medical Women's Association, 33*, 215–219.

Beutel, A.M., and M.M. Marini (1995). Gender and values. *American Sociological Review, 60*, 436–448.

Birkbeck, C., and G. L. LaFree (1993). The situational analysis of crime and deviance. *Annual Review of Sociology, 19*, 113–137.

Blackman, J. (1988). Exploring the impacts of poverty on battered women who kill their abusers. A paper presented at the American Psychological Association meeting in Atlanta, Georgia.

———. (1986). Potential uses for expert testimony: Ideas toward the representation of battered women who kill. *Women's Rights Law Reporter, 9(3–4)*, 227–238.

Bottcher, J. (1995). Gender as social control: A qualitative study of incarcerated youths and their siblings in greater Sacramento. *Justice Quarterly, 12*, 33–57.

Broidy, L., and R. Agnew (1997). Gender and crime: A general strain theory perspective. *Journal of Research in Crime and Delinquency 34(3)*, 275–306.

Browne, A. (1987). *When battered women kill*. New York: The Free Press.

Browne, A., and K.R. Williams (1989). Exploring the effect of resource availability and the likelihood of female perpetrated homicides. *Law & Society Review, 23(1)*, 75–94.

Browning, J., and D. Dutton (1986). Assessment of wife assault with the conflict tactics scale: Using couple data to quantify the differential reporting effect. *Journal of Marriage and the Family, 48(2)*, 375–379.

Bunch, B.J., L.A. Foley, and S.P. Urbina (1983). The psychology of violent female offenders: A sex-role perspective. *The Prison Journal 63*, 66–79.

Bureau of Justice Statistics (1998). Violence by intimates: Analysis of data on crimes by current or former spouses, boyfriends, and girlfriends. (NCJ 167237).

———. (1993). Family violence: Interventions for the justice system. Washington, DC: U.S Department of Justice.

Campbell, A. (1993). *Men, women, and aggression*. New York: Basic Books.

Campbell, J.C. (1992). If I can't have you, no one can: Power and control in homicide of female partners. In J. Radford & D.E.H. Russell (Eds.), *Femicide: The politics of woman killing* (pp. 99–113). New York: Twayne Publishers.

Cardarelli, A.P. (1996). *Violence between intimate partners: Patterns, causes, and effects.* Needham Heights, MA: Allyn & Bacon.

Cernkovich, S.A., and P.C. Giordano (1979). Delinquency, opportunity, and gender. *Journal of Criminal Law and Criminology, 70,* 145–151.

Chesney-Lind, M., and R.G. Sheldon (1992). *Girls, delinquency, and juvenile justice.* Pacific Grove, CA: Brooks/Cole.

Coker, D.K. (1992). Heat of passion and wife killing: Men who batter/ men who kill. *Review of Law and Women's Studies 2,* 71–89.

Conger, R.D., F.O. Lorenz, G.H. Elder, Jr., R.L. Simons, and X. Ge (1993). Husband and wife differences in response to undesirable life events. *Journal of Health and Social Behavior, 34,* 71–88.

Copelon, R. (1994). Recognizing the egregious in the everyday: Domestic violence as torture. *Columbia Human Rights Law Review, 25(2),* 291–367.

Daly, K. (1992). Women's pathways to felony court: Feminist theories of lawbreaking and problems of representation. *Review of Law and Women's Studies, 2,* 11–52.

Dobash, R.E., and R.P. Dobash (1979). *Violence against wives: A case against the patriarchy.* New York: The Free Press.

———. (1978). Wives: The "appropriate" victims of marital violence. *Victimology, 2,* 426–439.

Dornfeld, M., and C. Kruttschnitt (1992). Do the stereotypes fit? Mapping offender-specific outcomes and risk factors. *Criminology, 30,* 397–419.

Douglas, H. (1991). Assessing violent couples. *Families in Society, 72,* 525–535.

Downs, D.A. (1996). *More than victims.* Chicago: University of Chicago Press.

Egerton, M. (1988). Passionate women and passionate men: Sex differences in accounting for angry weeping episodes. *British Journal of Social Psychology, 2,* 51–66.

Elk, R., and C.W. Johnson (1989). Police arrest in domestic violence. *Response to the victimization of women and children, 12(4),* 7–13.

Ewing, P. (1987). *Battered women who kill: Psychological self-defense as legal justification.* Lexington, MA: D.C. Heath.

Fagan, J. (1989). Cessation of family violence: Deterrence and dissuasion. In L. Ohlin and M. Tonry (Eds.), pp. 377–425, *Family violence: An annual review of research,* vol. II (pp. 377–425). Chicago: University of Chicago Press.

Federal Bureau of Investigation (1993). *Uniform crime reports: Crime in the U.S. 1992.* Washington, D.C.: Federal Bureau of Investigation.

Feld, S.L., and M.A. Straus (1990). Escalation and desistance from wife assault in marriage. *Criminology, 27(1),* 141–161.

Felder, R., and B. Victor (1996). *Getting away with murder: Weapons for the war against domestic violence.* New York: Simon and Schuster.

Finkel, N. (1991). The self-defense defense and community standards. *Law and Human Behavior, 15,* 585–603.

Frieze, I.H. and A. Browne (1989). Violence in marriage. In L. Ohlin and M. Tonry (Eds.), *Family violence: An annual review of research*, vol. II (pp. 163–218). Chicago: University of Chicago Press.

Frost, W.D., and J.R. Averill (1982). Differences between men and women in the everyday experience of anger. In J.R. Averill (Ed.), *Anger and aggression* (pp. 281–315). New York: Springer-Verlag.

Giles-Sims, J. (1985). A longitudinal study of battered children of battered wives. *Family Relations 34(April)*, 205–210.

Gillespie, C. (1989). *Justifiable homicide: Battered women, self-defense, and the law*. Columbus, OH: Ohio State University Press.

Gilligan, C. (1982). *In a different voice*. Cambridge, MA: Harvard University Press.

Gilligan, C., N.T. Lyons, and T.J. Hanmer (1989). *Making connections*. Troy, NY: Emma Willard School.

Goetting, A. (1988). Patterns of homicide among women. *Journal of Interpersonal Violence, 3*, 3–20.

Gondolf, E.W., E. Fisher, and J.R. McFerron (1991). Racial differences among shelter residents: A comparison of Anglo, Black, and Hispanic battered women. In R.L. Hampton (Ed.), *Black family violence* (pp. 103–113). Lexington, MA: Lexington Books.

Grossman, J. (1985). *Domestic violence and incarcerated women: Survey results*. New York: New York State Department of Correctional Services.

Hart, B. (1991). *Testimony on the family violence prevention and services act*. Reauthorizing Hearing, July 1991.

Johnson, M.P. (1995). Patriarchal terrorism and common couple violence: Two forms of violence against women. *Journal of Marriage and the Family, 57(May 1995)*, 283–294.

Jones, A. (1980). *Women who kill*. New York: Holt, Rinehart, and Winston.

Jordon, J.V. (1995). A relational approach to psychotherapy. *Women and Therapy, 16*, 51–61.

Kahn, A.S. (1984). The power war: Male responses to power loss underequality. *Psychology of Women Quarterly, 6*, 234–247.

Kansas Insurance Department (1995). *Insurance companies underwriting practice as it relates to victims of domestic violence: A survey of life, accident, and health insurers*. Topeka, KS: Kansas Insurance Department.

Katz, J. (1988). *Seductions of crime: Moral and sensual attractions in doing evil*. New York: Basic Books.

Kaufman-Kantor, G., and J. Jasinski (1998). Dynamics and risk factors in partner violence. In J.L. Jasinski and L.M. Williams (Eds.), *Partner violence: A comprehensive review of 20 years of research* (pp. 1–43). Thousand Oaks, CA: Sage.

Klein, A.R. (1996). Re-abuse in a population of court-restrained male batterers: Why restraining orders don't work. In E.S. Buzawa and C.G. Buzawa

(Eds.), *Do arrests and restraining orders work?* (pp. 192–213). Thousand Oaks, CA: Sage.

Klein, D. (1973). The etiology of female crime: A review of the literature. *Issues in Criminology 8*, 3–30.

Kopper, B.A., and D.L. Epperson (1991). Women and anger. *Psychology of Women Quarterly 15*, 7–14.

Kurz, D., and E. Stark (1988). Not-so-benign neglect: The medical response to battering. In K. Yllo and M. Bograd (Eds.), *Feminist perspectives on wife abuse* (pp. 249–266). Newbury Park, CA: Sage.

Lerner, H.G. (1980). Internal prohibitions against female anger. *The American Journal of Psychoanalysis 40*, 137–147.

Luckenbill, D. F. (1977). Criminal homicide as a situated transaction. *Social Problems, 25*, 176–186.

Maguigan, H. (1998). It's time to move beyond battered woman syndrome [Review of the book]. *More than victims: Battered women, the syndrome society, and the law]. Criminal Justice Ethics, 17(1, winter/spring)*, 50–57.

Mahoney, M. (1991). Legal images of battered women: Redefining the issue of separation. *Michigan Law Review, 90(1)*, 1–94.

Mann, C.R. (1996). *When women kill*. Albany, NY: State University of New York Press.

Messerschmidt, J.W. (1993). *Masculinities and crime*. Lanham, MD: Rowman & Littlefield.

Miller, E.M. (1986). *Street woman*. Philadelphia: Temple University Press.

Miller, J.B. (1986). *Toward a new psychology of women*. Boston: Beacon.

Mirowsky, J., and C.E. Ross (1995). Sex differences in distress: Real or artifact? *American Sociological Review, 60*, 449–468.

Morris, A. (1987). *Women, crime, and criminal justice*. Oxford, England: Basil Blackwell.

Naffine, N. (1987). *Female crime: The construction of women in criminology*. Sydney: Allen & Unwin.

Novello, A.C. (1992). From the surgeon general, U.S. public health service, A medical response to domestic violence. *Journal of the American Medical Association 267(23, June 17)*, 3132.

Ogle, R.S., D. Maier-Katkin, and T.J. Bernard (1995). A theory of homicidal behavior among women. *Criminology, 33(2)*, 173–193.

Piven, F.F., and R.A. Cloward (1979). Hidden protests: The channeling of female innovation and resistance. *Signs: Journal of Women in Culture and Society, 4*, 461–487.

The Police Foundation (1977). *Domestic violence and the police studies in Detroit and Kansas City*. Washington DC: National Institute of Justice.

Prince, J.E., and I. Arias (1994). The role of perceived control and the desirability of control among abusive and nonabusive husbands. *American Journal of Family Therapy, 22(2)*, 126–134.

Ptacek, J. (1988). Why do men batter their wives? In Yllo, K. and M. Bograd (Eds.), *Feminist perspectives on wife abuse* (pp. 133–157). Newbury Park, CA: Sage.

Rasche, C.E. (1988). Minority women and domestic violence: The unique dilemmas of battered women of color. *Journal of Contemporary Criminal Justice, 4*, 150–171.

Renzetti, C. M. (1992). *Violent betrayal: Partner abuse in lesbian relationships.* Newbury Park, CA: Sage.

Roberts, A.R. (1996). Introduction. In A.R. Roberts (Ed. 1996), *Helping battered women: New perspectives and remedies.* New York: Oxford University Press.

Schechter, S. (1982). *Women and male violence.* Boston: South End Press.

Senate Judiciary Committee (1992). *Violence against women: A week in the life of America.* 102nd Congress, 2d sess. S. Rept. 118, 26.

Sheehy, E., J. Stubbs, and J. Tolmie (1992). Defending battered women on trial: The battered woman syndrome and its limitations. *Criminal Law Review, 16*(6), 369–394.

Sommers, I., and D.R. Baskin (1993). The situational context of violent female offending. *Journal of Research in Crime and Delinquency, 30*, 136–162.

Sonkin, D.J., D. Martin, and L. Walker (1985). *The male batterer: A treatment approach.* New York: Springer.

Stanko, E.A. (1988). Fear of crime and the myth of the safe home. In K. Yllo and M. Bograd (Eds.), *Feminist perspectives on wife abuse* (pp. 75–88). Newbury Park, CA: Sage.

Stark, E. (1995). Re-presenting woman battering: From battered woman's syndrome to coercive control. *Albany Law Review, 58*, 973–1026.

Stark, L.J, A. Spirito, C.A. Williams, and D.C. Guevremont (1989). Common problems and coping strategies: Findings with normal adolescents. *Journal of Abnormal Child Psychology, 17*, 203–221.

Steffensmeier, D., and E. Allan (1995). Criminal behavior: Gender and age. In J.F. Sheley (Ed.), *Criminology: A contemporary handbook* (pp. 83–113). Belmont, CA: Wadsworth.

Steinmetz, S.K. (1977). *The cycle of violence: Assertive, aggressive, and abusive family interaction.* New York: Praeger.

Thoits, P.A. (1982). Life stress, social support, and psychological vulnerability: Epidemiological considerations. *Journal of Community Psychology, 10*, 341–362.

Totman, J. (1978). *The murderess: A psychological study of criminal homicide.* San Francisco: R and E Research Associates.

Turner, R.J., B. Wheaton, and D.A. Lloyd (1995). The epidemiology of social stress. *American Sociological Review, 60*, 104–125.

Walker, L. (1989). *Terrifying love: Why battered woman kill and how society responds.* New York: HarperCollins.

———. (1984). *The battered woman syndrome.* New York: Springer.

————. (1979). *The battered woman*. New York: Harper & Row.

Wethington, D., J.D. McLeod, and R.C. Kessler (1987). The importance of life events for explaining sex differences in psychological distress. In R.C. Barnett, L. Biener, and G.K. Baruch (Eds.), *Gender and stress* (pp. 144–158). New York: Free Press.

Widom, C.S. (1979). Female offenders: Three assumptions about self-esteem, sex role identity, and feminism. *Criminal Justice and Behavior, 6*, 365–382.

Wolfgang, M.E. (1958). *Patterns of criminal homicide*. Philadelphia, PA: University of Pennsylvania Press.

Chapter 4

The Law of Self-Defense and the Battered Woman

In this chapter, we explore the law of self-defense. As an initial matter, it is good to be reminded that there is not a single "law of self-defense." Each state recognizes the defense, but our federalist system allows each to define and understand it differently. Given the variety, indeed the discrepancy, of understandings, it is difficult to draw meaningful generalizations. Therefore, we have chosen to organize these materials by broad substantive topics, discussing the general nature of self-defense and then illustrating and critiquing, where appropriate, some of its dominant variations. We have chosen this approach because it makes little sense to suggest that counsel in any given case will set out to use that case to change the law; counsel is required to represent her client within the bounds of the law and to work with the law as it is in the jurisdiction. Virtually no lawyer would ignore the law of the jurisdiction in favor of sacrificing the client toward the end of modifying some legal standard. At most, if defense of the client fails, an appellate court may be persuaded to modify legal understandings. But for the most part, real change in the law comes from the legislature and those changes are slow to be realized.

In these materials, then, we take the law as it is and find that, in some important respects, it is evolving fairly well; that is, some important concepts defining self-defense are becoming more broadly understood, hence the defense is not as narrowly available as it once was. Beyond that, we discover that changes in the rules of evidence governing the admission of expert and lay evidence may well operate to favor increased admissibility of testimony about battering relationships, an evolution that will surely favor battered women who are criminally charged with murder of their batterers. Having said that, however, the reality of these cases is, very simply, that they are hard to win. Self-defense may be a complete defense, capable of providing acquittal to a defendant, but it rarely operates in that complete fashion in battered women cases. And it is especially unsuccessful in nonconfrontational cases, in which the battered woman kills her batterer during a lull in the violence. So, while the law may be moving in directions that favor the application of this defense in battered women cases, there are still some cases out there that just make us stand up and take notice and wonder if we can't find more persuasive ways to explain to judges and juries just what these battering relationships, that finally dissolve to the point of death, are like. We begin with a summary of two of these cases, one a confrontational case and the other a nonconfrontational case, that illustrate some of the important concepts we examine in this chapter on self-defense.

The confrontational case is *Commonwealth v. Stonehouse* (Pa. 1989). This case presents a factual horror story, exacerbated by police who did not assist, prosecutorial arguments that exploited common myths about battering, and ineffective defense counsel. Carol Stonehouse killed William Welsh after a series of events that the appellate court characterized as "bizarre" but believable because they were corroborated by disinterested witnesses and not unlike those in other battered women cases. The facts set out here are severely cut and are organized topically.

Stonehouse and Welsh were both police officers. They met in 1980, just after Stonehouse had completed her cadet training; when they met, Welsh was married and Stonehouse was twice divorced. They began dating shortly after they met.

The evidence of battering and abuse. The appellate court devoted a full five and one-half pages to recitation of the facts in this case, in detail almost unheard of in reported cases. Without meaning to discredit the significance of the history of abusive behavior, we offer only a paragraph or two here.

Welsh was "possessive and demanding." He put sugar in the gas tank and would let the air out of the tires on the defendant's car when she did not do as she had been told, as often as two or three times a week according to the evidence. One time after an argument, Welsh was able to enter the defendant's secured apartment building and put flowers inside her apartment; he admitted that, and told her they were for her funeral. He kicked in the doors to her apartment and, on other occasions, he broke into her apartment when she was absent (even after she had changed the locks) and took things, threw food around, cut up her clothing, urinated on her bed, soaked her shoes in water and her clothes in beet juice. On one occasion he broke in when she was at home and dumped a bucket of ice water on her in the middle of the night. He threw a brick through the window of her apartment. He parked outside her apartment building for long periods. He left notes for her at work, in her car, at the spa, and he began following her. He tapped her telephone, physically removed her from a friend's home, ran her car off the road, beat her head against the inside of her car, and spit on her.

Reports to the police were ineffective. The evidence showed that within three months after their relationship began, Welsh had broken into the defendant's home and made such a nuisance of himself that the defendant had called the police. Her call was treated as a "domestic" by the officers who knew Welsh, and no police report was filed. When the defendant returned home to discover the premises vandalized, she did not call the police because she did not think she could prove who had been responsible; but later that night Welsh returned and, when he refused to leave, she did call for assistance. The police knew Welsh and they did not make a report; instead, they insisted that the defendant serve as her own arresting officer. So the defendant wrote the report, approached Internal Affairs with the problem, all with no result. She filed a formal complaint with a magistrate regarding this incident. Welsh was ordered to stay away from the defendant for 30 days, after helping to clean her apartment, and he was ordered to replace her clothes and drapes and repay the money he had taken.

The next encounter with the police came after Welsh dragged the defendant out of the car in the parking lot of a shopping center, attempted to run over her, broke her nose, and rendered her semiconscious. The defendant recalled seeing flashing lights at the scene, but no arrest was made of Welsh at that time. In the fall of 1981, the defendant called the police after Welsh broke into her apartment during the night. Police officers found the apartment door splintered from a forced entry; as they were questioning the defendant about the incident, Welsh called to say he would break the windshield of her car, which he proceeded to do while police were still on the scene. Welsh was arrested, but the defendant did not press charges after police reminded her that she was not living in the city limits. In May 1982, the defendant moved into the city and testified that she did so in order to be able to report Welsh's acts of harassment to the police. Neighbors testified to acts of harassment at the new residence; one neighbor testified that, although the police were notified, an officer told her it was just a "domestic matter." In July 1982, Welsh stole the defendant's car and she filed a report with the police; the car was later found in front of her apartment, scratched but operable. In September 1982, the defendant filed harassment charges against Welsh and, at the hearing, testified that he broke her apartment doors, followed her, and appeared uninvited at social events. Welsh admitted to the harassment and to breaking the defendant's nose. He was ordered to stay away from her for 60 days.

During that period, when the defendant dated another man, Welsh threatened the man's estranged wife and threatened the defendant's date with a gun. At the next hearing on the restraining order, in November 1982, the charges were dismissed because the court found Welsh had not been harassing the defendant. In December 1982, the defendant fled to a friend's home to escape Welsh, but he found her there and forced his way into the home, assaulted the defendant, and spat on her. The defendant's friend called the police who were not going to file a report until the friend insisted on it.

In February 1983, Welsh telephoned the defendant and threatened to throw acid in her face. Distraught, she went to his residence to tell him to stop, to tell him she could not take it any more; he laughed and she ran out of the residence without her coat and keys. They struggled on the steps, and then he sat in his van while she tried in vain to get in to recover her keys and coat. "Because she was freezing, [defendant] broke the door glass to get her coat and purse. Welsh called the police, who filed a report over the incident" (*Commonwealth v. Stonehouse*, p. 779).

The killing. On the night she killed Welsh, the defendant was at home with a friend when Welsh began kicking at her front and back doors. Because she believed he could kick in the back door, she went to the door holding a gun at her side, and let him in. They struggled for the gun; Welsh got it, but the defendant and her friend were able to retrieve it from Welsh. Welsh immediately left and threw a brick through the window of the defendant's car. She called the police. As they waited for the police to arrive, her friend left. The back door was still open, and the defendant was standing at the kitchen sink when Welsh suddenly appeared in the kitchen. He pointed a .357 Magnum revolver within six inches of the defendant's face. He told her she was going to die and, as she begged him not to kill her, she tried to get the gun. A struggle ensued in the kitchen and the bedroom. The defendant was able to locate her gun, and Welsh disappeared.

[Defendant] knew Welsh would return because he always returned, so she stepped out onto the back porch to look for him, not wanting to be caught with her guard down. As she leaned over the railing, [defendant] saw Welsh on the ground below aiming his gun at her. Believing that she heard a shot, [defendant] fired her gun twice. One of the bullets entered Welsh at the top of his right shoulder and exited near his clavicle, severing a major artery. At the time of his death, Welsh's blood alcohol level was .14. (*Commonwealth v. Stonehouse*, p. 780)

The defendant was charged with criminal homicide, convicted of third-degree homicide, and sentenced to seven to fourteen years imprisonment. She appealed, based on ineffective assistance of counsel.

The instructions to the jury. At trial the jurors were given a self-defense instruction that directed them to find the defendant guilty only if they were satisfied beyond a reasonable doubt that she did not reasonably believe that the use of deadly force was necessary to protect herself against death or serious bodily injury. They were further instructed that if they found she was not reasonable in her belief that deadly force was necessary to protect her from death or serious bodily injury, they could find her guilty. If they found that she believed it was necessary to use deadly force to protect herself, but that her belief was unreasonable, they could find her guilty of voluntary manslaughter.

The prosecutor's arguments. The prosecutor attempted to show that the defendant deliberately provoked Welsh's attacks by talking with and dating other men. He exploited the myth that battered women are masochists who find pleasure in their abuse, asking the defendant on cross-examination if she was "a willing participant in the activities that went on between [her] and William Welsh" and, during his final argument, when he stressed that if the defendant had truly been an "innocent victim," she could have put an end to the relationship. According to the appellate court, the prosecutor took advantage of the myths that battered women are uneducated with few skills and that police can protect them, when he introduced evidence detailing the police training the defendant had received, "implying that her training made her incapable of being victimized by a batterer." He then argued to the jury that she could have been rescued, if she had really wanted to be rescued, by a law enforcement system that was ready, willing, and able to protect women who are victims of domestic violence.

The inactivity of defense counsel. The defendant was represented by retained counsel at trial and by the public defender's office on appeal when the issue of ineffective assistance of counsel was raised. The claim was based, in part, on the fact that trial counsel never requested jury instructions that would require the jury to consider the abuse suffered by the defendant as an element in their determination of the reasonableness of her beliefs and actions. The appellate court found failure to request such an instruction to be clearly erroneous. Beyond that, trial counsel did not request an instruction, available under Pennsylvania law, telling the jury that reasonable provocation (that would reduce murder to manslaughter) could be found in a series of related events; provocation would not have to be found, entirely, in the events immediately surrounding the killing. That, too, was found to be error. Finally, defendant complained that trial counsel was deficient in failing to present expert testimony regarding battering. That, too, was error.

On appeal, Stonehouse's conviction was reversed and the case was remanded for a new trial. Two judges dissented, contending that the issue of battering was not properly before the court, hence trial counsel's failure to pursue it should not have been considered.

The second case we offer for initial consideration was a nonconfrontational case, *People v. Aris* (Cal. 1989), in which the jury was never allowed to consider whether the defendant killed her sleeping husband in self-defense. The case raises issues surrounding the meaning of "imminent" harm and the difference between a perfect and an imperfect defense, illustrates an instance in which the trial court's refusal to allow expert testimony on battering is declared to be "harmless error," and shows a court's somewhat cavalier attention to options a battered woman may have for safety.

In this case, the defendant was convicted of second-degree murder of her husband for which she was sentenced to 15 years to life, and that conviction was affirmed on appeal. At trial, Mrs. Aris testified that her husband had beaten her severely and often during their ten-year marriage and that she had left him on many occasions, always returning after he convinced her to take him back. Her testimony of abuse was corroborated by numerous witnesses. The appellate court summarized the evidence of the shooting:

On the night of the killing, defendant testified that her husband beat her and threatened that "he didn't think he was going to let me live till the morning. She believed he was "very serious." She waited about ten minutes to make sure he was asleep, then went next door to get some ice to ease the pain of the blows to her face. She found a handgun on the top of the refrigerator and took it "for protection." She testified she thought she needed it for protection because "I felt when I got back . . . he'd probably be awake and he would start hitting me again." Walking back to her residence she was thinking, "that I was tired of it. I'd had it." She denied intending to kill her husband at that time. When she returned to the bedroom, "I then sat down on the bed and I felt that I had to do it. It would be worse when he woke up." She testified that she had to do it "because I felt when he woke up that he was then going to hurt me very badly or even kill me."

Defendant then shot her husband five times in the back while he was asleep in the bed on his side. The victim died of the gunshot wounds. (*People v. Aris*, p. 171)

The difference between a "perfect" and an "imperfect" self-defense. Perfect self-defense requires both subjective honesty on the part of the defendant and objective reasonableness. That is, it requires the defendant to actually and honestly believe that deadly force is necessary for her protection. Beyond that, it requires a finding that her belief was objectively reasonable. If both the subjective and objective elements are present, the accused may be completely exonerated. If, however, only the subjective element is present if the defendant actually believes she needs to use deadly force to protect herself, and if that belief is unreasonable under the circumstances, then we have imperfect self-defense, and homicide is reduced to manslaughter. In this case, the defendant contended that she presented facts that qualified as perfect self-defense.

The meaning of "imminence." California law required a showing for perfect self-defense that the defendant actually and reasonably believed the danger was "imminent," and the jury was so instructed. Throughout deliberations, however, the jury requested clarification of the term "imminent." After several inquiries from the jury, and after consultation with counsel (and over objection by defense counsel), the court offered this clarifying instruction to the jury:

"Imminent peril," as used in these instructions, means that the peril must have existed or appeared to the defendant to have existed at the very time the fatal shot was fired. In other words, the peril must appear to the defendant as immediate and present and not prospective or even in the near future. An imminent peril is one that, from appearances, must be instantly dealt with. (*People v. Aris*, p. 172)

Defense counsel objected because the words "imminent" and "immediate" were used interchangeably. The appellate court found no flaw in the definition given, especially in light of the fact that the court had given another instruction, requested by the defendant, allowing the jury to consider past incidents of threatening or assaulting behavior in determining her state of mind and her perception of danger on the night of the killing.

The objective standard in determining reasonableness. The question in this case was not the reasonableness of the defendant's mental processes. The question was what a hypothetical reasonable person would have done. That determination is for the jury alone.

Failure to allow expert testimony was only harmless error. The trial court allowed testimony about Battered Woman Syndrome in general, but refused to allow the expert to testify that the defendant was, in fact, a battered woman. Neither was the expert allowed to explain how the psychological impact of being a battered woman affected the defendant's perception of danger. In this case, in which the victim was sleeping at the time he was shot, the court decided it really did not matter much that the expert was not allowed to testify that the defendant honestly perceived imminent danger. As the court explained it:

Shooting a sleeping potential attacker is very close to killing an actual attacker after having rendered the attacker incapable of continuing the assault. . . . In this case also the danger did not exist at the time of the assault, although it probably would in the future. No matter what the expert testimony, it is not reasonably probable that a jury would find defendant actually believed she was in imminent danger. (*People v. Aris*, p. 181)

Options available for battered woman's safety. Self-defense is only designed to be used defensively, never as an offensive weapon. Beyond that, if there are other means of protection available, the law directs us to use those rather than choosing to defend with deadly force. In this case, Mrs. Aris contended she was justified because her belief in the threat of deadly harm was both honestly held and reasonable. The trial and appellate courts disagreed:

The law of self-defense, whether perfect or imperfect, does not provide an alternative means of resolving the battered woman's problem. For resolution of that problem, a battered woman must look to other means provided by her family, friends, and society in general such as restraining orders, shelters, and criminal prosecution of the batterer. While these means have proved tragically inadequate in some cases, the solution is to improve those means, not to lessen our standards of protection against the unjustified and unexcused taking of life. (*People v. Aris*, p. 174)

Each of the themes summarized in these two cases is dealt with at greater length in this chapter.

SELF-DEFENSE GENERALLY

As its history was traced by the court in *State v. Goldberg* (N.J., 1951), self-defense was established in England in 1534 and became one of those tenets of English law adopted by the colonists. It was a defense in which both parties were thought to share fault, as in a sudden brawl. Consideration of strength differential did not typically play a part in the analysis, since the defense was generally raised in cases in which two relatively equally matched men fought.

As the law of self-defense has evolved, it has become a recognition of our right to defend ourselves with lethal force when we reasonably believe we are confronted with an imminent threat, which threat we did not create and from which we cannot retreat with safety. Under those circumstances, the law is prepared to justify, as self-defense, conduct that otherwise would be considered criminal.

SELF-DEFENSE AS A JUSTIFICATION

The law offers two kinds of defenses: justifications and excuses. A defense that justifies conduct is one in which the defendant says, in essence: The state may be able to prove beyond a reasonable doubt that I did the criminal act and intended to do it; but, even so, I was justified so I should not be held criminally responsible. For example, I shot him, but I was justified in doing so because I was acting in self-defense. In other cases, criminal conduct may be justified if the defendant was acting to defend another, or to protect property from unlawful taking or damage; likewise, the defendant who chooses the lesser of two evils (even though the conduct is actually a criminal act) may be justified for acting out of necessity. In cases in which these defenses are raised, the defendant contends the "criminal" behavior was appropriate under the circumstances and should not be punished as a form of illegality, but instead, taking into account the context in which the act occurred, the defendant should be exonerated. In these cases, the law declares that the defendant was justified in committing an act that, in other circumstances, would have been a crime.

Other defenses do not justify conduct, but instead excuse it. Criminal conduct may be excused if the defendant, even having committed a criminal act and having intended to commit that act, is shown to have been insane, or to have acted under duress (the gun-to-the-head defense). In other cases, criminal conduct may be excused if the defendant was entrapped by the government, or if the criminal act was produced by involuntary intoxication. In those cases, the law recognizes that the defendant has broken the law, but has done so under circumstances or conditions for which the defendant really cannot be held personally responsible; therefore, the conduct should be excused.

The distinction between justification and excuse may not seem important. Some commentators relegate it to a mere academic distinction (Greenawalt, 1984). Some declare it academic and without practical import in a particular case, but still theoretically important and not to be ignored (*State v. Leidholm*, N. D. 1983); and others advocate abandoning it altogether (Corrado, 1991). Certainly, the distinction makes no difference to jurors who are unaware of it; in that respect, it may appear not to play any part in cases as they are actually tried and decided. But, theoretically and philosophically, the distinction is an important one. It has serious theoretical implications in battered women cases. The question it thrusts upon us—the question that makes it an important issue to consider—is this: Are we prepared to justify, hence in essence to positively sanction, homicide on the part of the battered woman who kills her batterer; or will we at most just excuse the act as one for which she should not be held responsible for murder? If we are prepared to justify lethal force used by an abused woman against her abuser, then self-defense should be seriously examined and refined to allow it to be presented and to operate as a complete defense in these cases. As our review of the cases reveals in the material that follows, self-defense often does not operate successfully in abused women cases because it is simply presented in its most traditional form. That form does not allow the use of lethal force inflicted on an abuser under the conditions in which battered women typically defend themselves.

The justification/excuse distinction has been blurred in trials of battered women because most of them have arisen in the context of Battered Woman Syndrome. Self-defense is really a justification defense, but reliance on Battered Woman Syndrome tends to present the lethal response to battering more often as an excuse, an attempt to explain why a battered woman should be excused from the legal consequences of homicide.

Since self-defense is really more than an excuse, since in its historical and theoretical development it really is a justification, any approach that leans toward only excusing the conduct often falls short of persuading the trier of fact that self-defense applies. The approach taken here, however, is one that places the homicidal act in a broader context that is more likely to illustrate that the homicide was actually committed in self-defense, and hence was justified. In this respect, our approach addresses the justification of the act in a fashion more true to the underpinnings of the defense. This theoretical approach to understanding battering as a slow homicidal process promises to advance self-defense as a viable defense for battered women, especially in nonconfrontational cases.

In one of the most insightful and thorough articles on self-defense for battered women, Schopp, Sturgis, and Sullivan (1994) outline three different kinds of cases that produce different results depending on whether self-defense is seen as a justification or as an excuse. In the first, we have a case in which the evidence shows that legal protection was available and the defendant was aware of it; nonetheless, the defendant resorted to violence rather than take advantage of that legal protection. In that case, self-defense probably would not operate successfully as a defense, nor should it. At most, if there were provocation, a murder charge would be reduced to manslaughter.

In the second instance, we have a case in which legal protection was available but the defendant was not aware of it. In this case, the defendant believed force was necessary but, in fact, it was not. If self-defense is available only when it is justified, the court in this case must inquire into whether the defendant's mistake was a reasonable one. If it was a reasonable mistake, the law will generally forgive it and self-defense could still be raised successfully. Evidence as to the availability of protection would be admissible, but Schopp et al. note that the difficulty encountered here may well be the court's greater ability to gather and weigh this evidence, relative to that of the defendant who, at the time, did not have the same chance to research and consider the information and who had to act in the immediacy of a threatening situation. Nonetheless, they correctly observe that the stronger the evidence of availability of these resources, the stronger the inference the defendant's belief in the necessity of force was not justified.

In this kind of case, in which the focus is on justifying the defendant's chosen act by showing it to have been reasonable, Battered Woman Syndrome is only a useful construct in those jurisdictions that allow psychological testimony as a foundation for reasonableness of the defendant's belief. That is, Battered Woman Syndrome is a psychological framework for understanding battering, as opposed to a sociological perspective that addresses the battering relationship. Psychological testimony goes to explaining what the battered woman perceived and why; it does not go to the reasonableness of that perception.

The learned helplessness portion of Walker's theory may be useful to help persuade the jury that the defendant's action was understandable, but "understandable" is not the same as "reasonable" under the law. If, however, self-defense is seen as an excuse, then Battered Woman Syndrome may be useful in persuading the jury that although the defendant was wrong in resorting to violence, she is not so culpable as to warrant the full punishment of the law. That is, learned helplessness (if it exists as Walker posited it) may be seen as a reason that excuses the defendant's failure to know and appreciate the legal protection that was available to her.

In the third kind of case discussed by Schopp et al. the court may not have reliable information about the options available to the defendant, perhaps because the record of police or judicial response in battering cases is just not clear. In these cases, if the promise of police or judicial protection is not clear to the court, chances are very good it would not have been clear to the battered woman at the time of the homicidal incident.

The fact that the availability of protective options is unclear may not work to the advantage of the battered woman who opted to use deadly force: The fact that she was not sure whether protection was available is not necessarily justification for assuming or believing that it was not available. Rather, the reasonable conclusion is that she did not know. That, of course, is a harsh result and one that Schopp et al. argue can be avoided by considering culpability and not just reasonableness. As they explain:

By addressing justification defenses and nonculpable mistakes regarding justification separately, the criminal law can accommodate these cases appropriately. . . .
Although these defendants lacked reliable information regarding legal alternatives, it remains true that in each case such alternatives either were available or
they were not. If they were not, the defensive force was justified by actual necessity.
If the alternatives were available but the defendant's Battered Woman Syndrome
or abuse-driven fear led them to believe that they were not, the juries would have
to determine for each defendant whether the severity of the syndrome or the abuse
was sufficient to render that defendant's mistake nonculpable rather than negligent or reckless. The former conclusion would generate exculpation under the excuse for nonculpable mistake regarding justification, and the latter would result in
liability for negligence or reckless homicide. (Schopp et al., 1994, p. 110)

Schopp et al. advocate maintaining a clear distinction between justification and excuse, arguing that the two can and should be separated by
consideration of actual necessity. This would enable the battered woman
who kills to take advantage of self-defense if legal protection was not available, but would not allow a defense to the battered woman who simply
chose not to avail herself of legal alternatives that would have provided
protection. In those difficult cases in the middle, those cases in which we
have serious questions of fact about what alternatives were known to be
available or questions about how effective they were, the defense may still
be raised.

The actual necessity standard Schopp et al. propose relies primarily on
evidence of the pattern of battering for its factual conclusions about the necessity of using lethal force at the time such force was employed. That being
the case, battered women who kill because killing was actually necessary
under the circumstances would be justified, exonerated, acquitted. Battered women who kill when they have made a mistake about the availability or viability of legal alternatives, or who kill under circumstances in
which they did not know whether viable alternatives were available to
them, may still be found less culpable than other murderers; and hence
would be excused. This would most likely encompass battered women who
kill in nonconfrontational situations. This approach, theoretically true to
the development of legal defenses generally, has the added advantage of allowing juries "to arrive at legally and morally defensible verdicts when presented with distinct claims of justification and excuse accompanied by
instructions and evidence clearly identified with each" (Fn. omitted.
Schopp et al., 1994, pp. 111–112).

To illustrate how courts have struggled with the distinction between
self-defense as a justification of conduct or simply as a means of excusing it
(and how they have wondered if it really matters), consider *State v. Leidholm*

(N.D. 1983), a case in which the defendant stabbed her sleeping husband after he fell asleep following a violent argument. Prefacing its remarks with an apologia that this discussion required it "to venture briefly into the pathway of academicism," the court observed:

A defense of justification is the product of society's determination that the actual existence of certain circumstances will operate to make proper and legal what otherwise would be criminal conduct. A defense of excuse, contrarily, does not make legal and proper conduct which ordinarily would result in criminal liability; instead, it openly recognizes the criminality of the conduct but excuses it because the actor believed that circumstances actually existed which would justify his conduct when in fact they did not. In short, had the facts been as he supposed them to be, the actor's conduct would have been justified rather than excused.

In the context of self-defense, this means that a person who believes that the force he uses is necessary to prevent imminent unlawful harm is justified in using such force if his belief is a correct belief; that is to say, if his belief corresponds with what actually is the case. If on the other hand, a person reasonably but incorrectly believes that the force he uses is necessary to protect himself against imminent harm, his use of force is excused.

The distinction is arguably superfluous because whether a person's belief is correct and his conduct justified, or whether it is merely reasonable and his conduct excused, the end result is the same, namely, the person avoids punishment for his conduct. Furthermore, because a correct belief corresponds with an actual state of affairs, it will always be a reasonable belief, but a reasonable belief will not always be a correct belief, viz., a person may reasonably believe what is not actually the case. Therefore, the decisive issue under our law of self-defense is not whether a person's beliefs are correct, but rather whether they are reasonable and thereby excused or justified. . . .

If, therefore, a person has an actual and reasonable belief that force is necessary to protect himself against danger of imminent unlawful harm, his conduct is justified or excused. If, on the other hand, a person's actual belief in the necessity of using force to prevent imminent unlawful harm is unreasonable, his conduct will not be justified or excused. Instead, he will be guilty of an offense for which negligence or recklessness suffices to establish culpability. For example, if a person recklessly believes that the use of force upon another person is necessary to protect himself against unlawful imminent serious bodily injury and the force he uses causes the death of the other person, he is guilty of manslaughter. (Citations omitted. *State v. Leidholm*, pp. 814–815)

The court here declared the distinction between justification and excuse to be an important one, but one that did not impact the outcome of the case. Instead, the court argued that jurors' attention must be carefully directed to the issue of reasonableness.

Reasonableness is one of the traditional elements of self-defense. We argue that it is the most important element in self-defense in battered women cases (although the case law shows greater preoccupation with the requirement of imminent harm, especially in nonconfrontational cases).

TRADITIONAL ELEMENTS OF SELF-DEFENSE

Self-defense is available as a complete defense, even to murder, in cases in which the defendant reasonably believes he is confronted with imminent harm, which harm he did not create and from which he cannot reasonably retreat. If the harm is serious enough to threaten serious bodily harm or death, the defendant is justified in using lethal force to avoid it; if the harm threatened is not lethal, the defensive force cannot be lethal force. If the defendant is in his home or other protected space, retreat is not required; likewise, if retreat cannot be made in safety, it is not required.

Self-defense is designed to operate as a shield, not a sword. For that reason, rules have developed historically requiring a showing that the person claiming to have employed self-defense was not acting as the aggressor but was, instead, defending against imminent attack. It is virtually indisputable that as a general rule one should not be allowed exoneration by striking out preemptively, claiming that a future attack would have occurred had it not been thwarted. But battered women cases force us to reexamine the rules that have grown up to support the principle that self-defense is only defensive in that strict temporal sense.

We begin our analysis of the defense with a statement of each element of the general rule; we then proceed to critical examination of each element as it operates, and as we believe it should operate in battered women cases.

Reasonableness

Self-defense requires a reasonable perception of impending harm.

By What Standard Do We Measure Reasonableness?

The literature on self-defense distinguishes between an objective standard and a subjective standard to evaluate the reasonableness of behavior. Although it is difficult to find examples of either standard in its "pure" form, it is probably fair to say that courts know what this distinction means and their decisions in self-defense cases are designed to fall toward one end of the continuum or the other. An objective standard is the "reasonable man" standard. (In these more enlightened and politically correct days, one might be inclined to say "reasonable person" standard. But the law typically does not and, in battered women cases especially, that bit of tradition is mightily important.) The reasonable man standard is one in which we compare the defendant's behavior to the behavior we would expect of a "reasonable man." If the two are compatible, we deem the defendant's behavior reasonable; if they are not, we declare the defendant's behavior unreasonable. In the case of self-defense, a finding that the defendant did not behave reasonably would mean we would not consider the defense further, because self-defense requires that the defendant reasonably believed he was faced with imminent harm requiring defensive action.

A subjective standard is one in which we query whether the defendant, in fact, believed what he says he believed. In the case of self-defense, if we used a subjective test, we would be asking whether the defendant, in fact, believed he was faced with imminent harm. Although there is relatively little case law employing this test (the objective test being much more widely used), it is the standard that was reflected in the English common law and the American states initially adopted it as well. Indeed, it is the standard reflected in the Model Penal Code's 1958 formulation of self-defense. (Model Penal Code § 3.04[1]. See Model Penal Code § 3.04, Comment [Tent. Draft No. 8, 1958]). Later drafts of the Code moved toward a more central and less subjective position, but still reflected the drafters' concern with the possible unfair results that may be obtained by rigid application of an objective standard (Model Penal Code, Official Draft, 1962). Of course, utilizing an entirely subjective standard invites a different problem and one the criminal law is anxious to avoid: It would allow self-defense to be claimed on the defendant's word alone. If the finder of fact believed the defendant (i.e., if the jury believed the defendant was telling the truth, irrespective of how wrong or unreasonable the defendant's belief was), self-defense could be claimed and the behavior that would otherwise be punishable as a crime would be justified; the defendant would go free.

Given that, it is not surprising that as the American law of self-defense developed, it moved toward an objective standard. Recently, however, there is some trend toward blending the tests, toward allowing greater particularization (Singer 1987), a jurisprudential shift that promises to be enormously useful in cases in which we scrutinize the reasonableness of a battered woman's assessment of imminent danger.

Because the test employed by the court will determine the kinds of evidence admissible to support proof relevant to it, it is useful to examine some cases to understand just how each of these tests operates. Beyond that, the case law illustrates how the law is changing in ways that allow battered women more latitude in presenting the facts of their cases.

The Objective Test

The objective test measures behavior against that expected of a reason-able man. It is designed to measure everyone by the same standard, argu-ably toward the end of fairness. Perhaps the most notorious, recent case illustrating the objective standard is *People v. Goetz* (N.Y. 1986). Bernard Goetz was the man on the New York subway who shot four young men after one of them approached him and said, "give me $5." Goetz said he feared they would hurt him, so he shot in self-defense. The case went to a grand jury that was instructed that self-defense applies if a person "reasonably be-lieves" he is faced with imminent danger. Applying that objective stan-dard, the grand jury indicted Goetz. When the case went to trial after that grand jury indictment, the trial court dismissed, holding that it was error to use an objective standard. The trial court concluded that whether self-de-fense requires deadly force is an entirely subjective matter. That decision was appealed, and the appellate division agreed that the subjective test is correct, basing its decision on statutory language that referred to whether "[the defendant] reasonably believes"; the court decided that meant the in-quiry should focus on whether the decision to use deadly force is "reason-able to [the defendant]." That decision was further appealed to the New York Court of Appeals. At that point, the last stopping point for the Goetz case, the court determined that the proper test in self-defense cases is the objective one. Bernard Goetz's behavior should be evaluated relative to what a "reasonable man" would have done.

Goetz had argued, as many battered women argue, that the objective test will preclude a jury from considering factors such as the defendant's prior experiences, and thus require the jury to make a determination of rea-sonableness without regard to the actual circumstances of a particular inci-dent. The court declared, however, that Goetz misunderstood the objective standard:

[W]e have frequently noted that a determination of reasonableness must be based on the "circumstances" facing a defendant or his "situation" . . . Such terms encom-pass more than the physical movements of the potential assailant. . . . [T]hese terms include any relevant knowledge the defendant had about that person. They also necessarily bring in the physical attributes of all persons involved, including the defendant. Furthermore, the defendant's circumstances encompass any prior experiences he had which could provide a reasonable basis for a belief that another person's intentions were to injure or rob him or that the use of deadly force was nec-essary under the circumstances. . . . The jury must first determine whether the de-fendant . . . believed deadly force was necessary to avert the imminent use of deadly force. . . . [T]hen the jury must also consider whether these beliefs were reasonable.

The jury would have to determine, in light of all the "circumstances" . . . if a reasonable person could have had these beliefs. (*People v. Goetz,* p. 506, N.Y.S.2d 29)

In the context of battered women cases, the objective test is illustrated by *State v. Stewart* (Kan. 1988), a case in which a wife killed her abusive husband. The Stewart marriage presented a long history of mental and physical abuse. Mr. Stewart had beat his wife, kicking her in the chest and ribs so violently that she had to be hospitalized; he had killed her pet and then held a gun to her head and threatened to kill her. At one point, she institutionalized herself because she had become suicidal, but her husband retrieved her from the hospital. After he brought her home, he forced her to perform oral sex several times and threatened to kill her if she ever ran away again. She found a loaded gun and testified that she was afraid of what he would do with it, so she hid it under the mattress of a bed in a spare room. Later that morning, as she was cleaning the house, her husband told her that she should not bother because she would not be there long. After forcing her to have oral sex again, he went to sleep. The court noted that, at that time, there were two vehicles in the driveway and that the defendant had access to the car keys. While her husband slept, Mrs. Stewart retrieved the gun from under the mattress and killed him.

The trial court allowed testimony detailing the abusive history of the marriage and the appellate court approved that as a means of helping the trier of fact determine whether the defendant's perception of danger was reasonable. But the appellate court criticized the self-defense instruction the trial court gave because it was not sufficiently objective. The jury had been instructed:

A person is justified in the use of force against an aggressor when and to the extent it appears to him and he reasonably believes that such conduct is necessary to defend himself or another against such aggressor's imminent use of unlawful force. Such justification requires both a belief on the part of the defendant and the existence of facts that would persuade a reasonable person to that belief. You must determine, from the viewpoint of the defendant's mental state, whether the defendant's belief in the need to defend herself was reasonable in light of her subjective impressions and the facts and circumstances known to her. (*State v. Stewart,* p. 579)

Declaring Kansas to be a state in which the reasonableness of a belief that self-defense is necessary will be measured by an objective standard, the Kansas Supreme Court explained: "Our test for self-defense is a two-pronged one. We first use a subjective standard to determine whether the defendant sincerely and honestly believed it necessary to kill in order to defend. We then use an objective standard to determine whether defendant's belief was reasonable—specifically, whether a reasonable person in defendant's circumstances would have perceived self-defense as necessary."

The language chosen by the court in this particular passage could lead one to argue that the court has not set out an entirely objective test here, but has blended the standards by suggesting that we should be comparing the defendant's conclusion to that reached by a reasonable person who had suffered the history of abuse and who had suffered abuse on the day of the killing that the defendant had suffered. But in *Stewart*, the Kansas Supreme Court did not send the case back for a new trial with a different self-defense instruction. Instead, it declared that in a nonconfrontational case such as this, self-defense could never be found:

> [T]he giving of the self-defense instruction was erroneous. Under such circumstances, *a battered woman cannot reasonably fear imminent life-threatening danger from her sleeping spouse....* We must ... hold that *when a battered woman kills her sleeping spouse when there is no imminent danger, the killing is not reasonably necessary and a self-defense instruction may not be given. To hold otherwise in this case would in effect allow the execution of the abuser for past or future acts and conduct.* (*State v. Stewart*, pp. 578–579, emphasis supplied)

A few years later, in another battered woman homicide case in Kansas, a jury had trouble knowing just what the standard was for determining whether the defendant's belief was reasonable. During its deliberations, the jury sent this question out to the judge: "Does this mean (1) that a reasonable person, in the same situation, would choose the same, or (2) that a reasonable person would believe that she believed that was her only option?" (*State v. Cramer* [Kan.Ct.App. 1993]). After conferring with counsel for the prosecution and defense, the trial court responded to the jury's question by quoting that portion of the *Stewart* opinion set out above that explains the two-pronged test, subjective then objective.

On appeal the defense argued that the jury should have been advised that the objective test is one in which the jury considers whether "a reasonably prudent battered woman would have perceived self-defense as necessary." The appellate court rejected this argument:

> [O]ur reading of the Supreme Court decisions concerning battered women reveals no requirement that a jury be advised that it must employ an objective test based on how a "reasonably prudent battered woman" would react to a threat. Indeed, to employ such language would modify the law of self-defense to be more generous to one suffering from the battered woman's syndrome [*sic*] than to any other defendant relying on self-defense. (*State v. Cramer*, p. 1118)

The Subjective Test

In deciding whether the defendant acted reasonably in delivering a fatal blow, other courts have elected to focus on the circumstances as the defendant perceived them. An example is *Smith v. State* (Ga. 1997), a case in which the defendant had the advantage of a state statute designed specifically for battered spouse cases. The Georgia legislature amended the self-defense statute to provide that if a defendant raises a defense of justification (self-defense), the defendant may offer evidence that the defendant had been the victim of acts of family violence or child abuse committed by the deceased.

The defendant wife testified that her husband had beaten her repeatedly during their 18-month marriage, that he had frequently held a gun to her head and threatened to kill her and abscond with their child, that on one occasion he had choked her until she lost consciousness. On another occasion, he had wrapped a lamp cord around her neck and had stopped only when her brother rescued her. The evidence showed that she had called the police on a dozen occasions and had left her husband twice because of the abuse, but each time he was remorseful and promised to reform and she returned. In addition to the wife's testimony of abuse, several other witnesses testified about his abusive conduct toward her and to the beatings and threats he inflicted on the defendant.

On the day of the shooting, Mr. Smith became enraged because he had observed his wife out visiting with friends. When she returned home, they argued about this and he struck her in the face, causing her mouth to bleed. He continued to hit her and held a metal can over his head in a manner threatening to her. She grabbed a pistol and fired one shot into his chest. They both ran out of the house. She offered to get medical help and he responded: "Bitch, you're dead." He died sometime later as a result of the gunshot.

Mrs. Smith was charged with murder and convicted of a lesser charge of voluntary manslaughter. On appeal, her conviction was reversed because the trial court had refused her requested jury instruction to explain the relevancy of the evidence of battering. She had requested a specific instruction related to the reasonableness of her belief that the use of deadly force was immediately necessary to defend herself against her husband's imminent use of unlawful force. In light of the Georgia statute, she was entitled to that. In ordering the new trial, the court explained:

The issue in a battered person defense "is not whether the danger was in fact imminent, but whether, given the circumstances as [the defendant] perceived them, the defendant's belief was reasonable that the danger was imminent." (*Smith v. State*, p. 823, quoting *Bechtel v. State* [Okla. Crim. App. 1992])

North Dakota champions the subjective test as well, describing it in its purest form as a test in which

the issue is not whether the circumstances attending the accused's use of force would be sufficient to create in the mind of a reasonable and prudent person the belief that the use of force is necessary to protect himself against immediate unlawful harm, but rather whether the circumstances are sufficient to induce in the accused an honest and reasonable belief that he must use force to defend himself against imminent harm. (*State v. Leidholm*, N.D. 1983, p. 817)

The North Dakota court explained that the significance of the difference between the objective and subjective tests is that the subjective test allows consideration of the unique physical and psychological characteristics of an accused, and it allows the jury to judge the reasonableness of the defendant's actions against *her* subjective impressions of the need for use of force, rather than against the impressions which a jury determines a hypothetical reasonably cautious person would have under similar circumstances. Utilizing language that is especially helpful in understanding just how valuable this test is in battered women cases, but couched in language that makes it more palliative, the court offered this example: "if the accused is a timid, diminutive male, the fact finder must consider these characteristics in assessing the reasonableness of his belief. If, on the other hand, the accused is a strong, courageous, and capable female, the fact finder must consider these characteristics in judging the reasonableness of her belief" (*State v. Leidholm*, p. 817).

Washington and Ohio also claim to use a subjective test to evaluate the reasonableness of a defendant's perceptions, although their tests tend toward some objective elements. A battered woman homicide case from Washington, for example, was reversed and remanded for a new trial because the language in the self-defense instruction did not adequately convey the subjective standard to the jury. The instruction, as originally given by the trial court, said that homicide was justifiable if the slayer had reasonable grounds to believe that the person slain intended to inflict death or great bodily harm and if it appeared to the slayer that she was in imminent danger of such harm. The court disapproved that language because "the jury was not instructed to evaluate self-defense in the light of all circumstances known to the defendant, including those known before the homicide" *State v. Allery* (Wash. 1984, p. 314). The court made it clear that self-defense must be judged from the perspective of the defendant, evaluating conditions as they appeared to her at the time of the act in question. "The jurors must understand that, in considering the issue of self-defense, they must place themselves in the shoes of the defendant and judge the legitimacy of her act in light of all that she knew at the time."

Ohio also claims a subjective test as illustrated in *State v. Daws* (Ohio App. 1994): "In any case involving self-defense, the trier of fact is called upon to determine whether the accused had an honest belief that she was in imminent danger of death or great bodily harm and that the use of force was her only means of escape. This test is subjective, and the jury must consider the circumstances of the accused and determine whether her actions were reasonable given those circumstances" (*State v. Daws*, pp. 810–811, citations omitted). A subsequent case makes it clear that Ohio is serious about the subjectivity of its measure of reasonableness. In *State v. Sallie* (Ohio 1998) the Ohio Supreme Court clearly stated: "Ohio has adopted a subjective test to determine whether a defendant properly acted in self-defense. If the defendant honestly believes that death or great bodily harm is imminent and that the only means of escape from such danger is in the use of deadly force, then the defendant has acted in self-defense" (*State v. Sallie*, pp. 675, 270).[1]

The subjective test is a weak one, giving great latitude to the defendant's perceptions if the jury simply believes that the defendant perceived things as she testified she did. The objective test can be a harsh one, holding a battered woman to the standard of a "reasonable man" who has never experienced the pattern of abuse she has. Given the inadequacies in each traditional test, it is not surprising to find that states are moving toward blending these tests, toward the end of eliminating the sharp distinction between objective and subjective standards.

The Blending of Objective and Subjective Tests

There is some significant movement in the courts to establish a test for reasonableness that will allow the trier of fact to take into account the circumstances as they appeared to the defendant at the time of the homicidal incident. The trend is not a universal one by any means, but it is hopeful. This blending takes at least two forms. In the first, courts are allowing greater particularization in the proof of reasonableness. That is, these courts are granting greater leeway for defense counsel to offer evidence of battering, toward the end of assisting the jury to judge the facts from the defendant's perspective. In the second, a "reasonable battered woman" standard is employed.

Greater Particularization. Courts adopting this position agree that, in determining objective reasonableness, a jury must be allowed to view the situation from the defendant's perspective. An example is *People v. Humphrey* (Cal. 1996), a case in which the defendant-wife admitted to police as soon as they arrived that she had shot her husband, after which she led them into the house and showed them the revolver she had used. She was charged with murder, but the trial court acquitted her of that charge, sending three less serious charges of second-degree murder, voluntary manslaughter, and involuntary manslaughter to the jury for consideration. The court instructed on self-defense, telling the jury that in order to find the defendant acted in self-defense it must find that she had an "actual and reasonable belief that the killing was necessary." The jury was further instructed that in determining reasonableness, it was to consider what "would appear to be necessary to a reasonable person in a similar situation and with similar knowledge." (*People v. Humphrey*, p. 147) During deliberations, the jury asked for and received clarification of the terms "subjectively honest and objectively reasonable." Thereafter, they returned a verdict of voluntary manslaughter, from which the defendant appealed.

The trial court had allowed evidence of the history of battering throughout the marriage and evidence of Battered Woman Syndrome for the purpose of determining whether the defendant actually believed she needed to kill in self-defense. The question on appeal was whether that evidence could also be considered to establish the reasonableness of the defendant's perceptions. The state attorney general conceded that history of violence in the marriage would be relevant, but he argued that expert testimony about its effects on the defendant should not be admitted because that testimony went to credibility of the defendant's testimony. The California Supreme Court disagreed. According to the court, it is appropriate to consider both kinds of evidence for the purpose of establishing reasonableness, because, "although the ultimate test of reasonableness is objective, in determining whether a reasonable person in defendant's position would have believed in the need to defend, the jury must consider all of the relevant circumstances in which defendant found herself" (*People v. Humphrey*, pp. 1083, 7, 148).

Missouri is in accord, holding that evidence of battered spouse syndrome may explain what might otherwise be inexplicable: why a woman perceives the necessity of using lethal force when a "reasonable person" would have chosen to leave the relationship (*State v. Pisciotta*, Mo. 1998). Likewise the courts in Georgia (*Smith v. State*, 1997) and New Mexico (*State v. Gallegos*, 1986) have approved hybrid tests, incorporating both objective and subjective standards.

"*Reasonable Battered Woman.*" This standard was first advocated by Kinports in 1988. "Some commentators contend it is an unfortunate term because it is not a new standard, but really only reflects particularization of the objective standard to the specific facts in the defendant's situation" (see, e.g., Heller, 1998; Cahn, 1992). Others question whether a "reasonable battered woman" really exists (Saitow, 1993).

The first court to change its jury instructions to acknowledge that what is reasonable to a battered woman may legitimately differ from what is deemed reasonable to the hypothetical reasonable man was Oklahoma in *Bechtel v. State* (Okla. Crim. App. 1992). In a case remanded for a third trial on homicide charges, the court adopted this instruction to be given in all cases in which Battered Woman Syndrome was admitted as evidence:

Under our present instructions, a fact finder conceivably may ponder whether the battered woman's perceptions should be viewed from the standpoint of a reasonable person in the circumstances of the battered woman or from the standpoint of a reasonable battered woman. (*Bechtel v. State*, p. 11)

That instruction replaced one that allowed deadly force in self-defense only in cases in which the defendant reasonably believed that such force was necessary to protect herself from "imminent danger." In support of its amended instruction, the court explained that the former instruction was a hybrid, requiring the jury to assess the reasonableness of the defendant's belief (i.e., subjective) and also to determine whether that viewpoint was that of a reasonable person in similar circumstances and with the same perceptions (i.e., objective). Although that instruction had withstood prior judicial scrutiny in response to charges that it was ultimately an objective, reasonable person standard, the court changed it in *Bechtel* in light of its decision to allow Battered Woman Syndrome testimony, and in light of the jury's question during deliberations in the case. The jury had been instructed that:

Self-defense is permitted a person solely because of necessity. Self-defense is not available to a person who was the aggressor, no matter how great the danger to personal security became during the altercation. (*Bechtel v. State*, p. 14, fn. 17)

Confused as to its meaning, the jury sent this question out to the court during its deliberations:

1. Does this mean or imply when no other options are available; or from
2. Defendant's viewpoint & circumstances. (*Bechtel v. State*)

After consultation with the attorneys, the judge sent a note back to the jurors saying, "You have everything before you that you are permitted to have." The defendant objected to the response and made a record requesting a different instruction. The jury returned a verdict of guilty.

On appeal, the court decided to modify the instruction and to include reference to the "reasonable battered woman," because battered women develop a heightened sensitivity to danger, resulting from the intimacy and the history of violence in the relationship. Indeed, in *Bechtel*, Dr. Walker had testified to that pattern as part of the cycle of violence. Sensitive to that, the court acknowledged:

[T]he battered woman perceives danger faster and more accurately as she is more acutely aware that a new or escalated violent episode is about to occur. "What is or is not an overt demonstration of violence varies with the circumstances. Under some circumstances a slight movement may justify instant action because of reasonable apprehension of danger, under other circumstances this would not be so. And it is for the jury, and not for the judge passing upon the weight and effect of the evidence, to determine how this may be." (*Bechtel v. State*, p. 10, citations omitted)

We may not be able to associate with the thoughts and perceptions of a battered woman and decide if they are reasonable unless we have a notion that they may be, unless we have a notion that in fact a reasonable battered woman may exist. The Oklahoma court gives the jury permission to view the facts in that light if they find the testimony on battered women credible.

The South Dakota Supreme Court has adopted the same standard and has made it absolutely clear that there is such a thing as a "reasonable battered woman" in the eyes of the law and the jury is to judge a battered woman's actions relative to that standard. In *State v. Burtzlaff* (S.D. 1992), a battered woman who killed her husband during a period of confrontation appealed her manslaughter conviction. The trial court gave this instruction that was not objected to, hence not affirmed or rejected on appeal. It is set out here because it so clearly illustrates the "reasonable battered woman" standard:

Under certain circumstances, it is lawful to take the life of another. One who is acting in self-defense may take the life of an aggressor if the aggressor poses a serious risk of serious bodily injury or death. The risk of serious bodily injury or death must be imminent, that is it must be such that a reasonable and prudent person standing in the shoes of the Defendant, knowing what the Defendant knows and seeing what the Defendant sees, would believe that serious bodily injury or death would result immediately if the aggressor were not killed.

In the case wherein [a battering relationship] is raised, and if you in fact find that Defendant is a battered woman, you are to look at the evidence presented through the eyes of a reasonable and prudent battered woman. If a reasonable and prudent battered woman would have believed serious bodily injury or death was imminent, then the killing was lawful. But, if you find that a reasonable and prudent battered woman would not have believed serious bodily injury or death imminent, then the killing was unlawful. (*State v. Burtzlaff*, p. 9)

The Ohio Supreme Court essentially uses the reasonable battered woman label, but sets out the case for particularization in its subjective test, in *State v. Thomas* (1997, p. 1346):

[T]he jury first must consider the defendant's situation objectively, that is, whether, considering all of the defendant's particular characteristics, knowledge, or lack of knowledge, circumstances, history and conditions at the time of the attack, she reasonably believed she was in imminent danger. . . . This standard is sometimes labeled the "reasonable battered woman standard". . . . Then if the objective standard is met, the jury must determine if, subjectively, this particular defendant had an honest belief that she was in imminent danger. (Citations omitted).

Kansas, Pennsylvania and South Dakota (*State v. Burtzlaff*, S.D. 1992) are sometimes cited as having adopted the "reasonable battered woman" standard, but they have not. The Kansas Court of Appeals declined to find a mandate from the Kansas Supreme Court to use the words "reasonably prudent battered woman" in jury instructions, declaring the Kansas Supreme Court's use of that term to have been dicta, not part of its holding in any prior case (*State v. Cramer*, Kan. 1993).

Although there is language in *Commonwealth v. Stonehouse* (Pa. 1989) to suggest that Pennsylvania has adopted a reasonable battered woman standard to gauge reasonableness, that opinion was authored by one judge who was joined by enough others in concurrence to determine the result in the case, but the concurring judges disagreed with his reasoning; thus, the lead opinion containing the reasonable battered woman language did not gain a majority of the Pennsylvania Supreme Court and does not stand as precedent.

In sum, courts that reference the "reasonable battered woman" are probably not creating a new standard to measure reasonableness. Instead, they are more likely joining in the trend toward particularization, a trend by which we measure reasonableness of a defendant's perceptions and consequent actions by taking into account all of the facts and circumstances surrounding the defendant at the time of the act in question.

Reasonableness and the Model Penal Code

In its most recent revision, the Model Penal Code formulation of self-defense contains no reference to "reasonableness" on its face. In pertinent part, the Code (Section 3.04) sets out self-defense this way:

(1) Use of Force Justifiable for Protection of the Person. Subject to the provisions of this Section and of Section 3.09, the use of force upon or toward another person is justifiable when the actor believes that such force is immediately necessary for the purpose of protecting himself against the use of unlawful force by such other person on the present occasion. . . .

(b) The use of deadly force is not justifiable under this Section unless the actor believes that such force is necessary to protect himself against death, serious bodily harm, kidnapping or sexual intercourse compelled by force or threat; nor is it justifiable if:

(i) the actor, with the purpose of causing death or serious bodily harm, provoked the use of force against himself in the same encounter; or

(ii) the actor knows that he can avoid the necessity of using such force with complete safety by retreating or by surrendering possession of a thing to a person asserting a claim of right thereto or by complying with a demand that he abstain from any action which he has no duty to take, except that:

(1) the actor is not obliged to retreat from his dwelling or place of work, unless he was the initial aggressor or is assailed in his place of work by another person whose place of work the actor knows it to be. . . .

(c) Except as required by paragraph . . . (b) of this Subsection, a person employing protective force may estimate the necessity thereof under the circumstances as he believes them to be when the force is used, without retreating, surrendering possession, doing any other act which he has no legal duty to do or abstaining from an unlawful action. (Model Penal Code § 3.04 [Official Draft 1962])

This self-defense provision must be read in conjunction with Section 3.09 which provides:

(2) When the actor believes that the use of force upon or toward the person of another is necessary for any of the purposes for which such belief would establish a justification under Sections 3.03 to 3.08 but the actor is *reckless or negligent* in having such belief or in acquiring or failing to acquire any knowledge or belief which is material to the justifiability of his use of force, the justification *afforded by those Sections is unavailable in a prosecution* for an offense for which *recklessness or negligence, as the case may be, suffices to establish culpability*. (Model Penal Code § 3.09 [Official Draft 1962], emphasis supplied)

Therefore, if the defendant's belief is reckless or negligent (the Code's analog of "unreasonableness" in the common law tradition), the defendant will only have an imperfect defense available because she would be guilty of crimes for which recklessness or negligence would satisfy the culpability component (the Code's analog of the *mens rea*/intent component in the common law tradition).

The author of the self-defense chapter in American Law Reports 4th (Wagner 1989) argues that this reformulation, in which "reasonable" does not obviously appear, means that the Code no longer requires reasonableness as an element of self-defense. The New Jersey Supreme Court has referred to "this uncertainty in the Code"(*State v. Bowen*, N.J. 1987). New Jersey refused to find that self-defense no longer had to be reasonable; instead the court concluded that the legislature (in expressly repealing the word "reasonable" from the self-defense language) abolished imperfect self-defense. Nebraska dealt with the ambiguity in a case in which the defendant contended his testimony of his subjective belief that deadly force was necessary should be enough to warrant a self-defense instruction because the statutory language just provided the act was "justifiable when the actor believes." The Nebraska Supreme Court said that although the term "reasonableness" is absent from the Model Penal Code provision, the drafters of the Code made it clear that they did not intend that the defense of justification would be good if the actor behaved unreasonably in defending himself. Instead, the drafters of the Code were simply trying to ensure that convictions for mere negligence did not result (*State v. Eagle Thunder*, Neb. 1978).

The bottom line is this: The Model Penal Code is not binding on any state or on any court. It is a draft of the law, as some of the best legal minds in the country believe it should be. State legislatures may or may not choose to adopt these provisions; most have to one degree or another. On the self-defense front, the drafters of the Code in 1962 (the most recent complete reformulation), electing to omit specific reference to "reasonableness" as a requirement of self-defense, did not create a self-defense provision that ignores the requirement that the actor behave reasonably. In essence, the Model Penal Code structure provides a perfect defense (i.e., one that may result in acquittal because the fatal blow struck in self-defense is considered justified) when the requisite culpability for the offense is purposeful or knowing behavior. That is, when one is charged with murder committed purposefully and knowingly, self-defense may be raised toward the end of acquitting the defendant of criminal responsibility. On the other hand, the Code provides that self-defense is an imperfect defense (resulting in conviction of a lesser crime) when the requisite culpability is negligence or recklessness. Therefore, perfect self-defense (or justification) would not be available if the defendant's belief was honest but negligent, or unreasonable. Instead, the defendant would be entitled to a jury instruction on the lesser crime of negligent homicide, a felony in the third degree in most jurisdictions. As Schopp et al. (1994, p. 50) summarize it: "The Model Penal Code allows liability for negligent or reckless homicide for those who exer-

cise deadly defensive force on the basis of negligently or recklessly held beliefs about the necessity of using such force. A large majority of
jurisdictions require reasonable belief in the necessity of exercising deadly
force, either explicitly or through provisions similar to those of the Model
Penal Code."

Reasonableness remains an integral part of self-defense, its explicit
omission from the language of the Code notwithstanding. Killing another
will not be justified as self-defense (i.e., self-defense will not operate as a
perfect defense, potentially resulting in acquittal) unless the actor behaved
reasonably in inflicting the fatal blow.

Imminence

Traditionally, self-defense requires a finding that the defendant reasonably perceived a threat of imminent harm which required defensive action.
There is no single understanding definition of "imminent" harm; it varies
from jurisdiction to jurisdiction, but we attempt to bring some order to its
understanding here.

As a preliminary matter, it is probably good to recall the scenarios that
are generally present when battered women contend they have killed their
abusers in self-defense. The reported cases most often reflect an active confrontation in which the battered woman has killed her abuser at the time
he was attacking her; sometimes, she has killed during a lull in the violence
(e.g., when he is sleeping); in fewer instances, the battered woman has
hired a third party to kill her abuser.

In situations in which the battered woman has killed her batterer during
a violent confrontation, courts generally give a self-defense instruction and
allow the jury to consider that defense.

When the battered woman kills during a lull in the violence, there is a
split of authority on whether she is entitled to claim self-defense, and the
most important element in that determination has been the manner in
which the particular jurisdiction defines "imminent danger." Jurisdictions
that define "imminent" danger as "immediate" danger have generally refused to allow a self-defense instruction; that is, the jury has not been allowed to consider whether the defendant acted in self-defense (See *People
v. Aris* [Cal. 1989]; *State v. Norman* [N.C. 1989]; *State v. Stewart* [Kan.
1988]). Other jurisdictions that define "imminent" more broadly have held
that the battered woman is entitled to a self-defense instruction. See *State
v. Gallegos* [N.M. Ct. App. 1986]; *State v. Allery* [Wash. 1984]; *State v.
Leidholm* [N.D. 1983]).

The few cases in which murder-for-hire is alleged have not allowed self-defense claims to go to the jury. See *State v. Anderson* (Mo. App. 1990); *State v. Leaphart* (Tenn.Crim.App. 1983).

Given that there is not uniformity here, we begin with sorting out the most common understandings of "imminence," recognizing that this is going to be critically important in those most difficult cases in which the battered woman has killed during a lull in the violence.

What Is a "Threat of Imminent Harm"?

"Imminent harm" means more than fear. It must be induced by some overt act, a "gesture or word spoken by the deceased at the time the homicide occurred which would form a reasonable ground for the belief that the accused is about to suffer death or great bodily harm" (*Bechtel v. State*, Okla. Crim. App. 1992, p. 28). Just how overt those words or gestures may be, or how subtle they may be, is the tricky question. Some words or gestures are easy to understand. "I'm going to kill you now," or the cocking of a gun and pointing it at another person, for example, would arguably present a reasonable person with fear of imminent harm. But others are not as clear, and the collection of battered women homicide cases is replete with examples. As the Oklahoma Court of Criminal Appeals in *Bechtel* struggled with this problem, it was persuaded that battered women learn to identify signs that precede escalated violence:

She learns to distinguish subtle changes in tone of voice, facial expression, and levels of danger. She is in a position to know, perhaps with greater certainty than someone attacked by a stranger, that the batterer's threat is real and will be acted upon. (*Bechtel v. State*, p. 12, citing Elizabeth Bochnak, *Women's Self-Defense Cases: Theory and Practice* [1981])

Applying that insight, the court held:

A defendant must show that she had a reasonable belief as to the imminence of great bodily harm or death and as to the force necessary to compel it. Several of the psychological symptoms that develop in one suffering from the [battered woman] syndrome are particularly relevant to the standard of reasonableness in self-defense. One such symptom is a greater sensitivity to danger, which has come about because of the intimacy and history of the relationship. . . . It is during the tension-building period that the battered woman develops a heightened sensitivity to any kinds of cues of distress. Thus, because of her intimate knowledge of her batterer, the battered woman perceives danger faster and more accurately as she is more acutely aware that a new or escalated violent episode is about to occur. What is or is not an overt demonstration of violence varies with the circumstances. Under some circumstances a slight movement may justify instant action because of reasonable apprehension of danger, under other circumstances this would not be so. And it is for the jury, and not for the judge passing upon the weight of the evidence, to determine how this may be. (*Bechtel v. State*, pp. 9–10, citations omitted)

Illustrations of the variety of "overt demonstrations of violence" reported in the cases include the "look on his face" and his "heavy walk" reported in *People v. Humphrey* (Cal. 1996). In that case, the defendant shot the man who had been physically and verbally abusive to her for most of the year they had lived together. His threats of violence had become more frequent for several weeks prior to the evening he died. The defendant testified that the evening before she shot him, he was "getting crazy" and asked for a gun, which he then shot in her direction. She described him at that moment as having a "look on his face" that she had seen before "but not this bad"; he "wasn't the same person." On the day she killed him, they had driven through the mountains and he pointed to a spot he said would be a good place to kill her because no one would find the body for a while. When they got home, they argued and he had a gun within easy reach. During the course of the argument, "all of a sudden, he got quiet for a minute or two, and then, he just snapped." A few moments later, she testified, he moved from the kitchen toward the gun saying, "This time, bitch, when I shoot at you, I won't miss." At this point, she "knew he would shoot me" and was "scared to death" because of his prior threats and also because of his "very, very heavy" walk indicating he was "mad." She testified that she had no doubt he would kill her if she did not kill him first. They confronted each other in the kitchen and he "looked crazy." She grabbed the gun. She testified that she was holding him at bay when he reached for her arm and she shot him.

The court admitted that, absent an expert's explanation, the average juror might be very skeptical that a look, a footstep, or a tone of voice could signal grave danger, or that a reasonable person would think self-defensive action was necessary on this basis. But the court also recognized that, with the assistance of expert testimony about battering and the battering relationship, these clues could be put in a context that would assist the jury in determining whether it was reasonable to believe harm was imminent.

The cues were even more subtle in *People v. Garcia* (Colo. 1999), a case in which the defendant's husband had attempted to sexually assault her and had threatened to kill her just before she killed him. She testified that she had initially fought him off by hitting and biting him and pushing him back with her foot. But then, he gave her "a look like he used to give me in

Missouri and Kansas when I messed up, and I was going to get hurt pretty bad, and . . . I just snapped" (*People v. Garcia*, p. 5).

Battered women testify that subtle cues such as these informed their actions and led them to kill in self-defense. But it is not clear to what extent these factors will be taken seriously and will be understood by judges and juries. Beyond that, if "imminence" is defined too narrowly, the jury will not even be permitted to consider these factors because the court may determine, as a matter of law, that the perceived threat was too remote to be considered "imminent" for purposes of the defense.

In the cases reported here, neither the trial nor appellate courts ruled as a matter of law on whether these descriptions of clues are sufficient to justify the use of deadly force. Instead, they properly recognized that these cues are meaningful to the women who experienced them, meaningful enough that they should be considered by the jury in its determination of whether it was reasonable to believe harm was imminent. One state has determined as a matter of statutory law that "belief that danger is imminent can be inferred from a past pattern of repeated serious abuse" (Ky. Rev. Stat. 503.010[3]). In other states, authority rests in the common law and in our understanding of general self-defense principles. Examination of judicial decisions reveals that courts differ in their approaches and conclusions. In *Bechtel v. State*, the Oklahoma Court of Criminal Appeals recognized that because of her intimate knowledge of her batterer, the battered woman perceives danger faster and more accurately than others would and she is more acutely aware that a new or escalated violent episode is about to occur. But in *State v. Stewart* (Kan. 1988) the court made it clear that self-defense requires confrontation, and long-term abuse is no substitute for imminence as traditionally understood. The trial court in *State v. Gallegos* (N.M. Ct. App. 1986) took the same approach and refused to give a self-defense instruction because there was no obvious threat at the time of the murder and past violent conduct could not provide the basis for a self-defense instruction. *Gallegos* was reversed on appeal, however, and on remand the trial court was directed to give a self-defense instruction "whenever a defendant presents evidence sufficient to allow reasonable minds to differ as to all elements of the defense" (*State v. Gallegos*, p. 21).

Is "Imminent" Harm the Same as "Immediate" Harm?

Consider these facts: At trial the defense had called 15 witnesses, in addition to the defendant, who had testified about the violent nature of the deceased, and the numerous occasions on which he had brutalized his wife. The battering relationship had been present throughout their 10-year marriage. Abusive behavior had ranged from the husband preventing the defendant from taking her medication to diluting her insulin with water, knocking her down, choking her into unconsciousness, harassing her, and threatening to kill her and members of her family.

Approximately six weeks prior to the husband's death, the couple separated; the defendant moved to a motel to escape the violence. Her husband found her and made such threatening calls that she started carrying a gun. The defendant had testified that on the day she shot her husband, he told her he was going to come over and kill her. That night she was in the bathroom and she heard a thumping on her motel door. By the time she got out of the bathroom, he had broken down the door and was in the room. He hit her and choked her and threatened to kill her. Then he forced her to shower with him, at which time he crudely and violently shaved her pubic hair and afterward forced her to submit to sexual intercourse. After the sexual interlude, he continued to threaten the defendant; he pounded a beer bottle on the nightstand and threw a dollar bill toward the window, demanding that she get him some cigarettes. Instead, she pulled out the gun and demanded that he leave. When he saw the gun he laughed and said, "You are dead, bitch, now!" He reached for the beer bottle. She shut her eyes and fired. When the gun was seized, there were five spent shells in the chamber. At the time of the shooting, the deceased had his back to the defendant. The evidence showed that she was not physically blocked from going to the door and she was more than two feet away from the deceased when she fired.

Those were the facts as summarized by the court in *State v. Hundley* (Kan. 1985). The trial court instructed the jury that self-defense required a finding that the defendant was faced with "immediate" harm. Defendant appealed that instruction, arguing that requiring "immediate" rather than "imminent" harm prevented the jury from considering evidence of long-term violence of the victim toward the defendant.

The appellate court agreed that "imminent" is a broader and more inclusive term than "immediate," and that a jury focusing on "imminent" harm will not be bound by strict time limitations that are associated with "immediacy." In explaining the difference in the terms, the appellate court penned one of the most sensitive passages found in battered women homicide cases:

The issue is dramatized by the nature of this case. This is a textbook case of the battered wife, which is psychologically similar to hostage and prisoner of war cases. Betty Hundley had survived her husband's brutal beatings for ten years. Her bones had been broken, her teeth knocked out and repeated bruises inflicted, but she did not leave him. She called the police occasionally but would continue to stay with Carl Hundley. The mystery, as in all battered wife cases, is why she remained after the beatings. The answer to that question can only be gleaned from the compiled case histories of this malady. It is not a new phenomenon, having been recognized and justified since Old Testament times. It goes largely unreported, but is well documented. It is extremely widespread, estimated to affect between four and forty million women. . . .

Wife beating is steeped in the concept of marital privacy, and the belief wives are the personal property of the husband. In Blackstone's Commentaries the theory of coverture was advanced, making punishment for mistreatment of a wife impossible since husband and wife were considered one. . . . Even though wife beating is now recognized as a crime in all fifty states, all the traditional attitudes have made legal and actual recognition of wife beating's criminal nature slow in coming. Even after it is recognized as a crime, it is difficult to obtain even-handed enforcement. The misconceptions have affected the battered woman's perception of herself and reduced the options available to her.

Thus we can see from this brief synopsis that there is no easy answer to why battered women stay with their abusive husbands. Quite likely emotional and financial dependency and fear are the primary reasons for remaining in the household. They feel incapable of reaching out for help and justifiably fear reprisals from their angry husbands if they leave or call the police. The abuse is so severe, for so long a time, and the threat of great bodily harm so constant, it creates a standard mental attitude in its victims. Battered women are terror-stricken people whose mental state is distorted and bears a marked resemblance to that of a hostage or a prisoner of war. The horrible beatings they are subjected to brainwash them into believing there is nothing they can do. They live in constant fear of another eruption of violence. They become disturbed persons from the torture.

Under the facts of this case, after ten years of abuse, Betty finally became so desperate in her terror of Carl she fled. Her escape was to no avail; he followed her. Her fear was justified. He broke through the locked door of her motel room and started his abuse again. Carl's threat was no less life threatening with him sitting in the motel room tauntingly playing with his beer bottle than if he were advancing toward her. The objective test is how a reasonably prudent battered wife would perceive Carl's demeanor. Expert testimony is admissible to prove the nature and effect of wife beating just as it is admissible to prove the standard mental state of hostages, prisoners of war, and others under long-term life-threatening conditions. Thus, we can see the use of the word "immediate" in the instruction on self-defense places undue emphasis on the immediate action of the deceased, and obliterates the nature of the buildup of terror and fear which had been systematically created over a long period of time. "Imminent" describes the situation more accurately.

Appellant aptly makes the following analogy under a more normal situation which further demonstrates the difference in the definition of "imminent" and "immediate." An aggressor who is customarily armed and gets involved in a fight may present an imminent danger, justifying the use of force in self-defense, even though the aggressor is unarmed on the occasion. There may be no immediate danger, since the aggressor is in fact unarmed, but there is a reasonable apprehension of danger. In other words, the law of self-defense recognizes one may reasonably fear danger but be mistaken. (*State v. Hundley*, pp. 478–479, citations omitted)

Having declared a significant difference between the terms "imminent" and "immediate," the court reversed and ordered a new trial, because use of the word "immediate" instead of "imminent" precluded the jury's consideration of prior abuse. "We conclude that the trial court's use of [the word 'immediate'] impermissibly excluded from the jury's consideration the effect on the appellant of the history of violence toward her by the decedent. This consideration was critical to the appellant's perception of the need to defend herself in this case and thereby caused reversible error" (*State v. Hundley*, p. 480).

While the Kansas Supreme Court based its decision on the distinction between the terms, other courts use the terms interchangeably (*People v. Humphrey*, Cal. 1996; *State v. Anderson*, Mo. Ct. App. 1990; *State v. Gallegos*, N.M. Ct. App. 1986). In persuasive support of the latter position Schopp et al. (1994) argue that the law does not distinguish between the two terms. These authors use the terms interchangeably and find no statutory or theoretical reason to dwell on an artificially imposed difference. Having said that, however, they proceed to discuss the related and substantive distinction between "imminent danger" and "immediate danger, such as must be instantly met." They offer a beautiful hypothetical situation to illustrate the difference: Two hikers are in the desert. One of them is threatening to poison the water hole. Is the other in imminent danger?

If imminent danger means immediate danger in the temporal sense, the answer may be no. There is nothing in that factual statement to prove that the poisoning is about to occur on the present occasion. If imminent danger means immediate danger, the second hiker may not "defend" himself against the threat because it is not a sufficient danger at the moment to justify defensive action. How long must the second hiker wait? What signals will be sufficient to establish the imminence of the danger? These are the kinds of questions faced by battered women. These are the kinds of issues jurors must resolve in deciding whether battered women acted in self-defense.

The Model Penal Code (section 3.04[1]) allows a reasonable solution to this problem by requiring that defensive force be "immediately necessary . . . on the present occasion." With that restatement of the principle, the drafters have adopted "a standard addressing the relation between the time the defensive force is exercised and the time at which it must be used in order to prevent the unlawful harm." (Schopp et al., 1994, p. 67) Schullhofer (1990) praises that as a better standard to replace our traditional understanding of imminence but, as Rosen (1993) notes, Schullhofer does not explain how the two requirements really differ on a temporal scale, and Vanderbraak (1979) sees little difference between the Model Penal Code and the traditional imminence requirement.

Analyzing that revised standard promulgated by the Model Penal Code, Schopp et al. recognize its merit generally and argue that it will operate reasonably in battered women cases:

The central question involves the appropriate relationship between the necessity and imminence requirements. A standard allowing defensive force only when immediately necessary to prevent unlawful harm treats imminence of harm as a factor regarding necessity. That is, the defensive force is justified only if necessary to prevent an unlawful harm, and the imminence of that unlawful harm contributes to, but does not completely determine, the judgement of necessity. In unusual circumstances such as those confronted by the desert hiker or by some battered women, defensive force may be immediately necessary to prevent unlawful harm, although that harm is not yet imminent. In these cases, imminence of harm does not serve as a decisive factor in the determination of necessity. A standard allowing defensive force only when necessary to prevent an imminent harm, in contrast, treats imminence of harm as an independent requirement of justified force in that the force must be necessary and the unlawful harm must be immediately forthcoming. Such a standard does not allow defensive force necessary to prevent delayed unlawful aggression, even if the present situation represents the last opportunity to prevent such harm. (Schopp et al., 1994, pp. 67–68)

The merit of this position is perhaps best illustrated by contrasting it to the courts' simple black-and-white declarations in *People v. Humphrey* (Murray 1997) and *Stewart* that the imminence requirement of traditional self-defense can never be met when the man is sleeping. Never mind the other circumstances surrounding the homicidal act; a sleeping giant is not an imminent threat by definition. That was essentially the same position taken by the court in *Norman* (N.C. 1989), the case that prompted Rosen to argue so eloquently that necessity, rather than imminence understood in a simplistic temporal fashion, should be the defining factor in determining the propriety of engaging in defensive action.

The Model Penal Code reflects that thinking as well. Section 3.04 of the Official Draft 1962 provides that self-defense may be employed "when the actor believes that such force is immediately necessary for the purpose of protecting himself against the use of unlawful force by such other person on the present occasion." Two points should be emphasized. First, the Code provides solid support for the position taken here (and earlier by Schopp et al. and in essence by Rosen) that necessity is a critically important element in determining the propriety of self-defense on a given occasion. Second, reference to "the present occasion" arguably broadens the time frame "enough so that persons who have good reason to believe that an assailant is about to launch an attack . . . can attack before it is too late" (Gillespie, 1989, p. 186, quoted in Singer and Gardner, 1996, p. 781). Gillespie concludes that the reasoning appears to work well in states that have adopted this version of the Code.

Imminence Is Closely Related to Reasonableness

Traditionally self-defense has required not only that the actor be confronted with an imminent threat, but also that the perception of threat be a reasonable perception. The two are closely related and the relationship has been discussed with clarity in a few battered women cases. The court in *Bechtel* (Okla. 1992) paid homage to the traditional requirement, recognizing that the law generally requires a temporal requirement of imminence because it would be unreasonable to be provoked to the point of killing well after the provocation has occurred. The court went on to discuss the implications of this traditional understanding in the context of battered women cases:

For the battered woman, if there is no escape or sense of safety, then the next attack, which could be fatal or cause serious bodily harm, is imminent. Based on the traditionally accepted definition of imminence and its functional derivatives, a battered woman, to whom the threat of serious bodily harm or death is always imminent, would be precluded from asserting the defense of self-defense. . . . Thus . . . an abused woman may kill her mate during the period of threat that precedes a violent incident, right before the violence escalates to the more dangerous levels of an acute battering episode. Or, she may take action against him during a lull in an assaultive incident, or after it has culminated, in an effort to prevent a recurrence of the violence. And so, the issue is not whether the danger was in fact imminent, but whether, given the circumstances as she perceived them, the defendant's belief was reasonable that the danger was imminent. (*Bechtel v. State*, p. 12)

That is in accord with the court in *Gallegos* (N.M. Ct. App. 1986, p. 22): "To require the battered person to await a blatant deadly assault before she acts in defense of herself would not only ignore unpleasant reality, but would amount to sentencing her to 'murder by installment.' "

The battered woman should not have to show actual physical assault on the date and occasion of her claimed defensive action. She must establish some showing of impending danger prior to her use of force, impending danger exhibited by threatening acts or words. History of physical abuse should come into evidence to illustrate the context in which these acts or words were experienced and to establish reasonableness of her perceptions. That history of violence, standing alone, does not justify the killing. But it is one element that should be available to prove the defendant's state of mind and the reasonableness of her perception that she was in imminent danger.

Finally, in establishing self-defense and recognizing the close relationship between threat of imminent harm and reasonableness of that perception, it is important to recognize that reasonableness is the more important of those two inquiries. On the defense side of the coin, emphasis on reasonableness enables the finder of fact to be released from the binding temporal quality that might otherwise surround the imminence requirement. On the prosecutorial side of the coin, emphasis on reasonableness enables us to question, even if the threat was immediate, whether the response was one reasonably calculated to be defensive.

LAW OF SELF-DEFENSE IS ADVANCED BY RELIANCE ON PROOF OF NECESSITY

Imminence of the threat of harm is not irrelevant, but it must not be allowed to take on a life of its own and become the defining element of self-defense in battered women (or other) cases. If we restrict self-defense to those cases in which the expected harm is immediate, we remove it from those admittedly more unusual cases in which the defendant must employ force now in order to preclude harm in the future. This is not to say that self-defense should be redefined to enable force to be used preemptively and offensively. That is not the nature of the defense, nor should it be. But we must recognize that there are cases in which the threat of harm is reasonably perceived and it is necessary to forcefully prevent it—or it will not be preventable. The mechanism for allowing self-defense to operate and to be considered by the jury in these more difficult cases is to employ the concept of necessity. That is, we should not simply ask: Was harm imminent? We should ask instead: Was it necessary to employ the force used in order to protect against the threat of harm? If it was necessary, self-defense may be considered.

Schopp et al. (1994) make the case for necessity this way:

The central question involves the appropriate relationship between the necessity and imminence requirements. A standard allowing defensive force only when immediately necessary to prevent unlawful harm treats imminence of harm as a factor regarding necessity. That is, the defensive force is justified only if necessary to prevent an unlawful harm, and the imminence of that unlawful harm contributes to, but does not completely determine, the judgment of necessity. In unusual circumstances such as those confronted by . . . some battered women, defensive force may be immediately necessary to prevent unlawful harm, although that harm is not yet imminent. In these cases, imminence of harm does not serve as a decisive factor in the determination of necessity. A standard allowing defensive force only when necessary to prevent an imminent harm, in contrast, treats imminence of harm as an independent requirement for justified force in that the force must be necessary and the unlawful harm must be immediately forthcoming. Such a standard does not allow defensive force necessary to prevent delayed unlawful aggression, even if the present situation represents the last opportunity to prevent such harm.

[S]ome writers interpret necessity as the core of self-defense doctrine. Imminence of harm remains consistent with this theoretical foundation when it serves as a factor regarding judgments of necessity because in most circumstances the judgment that no non-violent alternative will suffice is more likely to be accurate regarding imminent harm than a remote one. Imminence of harm can undermine these justificatory theories, however, if it is accepted as an independent requirement of the defense.

In short, imminence of harm can promote the underlying justifications of self-defense when it serves as a factor to be considered in making judgments of necessity, but it can undermine those justifications if it is accepted as an independent requirement in addition to necessity. For these reasons, the Model Penal Code and some commentators advocate some variation on the "immediately necessary" formulation rather than "necessity and imminence." (Schopp et al., 1994, pp. 67–69)

Rosen agrees. Rosen's (1993) article is probably the seminal piece on imminence in battered women cases. He questions whether the imminence requirement is essential to self-defense in battered women cases, especially in light of "continuing reports of jury nullification in prosecutions of battered women who kill their batterers, the exceptional number of grants of executive clemency to women who are convicted, and, in North Carolina, the case of Judy Norman . . ." (Rosen, 1993, p. 387). He argues that imminence of impending harm is really a "translator" for necessity, and when imminence and necessity conflict, necessity must prevail. Illustrative of his reasoning is this passage:

In self-defense, the concept of imminence has no significance independent of the notion of necessity. . . . [S]ociety does not require that the evil avoided be an imminent evil because it believes that an imminent evil is the only type of evil that should be avoided, nor because an imminent threatened harm is necessarily worse than a non-imminent one. Rather, imminence is required because, and only because, of the fear that without imminence there is no assurance that the defensive action is necessary to avoid the harm. (Rosen, 1993, p. 379, fn omitted)

Rosen argues for an instruction that imminence is required for self-defense unless the defendant presents evidence that she reasonably believed the killing was necessary (even if danger was not imminent). If that burden of production is met, the jury would get the case and would then be entitled to decide it on the issue of necessity as the primary element of self-defense.

To summarize and to illustrate how emphasis on necessity rather than imminence as traditionally understood is the superior and more fair reasoning, consider *People v. Aris* (Cal. Ct. App. 1989). This was a nonconfrontational case in which the defendant shot her abusive husband while he was sleeping. She testified that he had beaten her on the night of the killing and had threatened that, "he didn't think he was going to let me live till the morning." She thought he was "very serious." After he fell asleep, she went next door to get some ice for the pain from the blows he had inflicted to her face. She found a handgun on top of the refrigerator and took it "for protection," explaining that she thought she needed it for protection because "I felt when I got back . . . he'd probably be awake and he would start hitting me again." When she returned to the bedroom, "I then sat down on the bed and I felt that I had to do it. It would be worse when he woke up. . . . I felt when he woke up that he was then going to hurt me very badly or even kill me." She then shot her husband five times in the back while he was sleeping. He died of the gunshot wounds.

In this case, there was testimony about Battered Woman Syndrome and the court allowed that evidence to be considered in determining whether the defendant had a subjective belief that she was in danger. But the court refused to instruct on self-defense as a defense capable of entitling the defendant to acquittal, and it refused to allow Battered Woman Syndrome testimony to be considered to establish reasonableness of defendant's belief. (Note that the court's failure to allow this testimony to be considered with respect to reasonableness was overturned in *People v. Humphrey* in 1996.)

The jury returned a verdict of second-degree murder, failing to find evidence of an imminent attack, and failing to find that the defendant had an actual belief in the imminence of an attack.

The court declared the rationale of the verdict: "No jury composed of reasonable men could have concluded that a sleeping victim presents an imminent danger of great bodily harm, especially when the defendant was able to, and actually did, leave the bedroom, and subsequently returned to shoot him" (*People v. Aris*, p. 176).

Employing the traditional imminence requirement, that would be correct. But even if correct, it may not be the right decision. The jury is entitled to consider more and the defendant is entitled to have more considered. Employing a standard in which we emphasize proof of whether it was necessary for the defendant to act as she did on that occasion, we may have had a different conclusion. We certainly would have had a more thorough inquiry and deliberation.

Cases like this prompt the argument for a revised standard in self-defense that focuses on necessity, because serious consideration of whether the defensive action was "necessary" allows more comprehensive attention to the facts than when temporal restrictions surrounding imminence are in place.

LAW OF SELF-DEFENSE IS ADVANCED BY ALLOWING CONTEXTUAL EVIDENCE

If battered woman homicide cases are to be decided fairly, in consideration of the circumstances facing the defendant at the time she decided to use lethal force, those circumstances will have to be presented in context. It will be necessary to understand the history of the relationship, especially the history of the battering relationship; it will be critical to understand the events of the fatal day in the context of that battering relationship because reasonableness and imminence and the perceived necessity for lethal force can only be understood in the context in which the defendant acted. So, the question now becomes: How do we come to understand the context of the battering relationship that preceded the homicide? Stated differently and in the language so critical to traditional and modified notions of self-defense: How do we come to understand the facts of the homicide in context, so that we will be able to judge the reasonableness of the defendant's perception of impending harm (or, in its modified version, the perceived necessity for force) and the imminence of the threat? The rules of evidence allow this kind of contextual evidence to come from expert testimony as well as from lay testimony.

Expert Testimony to Establish the Context of Abuse

Rules of evidence govern the admissibility of expert testimony and those rules vary from state to state. A majority of states have adopted a rule patterned on the Federal Rule of Evidence 702 which provides that "if scientific, technical, or other specialized knowledge will assist the trier of fact to understand the evidence or to determine a fact in issue, a witness qualified as an expert by knowledge, skill, experience, training, or education may testify thereto in the form of an opinion or otherwise." Others have opted for different language but have not strayed far from the theme of the federal standard. A fairly typical example of the variant is Pennsylvania's rule which allows expert testimony when the court determines it can assist the jury by providing explanations and inferences that are not within the range of ordinary training, knowledge, intelligence, and experience (see, e.g., *Commonwealth v. Stonehouse*, Pa. 1989).

In battered women cases in which the defendant relies on self-defense, the expert testimony most often (and, to date, virtually exclusively) relied upon is the expert who will testify to the Battered Woman Syndrome. Lenore Walker (1984) brought the syndrome to academic and judicial attention, and she and her protégés are now accepted as legitimate expert witnesses in every jurisdiction in which the issue has been raised.

Walker's first reported entrance to the fray was in *Ibn-Tamas v. United States* (D.C. 1979). The trial court refused to allow Walker to testify because the methodology she had used to reach her conclusions did not satisfy the test set out in *Frye v. United States* (D.C. Cir. 1923). *Frye* required expert opinion to be based on scientific techniques that are "generally accepted" in their particular field as a prerequisite to admissibility. It is important to note that the trial court in *Ibn-Tamas* did not refuse Walker's testimony based on the conclusions she drew about battering or her theory of Battered Woman Syndrome; the refusal was based entirely on the methodology by which she had reached her conclusions. The defense appealed that refusal to allow the jury to hear Walker's opinion, and on appeal the court remanded the case back to the trial court to adduce more evidence on the methodology. After adducing additional information, the trial court again refused to allow the testimony because it determined that Walker's methodology failed the "general acceptance" test.

Determination of whether the methodology by which an expert reaches a conclusion reflects a generally accepted methodology is a question of law to be determined by the judge; it is not a question of fact to be determined by the jury. Beyond that, when courts determine whether to allow expert testimony, they must decide if the expert testimony is such that it would be helpful to the jury. That is, the court can find that the expert's methods are legitimate and that the expert has something of substance to say—nonetheless, the testimony may be inadmissible if the court determines that the opinion would not be useful to the jury (because, for example, it is a matter within the knowledge of the jury, hence not something the jury needs assistance understanding). It is not entirely surprising to discover that different courts reached different conclusions on these points early on.

After Walker's testimony was refused in 1979, defendants nonetheless continued to press for admission of expert testimony on Battered Woman Syndrome. In the early 1980s courts were split on its admissibility with decisions in Florida (*Hawthorne v. State*, 1982), Georgia (*Smith v. State*, 1981), New York (*People v. Torres*, 1985) and Maine (*State v. Anaya*, 1981) admitting it because they found Battered Woman Syndrome to be outside the knowledge of the jury; while courts in Ohio (*State v. Thomas*, 1981) and Wyoming (*Buhrle v. State*, 1981) refused it because they determined it would not be helpful to the jury and was not outside the ken of the average juror.

By the mid-1990s jurisdictions were nearly unanimous in allowing Battered Woman Syndrome testimony. Most of these decisions reflected judicial acceptance of the theory; in some states, however, admissibility of the evidence was assured by legislative mandate. Kentucky (Ky. Rev. Stat. § 503.050(3)), Wyoming (Wyo. Stat. § 6-1-203), and Ohio (Ohio Rev. Code § 2901.06) had statutes passed in the early 1990s that authorized evidence of Battered Woman Syndrome in self-defense cases.

Whether by judicial acceptance or legislative action, Battered Woman Syndrome found its way into self-defense cases in which battered women were charged with fatally attacking their batterers. That is not to say that any expert testimony will be allowed to assist the jury to understanding battering. New theoretical development will require demonstration of reliability in support of admissibility.

Broadening the scope of proffered expert testimony to include, for example, the theory set out here will require establishing the expertise of the witness to testify to this theory of the battering relationship. The question that arises is whether the battle over methodology that Walker began fighting in 1979 will have to be fought all over again. In other words, the question is whether the *Frye* test of generally accepted methodology is still intact. Exploration of that question requires a little historical context.

Frye was decided by the District of Columbia Court of Appeals, and thus had very limited binding authority; specifically it had no binding authority on any state court. Beyond that, it was decided in 1923 before the current Federal Rules of Evidence (and the state rules patterned after them) were adopted. Its significance really lies in the facts that it was the first decision to set out rules for admission of expert opinion evidence[2] and it led to a split in the circuit courts of appeals in the federal system. When the Federal Rules of Evidence were codified in 1975 and Rule 702 adopted, the vitality of *Frye* came into question. Neither the text of Rule 702 nor the Advisory Committee Notes mentioned the case, and some may have wondered if it was dead. But in 1979 the court in *Ibn-Tamas* clearly looked to *Frye* for guidance, as did many other courts, until the United States Supreme Court decided *Daubert v. Merrell Dow Pharmaceuticals, Inc.* in 1993 and declared that Federal Rule of Evidence 702 superseded *Frye*.

Rule 702 is plainly written but gives no detail as to how it is to be applied in practice. It simply instructs: "If scientific, technical, or other specialized knowledge will assist the trier of fact to understand the evidence or to determine a fact in issue, a witness qualified as an expert by knowledge, skill, experience, training, or education may testify thereto in the form of an opinion or otherwise." In *Daubert*, the Court derived a standard for reliability from the terms "scientific" and "knowledge" and enumerated several general considerations for applying the standard.[3] The *Daubert* test is generally thought to be less restrictive than the old *Frye* test, and it gives trial courts wide latitude in determining admissibility of expert testimony. If a party challenges the court's determination under *Daubert*, the court's determination will stand unless there is a showing that the trial court abused its discretion in admitting or failing to admit the proffered expert testimony (*General Electric v. Joiner*, U.S. 1997). "Abuse of discretion" is one of the lowest and most forgiving standards of review in the law. It is a standard that provides that the lower court's ruling will be affirmed and will not be interfered with unless the complaining party shows that the court abused the discretion granted to it in making that ruling. In establishing that standard of review, the Supreme Court not only made it clear that trial court decisions on admissibility of expert testimony would be respected, but it also stated clearly that the *Daubert* "gatekeeping" obligation of the trial court under Federal Rule of Evidence 702 applied to all expert testimony and not just to "scientific" testimony, and further that its abuse of discretion standard will be used to decide challenges to the trial court's decision of which of the five factors to use in its analysis (*Kumho Tire Co. v. Carmichael*, U.S. 1999).

The *Daubert* decision and its progeny means that *Frye* is "dead" at the federal level, but it may still be very much alive in state courts. Federal and state rules of evidence differ, and Congress does not have the power to set evidentiary rules for state courts. The general principles of federalism apply, so even if a state adopts a rule that is identical in its wording to Federal Rule of Evidence 702, the interpretation adopted by the state may be different than that adopted by the Supreme Court in interpreting Federal Rule 702 in federal courts. Presently, eleven states continue to govern admissibility of expert testimony by the test set out in *Frye*.[4] Seven states have adopted *Daubert*.[5] Nevada has adopted a wait-and-see attitude toward *Daubert*, characterizing it as a work in progress (*Dow Chemical v. Mahlum*, 1998). Finally, some states have adopted separate standards for scientific and experience-based expert testimony. Colorado has a statutory rule of evidence identical to Federal Rule 702, but Colorado adopted the *Frye* test subsequent to the enactment of that provision, so the reasoning of *Daubert* is inapposite. Colorado chooses to distinguish "hard science" from "social science" (*Brooks v. People*, 1999). The *Frye* test applies to "scientific devices or processes involving the evaluation of physical evidence" (e.g., DNA typing, blood typing, bite marks, gun residue) while Colorado Rule of Evidence 702 controls other expert testimony (e.g., Rape Trauma Syndrome and, presumably, expert testimony on battering relationships; *Fishback v. People*, 1993). Without elaborating, *Brooks* suggests that the focus for experience-based knowledge is whether the evidence is "reasonably reliable information that will assist the trier of fact" (*Fishback v. People*, p. 1114). In New York, *Frye* applies to novel scientific evidence, while the *Daubert-Kumho* formulation applies to experience-based expert testimony (*Wahl v. American Honda Motor Co.*, 1999). In Texas, *Daubert* applies to testimony based on scientific knowledge (*E.I. du Pont v. Robinson*, 1995), but a more general analysis applies if the testimony is based on knowledge obtained through observation, skill, or experience (*Gammill v. Jack Williams Chevrolet, Inc.*, 1998). Still other states reject both *Frye* and *Daubert*. Georgia rejects both rules and apparently places a great deal of discretion in the hands of the trial judge (see Johnson, Note, 1994). Wisconsin rejects both tests and falls back on a relevance test (*State v. Peters*, 1995). Oregon also rejects having a separate test for scientific evidence on top of the tests of relevancy and balancing unfair prejudice against probative value (*State v. Brown*, 1984).

In sum, the rules concerning admissibility of expert testimony vary according to jurisdiction and no general rule can be applied. Within a jurisdiction, it is important to realize that the type of knowledge serving as the basis for the expert's opinion may be critical, because the state may have separate analysis for "nonscientific" testimony such as is likely to arise in battered women homicide cases. Finally, as the rules are clarified at the federal level, states might adjust their own rules of evidence, so counsel is well advised to pay attention to changes on this front.

The point is that the decision as to whether an expert will be allowed to testify in a trial will be made by the trial judge, generally on the basis of the extent to which the testimony is outside the ken of the general lay jury and whether it will be useful to it to have this perspective for their consideration.

Use of Expert Testimony to Establish Reasonableness of Defendant's Belief in the Necessity of Self-Defense

In battered woman homicide cases, the only theory on which experts have offered evidence in support of self-defense thus far has been the Battered Woman Syndrome. Expert testimony on Battered Woman Syndrome is allowed in virtually every state. Louisiana is the lone holdout; there the court declared as a matter of law in *State v. Necaise* (La. Ct. App. 1985) that Battered Woman Syndrome testimony could only be associated with a diminished capacity defense (an excuse that essentially argues that the defendant was incapable of forming the necessary intent element of the offense, contrasted with self-defense which is an affirmative defense designed to justify the conduct).

We focus then on the admissibility of expert testimony to assist the jury in understanding battering and the circumstances that may lead a battered woman to believe it is necessary to use lethal force to protect herself. The cases illustrate a variety of reasons for admitting this testimony. Predominant among them is the effort to assist the jury to understand the reasonableness of a defendant's belief that she was in imminent danger and that lethal force was necessary to combat it. Taking clear exception to the Louisiana approach, the court in *Hawthorne v. State* (Fla.Dist.Ct.App. 1985) specifically cautioned that expert testimony on the Battered Woman Syndrome should not be categorized as an attempt to establish the defendant's diminished capacity and lack of responsibility for the shooting. Instead, such testimony "would be offered to show that because . . . [the defendant] suffered from the syndrome, it was reasonable for her to have remained in the home and . . . to have believed that her life and the lives of her children were in imminent danger." Thus, the expert testimony spoke directly to the self-defense doctrine's requirement that the defendant reasonably believed it was necessary to use deadly harm to prevent imminent death or great bodily harm. *Bonner v. State* (Ala.Crim.App. 1998) is in accord. There, defendant successfully appealed from a manslaughter conviction, arguing that the trial court improperly refused to allow expert testimony on the Battered Woman Syndrome. Interestingly, the trial court had declared that testimony relevant and material, but found it to be so prejudicial that the judge deemed it inadmissible.

In *Bonner*, the record reveals that defendant's husband subjected his wife and her children to mental and physical abuse before and during their marriage. On several occasions, the police responded to emergency calls that resulted from his physical beatings. There was evidence that the violence escalated during the marriage and included beating the defendant with fists and with a gun barrel and firing a gun at her. In response, she had fought back on occasion and had twice stabbed her husband during these altercations. Beyond that, she had requested the Department of Human Resources to provide legal aid to enable her to divorce her husband, but he had apologized for his behavior and persuaded her not to proceed with divorce. That pattern prompted the State to argue at trial that the defendant's claim of self-defense should be defeated because her decision to continue to remain in the allegedly abusive relationship created an inference that she was not afraid of her husband. It was especially in response to this prosecution argument that the appellate court reversed the conviction and ordered a new trial, admitting expert testimony of a social worker who regularly counsels battered women (but who had never counseled the defendant). His testimony was proffered not to illustrate that the defendant suffered from Battered Woman Syndrome, but to show the "psychological coping mechanisms of battered women and why they don't leave home and how they try to protect themselves." The trial court concluded that this testimony was unnecessary and would tend to confuse the jury. The appellate court rejected this attempt to protect the jury from additional evidence on battering, and explained: "Allowing the defense the opportunity to present expert testimony on the syndrome and the characteristics of a battered woman would not have confused the jury but instead would have given the jury and the trial court information beyond the understanding of the average layperson. Additionally, the introduction of expert testimony may have provided clarification on the issue of self-defense, i.e., whether the appellant acted reasonably under the circumstances" (*Bonner v. State*, p. 444).

Use of Expert Testimony to Dispel Myths About Battered Women and Battering

Other courts have emphasized the importance of allowing expert testimony to assist in dispelling myths, toward the end of helping the jury assess the reasonableness of a defendant's perceptions. The stereotype most often encountered is one that suggests a woman would have left her abuser if conditions were really as bad as she says they were (*State v. Hodges* [Kan. 1986]; *People v. Yaklich* [Colo. 1991]). This stereotype is most often encountered in prosecutorial questioning and argument. For example, in *Ibn-Tamas v. United States* (D.C. 1979) the prosecutor tried to discredit the defendant's testimony by suggesting that the violent nature of her relationship with her husband had been overdrawn, and he implied that the logical reaction of a woman who was truly frightened and on occasion brutalized by her husband would be to leave or at least call the police:

Q: And during the time in Miami, did you ever leave him?

A: No, I didn't.

Q: Did you ever call the police?

A: No, I didn't. He told me he would kill me if I called the police.

The prosecutor pressed the theme during his closing argument: "Maybe she put up with too much too long, although whose fault was that? She could have gotten out, you know."

That was the same argument made in *State v. Humphrey* (Cal. 1996) wherein the prosecutor urged the jury not to believe the defendant's testimony that her husband had shot at her the night before she killed him. The state's attorney argued that "if this defendant truly believed that [Hampton] had shot at her, on that night, I mean she would have left. . . . If she really believed that he had tried to shoot her, she would not have stayed" (*People v. Humphrey*, p. 151). The trial court did not allow expert testimony to explain why, in the expert's opinion, battered women do not leave. On appeal, the case was reversed and expert testimony declared admissible on retrial.

The value of expert testimony to explain why battered women do not leave is further illustrated in *Wieand v. Florida* (Fla. 1999), a case in which the defendant shot her husband during a violent argument and was charged with first-degree murder. Evidence at trial showed that her husband had beaten and choked her throughout the course of their three-year relationship and that he had threatened further violence if she left him. At trial, she claimed self-defense and presented expert testimony about the battered spouse syndrome, including expert testimony on reasons why she did not leave the apartment the night of the argument despite apparent opportunities to do so: She had just given birth seven weeks earlier; she had been choked unconscious; she was paralyzed with terror; experience had taught her that threats of leaving only made her husband more violent. The prosecutor capitalized on a common myth when she asked the jury why the defendant did not "go out the door" and why she did not "get in the car" before resorting to violence. Addressing this trial strategy and its concomitant invitation to allow expert testimony to combat it, the appellate court held that expert testimony should be admitted to rebut these kinds of common myths and to explain the very real dangers faced by women in battering relationships. "[T]here are many reasons battered women do not feel free to leave a battering relationship. The woman might have been isolated from her family by the abuser, she may not be able to afford to go, or she may realize that leaving is more dangerous than staying" (*Wieand v. Florida*, p. 1054).

The Texas Court of Criminal Appeals reached the same conclusion in *Fielder v. State* (1988) wherein the defendant testified she believed her husband would kill her if she did not kill him first. The trial court excluded testimony by a psychologist on why a woman would remain in an abusive situation. That exclusion was reversed on appeal and a new trial ordered because the appellate court found this information relevant to the central contested issue in the case: the reasonableness of the defendant's fear. The appellate court declared that the average layperson had no basis for understanding the conduct of an abused woman, and expert testimony on that issue could be of appreciable help to the trier of fact, especially in light of the fact that the prosecution argued that staying in the relationship was inconsistent with a claim of fear.

In that same vein, the Georgia court in *Smith v. State* (Ga. 1997) was concerned that myths might impede the jury's ability to fully assess reasonableness and declared that expert testimony should be available to help jurors determine whether the defendant had acted in self-defense. There the court reversed a conviction for voluntary manslaughter and directed that a clinical psychologist should be allowed to testify that a battered woman does not report the abuse to family members or friends for fear that they might take action and subsequently be injured; that it is not unusual for a battered woman who has been abused over a long period of time to remain in such a situation; that a battered woman typically believes that the man is not going to repeat the abuse when he promises not to; and that the battered woman becomes increasingly afraid for her own well-being so that her primary emotion is fear. The trial court had excluded that testimony on the grounds that the jurors could draw their own conclusions as to whether the defendant acted in fear of her life, but the appellate court disagreed, reasoning that the expert's testimony summarized above comprised conclusions that jurors could not ordinarily draw for themselves.

In *Smith*, the expert essentially testified to the profile of a battered woman and the appellate court declared that profile potentially useful to the jury. That approach was adopted by the appellate court in *State v. Richardson* (Wis. 1994) as well, in another case in which the trial court had refused to admit expert testimony designed to explain the profile of a battered woman offered to "assist the jury to evaluate the reasonableness of [the defendant's] fear." The defendant had killed her boyfriend who had beaten and threatened to kill her throughout their relationship. She testified that on the night of the killing he had kicked her, attempted to choke her, and threatened to kill her; she further testified that she was "terrified he would kill" her. The testimony excluded by the trial court

would have provided a context from which the jury could understand why [the defendant] might perceive herself to be in imminent danger at the time of the killing and could assess whether such a belief would have been reasonable. The confrontational nature of an incident where a battered woman kills her abuser might only become apparent when viewed in the context of a pattern of violent behavior rather than as an isolated incident. (*State v. Richardson*, p. 382)

That context is so critical to understanding these cases, and the *Richardson* court is absolutely right when it observes that without that evidence, an incident may appear to be an isolated one when, in fact, it is part of a pattern that is clear to the defendant and must be made clear to the jurors if they are to be enabled to fully understand and appreciate the circumstances in which the defendant operated at the time of the murder.

Finally, lest we think only prosecutors and jurors may fall into the stereotypical trap about the reality of battered women's lives and their options, it is clear that judges are not immune. The opinion in *Wieand v. Florida* (Fla. 1999, p. 1054) refers to the Gender Bias Report from Maryland and quotes a judge (whose anonymity is preserved) who expressed his disbelief of a battered woman's claimed defense:

The reason I don't believe it is because I don't believe anything like this could happen to me. If I was you and someone had threatened me with a gun, there is no way that I could continue to stay with them.

This kind of judicial myopia, although hopefully rare, was also reported in *United States v. Gaviria* (E.D.N.Y. 1992). Although not a self-defense case, it is reported here because the case involved a battered woman who sought to have her actions understood in the context of the battering relationship. There, the court rejected a battered woman's claim that she engaged in drug dealing under duress, explaining that her "status as a victim of systematic physical and emotional abuse substantially lessens her blameworthiness, notwithstanding her legal guilt." Having made this slight bow to an understanding of the woman's plight, the court ended with this astounding conclusion: "While it would have been an act of extraordinary courage and perhaps recklessness, she could have left her husband" (*United States v. Gaviria*, p. 481).

It probably goes without saying that defendants most likely run the risk that fact finders will engage in this kind of thinking and hold battered women to these "love them or leave them" standards in jurisdictions that rely on an objective measure of reasonableness, and that do not allow testimony on battering and the nature of the battering relationship.

Use of Expert Testimony to Show Typical Emotional and Behavioral Responses of Battered Women

Allowing contextual evidence may mean admitting evidence of prior violent acts and expert testimony on common patterns in abusive relationships. That was not done in *Commonwealth v. Rodriguez* (Mass. 1994), and the failure of the trial court to allow such evidence required reversal of the defendant's conviction. In that case, the defendant's boyfriend told her that she could not go to her friend's house; she went anyway and he came and retrieved her after arguing, slapping her, and pulling her hair. The quarrel continued after they got home. The boyfriend grabbed a knife and held it to the defendant's face and kicked her 11-year-old son. She told her daughter to call the police, but the boyfriend disabled the telephone. The defendant grabbed the knife off the table and tried to force the boyfriend out the door. He slapped her and she fatally stabbed him.

Declaring that the trial court should have allowed evidence of the boyfriend's prior violence, the appellate court explained:

We believe that the jury would have been aided considerably in determining the reasonableness of the defendant's use of deadly force if they had heard evidence of other violent acts recently committed by the victim against the defendant. We think this is so partly because much of the excluded evidence concerned acts of violence that were considerably more serious than those heard by the jury, and that those acts were committed against the defendant herself. . . . The excluded testimony would have enhanced the defendant's assertion of that defense so significantly that its exclusion constitutes reversible error. (*Commonwealth v. Rodriguez*, p. 1042, citations omitted)

The court made it clear that in cases like this, where self-defense is an issue, "expert testimony on common patterns in abusive relationships and the typical emotional and behavioral responses of persons who are battered may be admissible" (*Commonwealth v. Rodriguez*, p. 1042).

Expert Testimony Is Generally Not Admissible to Establish Defendant's State of Mind

When it comes to proving the defendant's state of mind, what she perceived, and how reasonable her beliefs were at the time of the alleged killing, the defendant is on her own. An expert cannot help and will not be allowed to offer evidence on these matters.

To illustrate the pattern of decisions and the rationale for them, consider *State v. Richardson* (Wis. 1994). In that case, the defendant did not dispute that she had stabbed and killed her boyfriend. She raised Battered Woman Syndrome as an element of her self-defense and sought to persuade the jury that on the night of her boyfriend's death, she was afraid he would kill her. An expert witness specializing in the treatment of battered women and other survivors of trauma was allowed to testify to the cycle of violence and learned helplessness; additionally she testified about common characteristics of battered women. The defendant testified that throughout her relationship of several years with her boyfriend, "he had beat" her and "threatened to kill" her. She also testified that on the night she killed him, he had kicked her, attempted to choke her, and threatened to kill her. She testified that she was terrified he would kill her.

The trial court refused to allow expert testimony comparing the defendant with the profile of a battered woman, and the appellate court found that to be error. The Wisconsin statute governing expert testimony provides that it should be allowed if it "assist[s] the trier of fact to understand the evidence or to determine a fact in issue" (W.S.A. § 907.02). Applying this standard, the Wisconsin Supreme Court determined that the profile evidence would assist the jury to evaluate the reasonableness of the defendant's fear, without invading the jury's province to determine the facts.

But a different conclusion was reached with respect to the defendant's contention that the expert should have been allowed to testify to her opinion of whether the defendant actually believed she was in danger, and the expert's opinion of whether that belief was reasonable. Rejecting that testimony, the trial and appellate courts emphasized that determination of the defendant's state of mind is for the jury to determine, and in this arena the expert has no more expertise than the jury.

The reason for allowing expert testimony about Battered Woman Syndrome is to assist the jury in an area where its knowledge may be mistaken but where the expert has special knowledge. The expert in Battered Woman Syndrome does not have special knowledge about the battered woman's state of mind during a homicidal act any more than the lay jurors. That a battered woman may exhibit certain characteristics from the psychological and physical abuse of battering is something that can be made known to the jury through the use of an expert witness. However, knowing those characteristics does not give the expert any special advantage in helping a jury determine whether the abuse cycle has escalated at the time of the homicidal act to a point at which the battered woman is in fear of imminent danger. (*State v. Richardson*, p. 383, citations omitted.)

In keeping with that decision and the rationale supporting it are *Witt v. State* (Wyo. 1995) and *State v. Griffiths* (Idaho 1980). In the same vein are cases in which the expert sought to offer an opinion as to whether the defendant actually suffered from Battered Woman Syndrome and whether her acts were the product of it. Those conclusions are variations on the "state of mind" theme and are routinely left for the jury alone,[6] without "assistance" from an expert (*People v. Wilson*, Mich. 1992; *State v. Burtzlaff*, S.D. 1992).

Lay Testimony to Establish the Context of Abuse

In addition to reliance upon expert testimony, lay testimony may be used to help the jury understand the battering context in which the fatal blow occurred. The law allows lay witnesses to testify to what they have seen in the past, and to what they have heard (subject to hearsay restrictions); and it may allow them to offer testimony on the conclusions they drew from these observations. Examination of the role of lay testimony in battered women cases focuses on the purpose for which it is offered.

Most often, lay testimony is offered to corroborate the testimony of the defendant. In some instances, it has been used to corroborate testimony of a history of abuse preceding that of her current husband or boyfriend (*Rogers v. State*, Fla. 1993).

Sometimes lay testimony is used as a means of giving independent accounts of abuse, so the jury can hear of these instances from someone other than the defendant. In these cases, the witnesses are not necessarily testifying to the same incidents related by the defendant; they are supplementing the abusive history with scenes they personally witnessed. For example, in *Commonwealth v. Stonehouse* (Pa. 1989) the defendant's neighbors testified that the deceased drove around the apartment with regularity and would awaken them when he pounded on the defendant's doors and shouted obscenities at her. Folks who lived within view of her apartment testified that the deceased would sit in his van and peer at the defendant's apartment through binoculars. The landlord testified that he often observed the deceased's van in the neighborhood, that once he found the deceased in the basement of the apartment building, and he saw folded pieces of paper stuck in the door jambs to appellant's apartment at odd hours. Another witness testified that she notified the police but was told that this was just a "domestic matter" and nothing could be done. This kind of evidence, not unlike that offered by the defendant, can be enormously persuasive, coming from witnesses who do not have a stake in the outcome of the litigation.

Another example is *Bonner v. State* (Ala. 1998), in which the defense employed lay testimony from police officers and children to corroborate the abuse reported by the defendant. A police officer testified that on several occasions he had responded to "911" calls made by the defendant as a result of beatings by the deceased. The defendant's ten-year-old son and her nine-year-old niece testified that at least three times a month the defendant's husband would beat the defendant with his fists and push her into the wall; they also testified that he had fired a gun at the defendant and had beaten her with the gun barrel. Both children further testified that on occasion the defendant had fought back and that on two of those occasions, she had stabbed her husband.

Most commonly, lay testimony is used to corroborate the defendant's accounts of abuse in the present relationship, abuse that finally culminated in the death of her abuser. The critical importance of that corroboration is illustrated by the court's opinion in *Wieand v. Florida* (Fla. 1999) in which the appellate court held that improper exclusion of eyewitness testimony to corroborate defendant's assertion of prior abuse by her husband was not harmless error. In that case, the defendant had shot her husband during a violent argument. At trial, she claimed self-defense and presented expert testimony on battered spouse syndrome. She testified that her husband had beaten and choked her throughout the course of their three-year relationship and that he had threatened further violence if she left him. She proffered lay testimony in the form of three eyewitnesses who had seen prior acts of abuse by her husband, directed toward the defendant. The trial court refused to allow that lay testimony.

The appellate court said that those lay witnesses should have been allowed to testify because they "would have provided the only direct testimony to support Wieand's claims of prior abuse and to corroborate the basis for the experts' opinions" (*Wieand v. State*, pp. 1057–1058). In light of the fact that experts were allowed to testify to prior abuse as reported to them by the defendant, the intermediate court of appeals had held that this failure to allow the lay testimony was only harmless error. The Florida Supreme Court disagreed, however, and found the exclusion of those lay witnesses was not harmless error. Courts may not be required to come to that conclusion in every case, but the mistaken exclusion was not harmless in this case because it opened the door for an unfair argument by the prosecutor, unfair because the prosecution knew that corroborating testimony of domestic violence had been excluded by the court and took advantage of it:

By excluding the witnesses in this case, the trial court deprived the defendant of eyewitness testimony. Furthermore, the exclusion of the three witnesses to prior incidents of domestic violence enabled the prosecutor to discredit Wieand's claims of abuse by arguing that no one had ever witnessed any injuries on Wieand or seen evidence of her husband's abuse of her: "Nobody saw any injuries to [Kathy] then. Nobody saw anything. . . . Anyhow do we know that she's not [a battered woman]? All we have to back her up is her own statements. . . . Nobody saw any injuries to her then. Nobody saw anything. . . . Co-workers didn't see injuries to her. Her mother-in-law didn't see the injuries to her. Her father-in-law didn't see the injuries to her. . . . Nobody sees any injuries to her. Nobody, nobody, ever." (*Wieand v. Florida*, p. 1058)

In that case, the prosecutor sought to take advantage of the absence of corroborative testimony. In *State v. Burtzlaff* (S.D. 1992) there was no suggestion of prosecutorial or other misconduct, but the appellate court commented on the advantage that might be gained by corroborative testimony. In this case, the defendant testified that the abuser had been drunk and physically abusive during the period of time preceding his death. On the night she killed him, he had been drinking and had "dragged [the defendant] into the family hot tub fully clothed and shoved her under the water several times." . . . [H]e then pulled her out of the tub, threw her on the floor, kicked her, and stated, "You think I'm going to kill you like this, don't you? I'm going to tell you right now it's not going to be this easy." The defendant testified that, after this threat, she left the room and got a shotgun. She found [the abuser] sitting on the couch with a drink in one hand and the television remote control in the other. She announced, "Larry, I'm going to kill you." He lifted his glass as if to toast her . . . then she fired. In her testimony, the defendant "alleged a history of mental, physical, and sexual abuse by her husband, especially during the preceding week."

The appellate court, in reviewing the record, observed that "despite his drinking and history of being a strict disciplinarian as a parent, no testimony other than Gloria Burtzlaff's could corroborate any history of violence."

The court says out loud what so many experience in these cases: The credibility of the abused woman who kills her abuser is always in play, especially so in cases in which that history of abuse was hidden, or is not obvious to the trier of fact. In these cases, lay testimony to corroborate the history of abuse is important. It may come from friends or family; indeed, those are probably the most common sources of corroboration. (See, for example, *People v. Humphrey*, Cal. 1996, in which several witnesses testified about the deceased's abusive conduct in general and his physical abuse of, and threats to, the defendant; *Rogers v. State*, Fla. 1993, where the defendant's mother corroborated the defendant's testimony of past abuse.) But, of course, the trier of fact may be suspicious of those witnesses, thinking perhaps that they are simply trying to help the defendant (in a word, thinking perhaps that they are lying). Additional sources of lay testimony should be considered and may be even more useful, for example, third parties who observed instances of threatening behavior or instances of controlling behavior that seemed disproportionate to the circumstances.

In some cases, the defense has attempted to introduce lay testimony to corroborate the defendant's testimony of an abusive relationship, but the trial court has refused the additional testimony on the grounds that it is cumulative. That was the case, for example, in *State v. Cramer* (Kan. 1993) and it was not reversed on appeal. Perhaps the most glaring example is *State v. Riley* (W. Va. 1997) in which the defendant had testified to the history of abuse and had described the events immediately preceding the shooting of her abuser, and an expert witness had testified about the Battered Woman Syndrome. But attempts to introduce evidence of the nature of prior abusive behavior were seriously restricted. The trial court refused to allow testimony by the defendant's daughter (who would have testified to abuse inflicted on the defendant by the deceased) because it would have been "cumulative" to that presented by the defendant and the expert. The trial court also restricted testimony by the defendant's son-in-law regarding abusive instances in which the defendant had contacted him for assistance; upholding prosecutorial objections of hearsay, the court allowed the son-in-law to testify to what he had seen but not to what he had heard. In addition, the trial court refused to allow a police officer and witness to testify regarding the abuser brandishing a gun upon the witness. The appellate court found no fault with these restrictions because it declared the proffered testimony would have been cumulative to the testimony of the defendant and her expert witness. But the trial court had already severely limited testimony by the expert witness and had not allowed "particular instances of abuse" based on the prosecutor's "concern that such hearsay evidence should be admissible only for a limited purpose" (*State v. Riley*, pp. 529–30). The defendant failed in her effort to persuade the court that this testimony would not be used for the prohibited purpose of demonstrating character,[7] but would have been used to show the defendant's state of mind. The appellate court noted in a footnote that "[e]vidence of battered spouse syndrome has been found to be admissible for a criminal defendant . . . to determine the defendant's mental state where self-defense is asserted" (*State v. Riley*, p. 529, note 6). The case nonetheless illustrates that the syndrome defense as presented through expert testimony may be severely limited, and the general defense of self-defense may be severely limited in instances such as this in which the court refuses credible evidence to establish the reasonableness of fear of imminent harm and the necessity of defense.

INSTRUCTING THE JURY ON SELF-DEFENSE

When Self-Defense Instruction Is Refused in Battered Woman Cases

As an initial matter, it is probably important to recognize a factual pattern in which many courts have held that a self-defense instruction is not warranted. These are the sleeping giant cases. That is, in cases in which the abuser was sleeping or otherwise incapacitated at the time the fatal blow is struck, courts employing traditional, objective notions of self-defense typically do not allow the jury even to consider self-defense. These courts generally decide *as a matter of law* that the blow was not struck in self-defense.

When a court decides an issue is a "matter of law," that means that it is not an issue to be decided by the fact finder. If the case is being heard by a jury, questions of law are decided by the judge; questions of fact are decided by the jury. Self-defense is generally considered a question of fact, to be decided by the jury as a factual matter. But before that defense gets to the jury for its consideration, the judge must determine that there is evidence on each element of the defense. If there is no evidence of self-defense, the jury is not entitled to consider it. In that case, the judge would determine as a matter of law that self-defense is not a question to be put before the jury. For example, if the court determines that a sleeping man cannot, by definition, pose an imminent threat, the court will refuse to allow the jury to determine whether the defendant who shot him acted in self-defense. Why? Because self-defense requires the finding of an imminent threat. If there was no imminent threat, there can be no claim of self-defense.

The best example of a case in which a battered woman raised self-defense but the trial court refused to allow the jury to consider the claim is *State v. Norman* (N.C. 1989). Ms. Norman was denied an instruction on self-defense because the court found, as a matter of law, that threatened harm was not imminent when she killed her sleeping husband. The facts of the case were summarized by Rosen (1993, pp. 392–393) succinctly:

J.T. Norman's abuse of his wife was prolonged and vicious. Over the years, whenever he was drunk, he brutally beat her, often inflicting serious injuries. He used his fists, bottles, ashtrays, and even a baseball bat. Mr. Norman forced his wife to prostitute herself to support him. When she was pregnant he kicked her down the stairs, causing the premature birth of her child. When she ran away, he tracked her, caught her, and beat her. He frequently threatened to kill her.

In the days immediately preceding the killing, the abuse Ms. Norman suffered became more constant and vicious, and the threats to kill her became more frequent and, by all accounts, more believable. Ms. Norman called the police. The officers told her that she would have to take out a warrant, but she told them that her husband would kill her if she did. The officers left, but returned when they received a call that she had taken an overdose of pills. When the ambulance arrived, Mr. Norman tried to interfere, saying, "Let the bitch die. . . . She ain't nothing but a dog. . . . She don't deserve to live," and threatened to kill her, her mother, and her grandmother.

The day after she was released from the hospital, Ms. Norman sought help at a counseling center. When she returned home and told her husband that he must stop drinking or she would have him committed; he told her that he would cut her throat if he saw someone coming for him. During the day, he threatened twice to cut off her breast, and his threats to kill her continued until he took a nap late that afternoon, forcing her to lie on the floor by the bed.

Ms. Norman sneaked out of the house while her husband slept. She went to her mother's home and retrieved her husband's gun from her mother's purse (her mother had taken the gun earlier in the day after Mr. Norman's serious threats). Ms. Norman then returned to her home and shot her husband three times while he slept.

On those facts, without the benefit of an instruction on self-defense, the jury found Ms. Norman guilty of manslaughter. She was sentenced to prison for six years. Her conviction and sentence was initially overturned on appeal, but it was ultimately reinstated and affirmed. The North Carolina courts found, as a matter of law, that Ms. Norman could not have acted in self-defense. The courts determined, as a matter of law, that Ms. Norman was not faced with an imminent threat of death or serious bodily harm from a man who was sleeping when she shot him. Since that was true as a matter of law, there was no factual issue of self-defense to be decided by the jury. Hence, no self-defense instruction was given.

Other courts reach the same conclusion and keep self-defense from the jury because they find, as a matter of law, that it was not reasonable to kill a sleeping abuser.

An example of refusing to give a self-defense instruction because the court found, as a matter of law, that it was unreasonable to kill a sleeping abuser is *State v. Stewart* (Kan. 1988). This case has found its way into a number of textbooks as a classic example of the failure of self-defense in battered women cases. The facts disclosed a long history of mental and physical abuse by the deceased, including beating the defendant, kicking her in the chest and ribs so violently that she had to be hospitalized, killing her pet and then holding a gun to her head and threatening to kill her, and kicking her juvenile child out of the house. At one point, the defendant institutionalized herself because she had become suicidal; the abuser retrieved her from the hospital, took her home and forced her to perform oral sex several times, and threatened to kill her if she ever ran away again. The defendant found a loaded gun in the house and feared what the abuser would do with it. She hid the gun under the mattress of a bed in a spare room. On the day she killed her abuser, as she was cleaning the house he made remarks that she should not bother because she would not be there long. After again forcing her to perform oral sex, he went to sleep. The court noted that, at that time, there were two vehicles in the driveway and the defendant had access to the car keys. While the abuser slept, the defendant retrieved the gun from beneath the mattress and killed the abuser while he slept.

The defendant asserted self-defense and the trial court instructed the jury that it should determine the reasonableness of the defendant's belief that she was in imminent danger from her individual subjective viewpoint rather than the viewpoint of a reasonable person in her circumstances. The appellate court did not dispute the violent relationship that preceded the killing, nor did it focus on the substance of the self-defense instruction. Instead, the court ruled that the jury should not have been allowed to consider self-defense:

[A] battered woman cannot reasonably fear imminent life-threatening danger from her sleeping spouse. . . . We must . . . hold that when a battered woman kills her sleeping spouse when there is no imminent danger, the killing is not reasonably necessary and a self-defense instruction may not be given. To hold otherwise in this case would in effect allow the execution of the abuser for past or future actions and conduct. (*State v. Stewart*, pp. 574, 578–579)

The bottom line is this: if self-defense is considered in the traditional fashion, the issue of whether the battered woman acted in self-defense may not ever get to the jury. If self-defense is considered and defined more broadly as we have argued here it should be, the issue of self-defense is much more likely to get to the jury, to be determined as a question of fact: Given the history of the battering relationship and the facts confronting the battered woman at the time she struck the fatal blow, did she reasonably believe it was necessary to defend herself with deadly force? If so, the law would permit acquittal or conviction of a lesser crime; if not, she will be convicted as charged.

If a change needs to be made in a state's understanding of self-defense, that change should be made at the legislative level. The state statute setting out self-defense should be changed to reflect the importance of considering contextual evidence, for example, in self-defense cases in which the facts establish a history of a battering relationship. This is the best way to deal with the matter because jury instructions typically reflect, and are patterned after, the language of the statute authorizing them.

When Self-Defense Instruction Is Given, It Generally Tracks Statutory Language

The law of self-defense varies from jurisdiction to jurisdiction. There is no uniform criminal law, nor is there any requirement that states interpret the commonalities in their statutes in the same way. Six states, for example, may choose to define self-defense as "defensive action employed as a reasonable response to imminent harm," and we may have six different definitions of "reasonable" and six different definitions of "imminent." In this federalist system, it is difficult to draw meaningful generalizations about the substance of the law, or about the instructions employed to help the jury apply it. Having said that, however, we can identify patterns in the appellate decisions that have ruled on instructions in these cases. Those patterns are useful in proposing instructions in future cases, as well as being useful tools in outlining arguments to assist the jury in following instructions that are given. Toward that end, we explore the cases that have focused on jury instructions in battered women homicide cases.

In the careful examination of jury instructions, it is good to recall that the language in the instruction will most often mirror the language of the state statute that authorizes it. To illustrate, *People v. Garcia* (Colo. 1999) was a case in which the defendant was convicted of second-degree murder for killing her husband with an axe. She testified that she killed him after he attempted to sexually assault her, and that he had verbally, physically, and sexually assaulted her frequently during their marriage. Colorado defines self-defense, in pertinent part, this way:

Deadly physical force may be used only if a person reasonably believes a lesser degree of force is inadequate and:

(a) The actor has reasonable grounds to believe, and does believe, that he or another person is in imminent danger of being killed or of receiving great bodily injury; or . . .

(c) The other person is committing or reasonably appears about to commit . . . sexual assault. . . . [Colo. Rev. Stat. § 18–1–704(2) (1988)]

The defendant requested an instruction that "her actions were to be measured by the conduct of a reasonable person in her position at that time." The trial court rejected that proffered instruction and, instead, instructed the jury in the language of the statute:

It is an affirmative defense . . . that the defendant used deadly physical force if:

1. She reasonably believed a lesser degree of force was inadequate, and
2. She had reasonable grounds to believe, and did believe, that she or another person was in imminent danger of being killed or of receiving great bodily injury.

Defendant objected to this instruction, contending that it was "incomplete and did not explain to the jury that evidence of Battered Woman

Syndrome could be used to gauge the reasonableness of her beliefs as they related to self-defense, nor did it explain that she had the right to act on appearances" (*People v. Garcia*, p. 7).

The appellate court approved the instruction given because it "tracked the text of both the pattern self-defense jury instruction and the self-defense statute." It informed the jury that it was to consider whether the defendant "reasonably believed a lesser degree of force was inadequate" and whether "she had reasonable grounds to believe, and did believe, that she or another person was in imminent danger of being killed or of receiving great bodily injury." The court concluded that "[a]n instruction in the language of the statute is generally considered to be sufficient" (*People v. Garcia*, p. 7).

The corollary of that, of course, is that if the instruction does not track the statutory language, it may be found to be an erroneous instruction. That was the case in *State v. Hundley* (Kan. 1985) where the issue was the use of the term "imminent" in the self-defense statute, as opposed to "immediate" in the instruction. The Kansas statute sets out self-defense as a justification when the defendant "reasonably believes that such conduct is necessary to defend himself or another against such aggressor's *imminent* use of unlawful force" (K. S. A. 21–3211, emphasis supplied). But the patterned jury instructions which the trial court used to instruct the jury provided that self-defense is justified when the defendant "reasonably believes that such conduct is necessary to defend himself or another against such aggressor's *immediate* use of unlawful force" (PIK Crim. 2d 54.17, emphasis supplied).

The appellate court reversed the verdict and insisted that the language in the jury instruction parallel the language of the statute. In so holding, the appellate court examined the pattern jury instruction to try to determine why the drafters varied its wording from the statutory language, and discovered that the drafters amended the wording because they thought "imminent" was a "better understood term" (PIK Crim. 2d 54.17, Comment; *State v. Hundley*, p. 466). The court rejected that rationale and held that the terms "imminent" and "immediate" are not interchangeable. Therefore, the case was reversed and remanded for a new trial in which the jury instructions would use the same language as the statute.

In the materials that follow, we examine cases that have specifically raised the issue of jury instructions. We try to organize these cases according to the substantive state law that controls them. Instructions in states evaluating reasonableness by an objective standard are contrasted with those employing a subjective standard and with those adhering to a hybrid standard. In this way, we hope to present these cases in the manner most useful to counsel.

When Self-Defense Instruction Is Given, It May Include Specific Reference to the Battering Relationship

We contend that in homicide cases in which a battered woman is charged with murder of her abuser, it is critically important that the jury be allowed to understand the entire context of the battering relationship. There is some precedent for allowing reference to that relationship in the instructions. The question is not so much whether battering can be mentioned in the instructions; the real question is how the jury is instructed with respect to what conclusions it may draw if it finds the battering relationship existed.

The Battering Relationship May Be Considered Along with Every Other Fact in Determining Self-Defense

In *People v. Garcia* (Colo. 1999) the trial court refused the defendant's requested instruction that included language instructing the jury that the defendant was a battered woman and that she had used deadly force while suffering from the Battered Woman Syndrome. Instead, the trial court gave a much more innocuous instruction, one approved by the appellate court, and one in keeping with the traditional law of self-defense:

The evidence in this case has raised an issue concerning the Battered Woman Syndrome. The Battered Woman Syndrome is not in and of itself a defense to a crime. However, if you find that the defendant did suffer from the syndrome, that is evidence which you can use in deciding the issues relating to the affirmative defense [of self-defense]. (*People v. Garcia*, p. 8)

This instruction is probably not objectionable in any jurisdiction allowing evidence of battering. It will probably be allowed in states employing the most traditional self-defense language because it does not expand the self-defense concept in the least. It simply reminds the jury that the battering relationship is a fact that may be taken into account to determine if the defendant acted defensively as permitted by law. Although the language of this particular instruction makes reference to the Battered Woman Syndrome, the substance of the instruction is not necessarily limited to that narrow scope of expert testimony; indeed, any evidence of battering and the effects of battering, as they may have influenced the defendant's actions, would lend itself to this instruction.

The Battering Relationship May Be Considered to Determine Whether the Defendant Honestly Believed She Was in Imminent Danger

In other cases, courts have allowed specific reference to battering to help the jury decide if the defendant had an honest belief that she was in imminent danger of death or serious bodily harm. Ohio is a state that employs a hybrid standard in self-defense cases and, in battered women cases, it recognizes a reasonable battered woman standard. The Ohio Supreme Court has approved this instruction (*State v. Thomas*, 1997; *State v. Koss*, 1990):

> In determining whether the Defendant had reasonable grounds for an honest belief that she was in imminent danger, you must put yourself in the position of the Defendant . . . You must consider the conduct of [the assailant] and determine if such acts and words caused the Defendant to reasonably and honestly believe that she was about to be killed or to receive great bodily harm. (*State v. Thomas*, p. 1345)

Thomas was another case in which the defendant sought more from the instructions. Specifically, she sought an instruction that attempted to more precisely define the Battered Woman Syndrome; beyond that, the proffered instruction required the jury to determine whether the defendant was a battered woman and then to use that determination to find that she believed she was in imminent danger. The trial and appellate courts refused that instruction, declaring that it would have set up an entirely separate defense, essentially a battered woman defense. Rejecting that defense, the court reiterated the importance of charging the jury to first determine objectively if the defendant reasonably believed she was in imminent danger. If so, the jury should be instructed to consider Battered Woman Syndrome in assessing the defendant's state of mind, in order to decide if, subjectively, she believed she was in imminent danger. Again, the import of these instructions does not hinge on evidence of Battered Woman Syndrome; the instructions lend themselves to use with any expert or other testimony of the battering relationship.

Another example of instructing the jury to consider the battering relationship in order to assess the defendant's belief that she was in imminent danger is *State v. Burtzlaff* (S.D. 1992). This is a case in which the instructions refer to a "reasonable battered woman" which may, in fact, be the standard in South Dakota. That issue was not before the court on appeal, however, so we cannot know if the state supreme court would approve it. With that caveat, this instruction is still helpful in a jurisdiction employing a hybrid standard for self-defense and is a lovely example of an instruction that focuses on the battering relationship as the context for determining the reasonableness and perception of imminent danger in a traditional understanding of self-defense:

Under certain circumstances, it is lawful to take the life of another. One who is acting in self-defense may take the life of an aggressor if the aggressor poses a risk of serious bodily injury or death. The risk of serious bodily injury or death must be imminent, that is it must be such that a reasonable and prudent person standing in the shoes of the Defendant, knowing what the Defendant knows and seeing what the Defendant sees, would believe that serious bodily injury or death would result immediately if the aggressor were not killed.

In the case wherein Battered Woman Syndrome is raised, and if you find in fact that Defendant is a battered woman, *you are to look at the evidence presented through the eyes of a reasonable and prudent battered woman. If a reasonable and prudent battered woman would have believed serious bodily injury or death was imminent, then the killing was lawful.* But, if you find that a reasonable and prudent battered woman would not have believed serious bodily injury or death imminent, then the killing was unlawful. (*State v. Burtzlaff*, pp. 8–9, emphasis supplied).

Again, this instruction may be tailored to cases in which there is evidence of battering relationships, separate and apart from the traditional "syndrome" evidence. If experts or other witnesses explain the battering relationship by the theory set forth in this volume or by other theoretical means, this instruction may still be used in hybrid jurisdictions.

The Battering Relationship May Be Considered to Determine If the Defendant Acted Reasonably

In other cases, courts struggling with how to incorporate evidence of battering into the traditional self-defense instructions have simply alerted the jury to the relevance of the battering, but have left it to the jury to determine just how it is relevant. The jury is entitled to more assistance than that. Consider, for example, *Smith v. State* (Ga. 1997). Georgia statutes reflect a traditional statement of self-defense, but the legislature added a section in 1993 specifically recognizing that in self-defense cases, the defendant may offer

(1) Relevant evidence that the defendant had been the victim of acts of family violence or child abuse committed by the deceased, and

(2) Relevant expert testimony regarding the condition of the mind of the defendant at the time of the offense, including those relevant facts and circumstances relating to the family violence or child abuse that are the bases of the expert's opinion. [OCGA § 16–3–21(d)].

If the jury believes that battering occurred, that factual finding could justify a finding that a reasonable person who had experienced abuse akin to that experienced by the defendant, would reasonably believe that the use of force was necessary in self-defense. Thus, the court held that in any case in which a battered person syndrome self-defense claim has been established (and the statutory language makes it clear that any competent evidence of battering would count, not just limited to or specifically including Battered Woman Syndrome), the court should give specific jury instructions on justification by self-defense. These jury instructions should be tailored to explain how the defendant's experiences as a battered person affected that defendant's state of mind at the time of the killing. The court, therefore, required that

a modified jury instruction be given in all battered person syndrome cases, when authorized by the evidence and requested by defendant, to assist the jury in evaluating the battered person's defense of self-defense. . . . It is suggested that such modified instruction read as follows: "I charge you that the evidence that the defendant suffers from battered person syndrome was admitted for your consideration in connection with the defendant's claim of self-defense and that such evidence relates to the issue of the reasonableness of the defendant's belief that the use of force was immediately necessary, even though no use of force against the defendant may have been, in fact, imminent. The standard is whether the circumstances were such as would excite the fears of a reasonable person possessing the same or similar psychological and physical characteristics as the defendant, and faced with the same circumstances surrounding the defendant at the time the defendant used force." (*Smith v. State*, pp. 823–24)

In that case, the court made it clear that the battered woman was entitled to a jury instruction to explain that the evidence of battering related to the reasonableness of her belief that the use of deadly force was immediately necessary to defend herself against her husband's imminent use of unlawful force. The court specifically held that the self-defense instruction should be modified in these cases "to permit juries to consider the reasonableness of the defendant's belief that the use of force was necessary in light of both [her] circumstances at the time [she] used force, and any psychological condition resulting from such circumstances" (*Smith v. State*, p. 823).

State v. Gartland (N.J. 1997) was another instance in which the court was sensitive to the fact that instructions should be tailored to reflect the facts of the case. This was an unfortunate case in the sense that the defendant had died by the time her conviction was reversed on appeal; nonetheless, the appellate court required contextual jury instructions in a way that will be helpful to other similarly situated defendants. Here, the defendant had shot her abuser when he came after her in her upstairs bedroom and the only means of retreat would have been through the door he blocked. The trial court used the model jury instruction and told the jury that "[a] reasonable belief is one which is to be held by a person of ordinary prudence and intelligence situated as Ms. Gartland was on [the date of the killing]." The court did not include any instruction that specifically apprised the jury that it could consider the 17 years of abuse suffered by the defendant in determining whether she actually and reasonably believed deadly force was necessary in self-defense. The jury asked twice during its deliberations for clarification. On each occasion, the court repeated its initial instructions.

The appellate court held that the jury instruction should have been tailored to the circumstances of the case, because the traditional self-defense standards fail to account for the perspective of abused women.

Any limitation of the jury's consideration of the surrounding acts and circumstances to those occurring at or immediately before the killing would be an erroneous statement of the applicable law.... At a minimum, the jury in Ellen Gartland's case should have been asked to consider whether, if it found such to be the case, a reasonable woman who had been the victim of years of domestic violence would have reasonably perceived on this occasion that the use of deadly force was necessary to protect herself from serious bodily injury. (State v. Gartland, p. 575)

Although most jurisdictions do not rely on a subjective test for determining self-defense, it is probably good to consider the instruction favored by a court from one of these jurisdictions. A case lending itself to careful exposition of proper instruction in a battered woman homicide case is State v. Leidholm (N.D. 1983), a manslaughter case in which the defendant was convicted for stabbing her husband after he fell asleep following a violent argument. The verdict was reversed and the case remanded for new trial because, among other errors, the trial court gave an erroneous instruction on self-defense. The subjective standard is one that requires the defendant's actions to be viewed and evaluated from "the standpoint of a person whose mental and physical characteristics are like the defendant's and who sees what the accused sees and knows what the accused knows" (State v. Leidholm, p. 818). That standard, by definition, requires the jury to consider the history of battering and to take into account the battering relationship as evidence of what has been presented at trial. With that understanding, the appellate court said it would never be necessary to include reference to battering in the jury instructions in a jurisdiction relying on a subjective standard, as long as the subjective standard is properly set out for the jury. The court offered this instruction, citing *State v. Hazlet* (N.D. 1907, p. 380):

A defendant's conduct is not to be judged by what a reasonably cautious person might or might not do or consider necessary to do under the like circumstances, but what he himself in good faith honestly believed and had reasonable ground to believe was necessary for him to do to protect himself from apprehended death or great bodily injury.

When reasonableness is measured objectively (i.e., reasonable is what a reasonably prudent person would do), a self-defense instruction is warranted whenever there is some evidence of the defendant's subjective belief that the use of deadly force was necessary to prevent death or great bodily harm. The critical question for the jury in these jurisdictions is whether the defendant's decision to use lethal force was reasonable. The jury is entitled to get to that question whenever the defendant achieves the threshold of showing that *she actually believed* it was necessary. If she actually believed it was necessary, the jury then decides if that belief was reasonable. If her belief was reasonable in the judgment of the jury, she may be declared to have acted in self-defense (assuming other requirements of the defense are also met). If her belief was not objectively reasonable, self-defense will fail. (*State v. Leidholm*, p. 818)

A case in point is *People v. Scott* (Ill. 1981), a case in which the trial court refused to instruct on self-defense. The case was reversed and remanded for a new trial in which the jury would have an opportunity to determine if the defendant's subjective belief in the necessity of lethal force was reasonable. In this case, the evidence of abuse was abundant but the question of whether the defendant killed in self-defense was a close one.

The man with whom the defendant lived was a correctional officer who mentally and physically abused her during the eight-year period they lived together. Often, he would handcuff her and beat her. On the evening the defendant killed her abuser, pursuant to the abuser's orders that the defendant never answer the door unarmed, she brought the abuser's .357 Magnum gun to the door when he knocked. After accusing the defendant of having an affair, he struck her across the face several times with a 9 mm gun and then with his fists. During his barrage, the abuser took the gun out of the defendant's hands and threw it on the bed. He then called his mistress on the telephone and said that the defendant would be gone in 45 minutes. The defendant walked around inside her house and tried to think of a way to leave with her youngest son without drawing the abuser's attention. While he was talking on the telephone, the abuser motioned to the defendant to get his handcuffs. Instead of getting the handcuffs, the defendant picked up the .357 Magnum off the bed, closed her eyes, and fired it. She testified that she "tried to fire once to scare him but the gun continued shooting" and she "heard it click over and over" (*People v. Scott*, pp. 71–72).

The appellate court held that "In order to support the giving of the [self-defense] instruction, there must be some evidence in the record revealing a *subjective belief* on the part of the defendant that the use of deadly force was necessary to *prevent imminent* death or great bodily harm" (*People v. Scott*, p. 72, emphasis supplied). The court added that it had previously held that "slight evidence of self-defense" will support giving a self-defense instruction.

The court declared this an "admittedly very close case" but observed that the record contained "sufficient evidence of defendant's subjective belief in the necessity of the use of force likely to cause death or serious bodily harm to warrant the giving of a self-defense instruction." The defendant had testified that on the night she killed her boyfriend, she was frightened that he was going to hurt her, even kill her, and that she picked up the .357 rather than complying with his demand of her to be handcuffed and she began shooting because she was frightened of what he would do to her. Whether this subjective belief that deadly force was necessary to deter the decedent from causing her great bodily harm or death was a reasonable belief was a question for the jury. "So long as some evidence is presented from which a jury could conclude that defendant had a subjective belief, the jury should determine if the belief existed and, if so, whether that belief was reasonable or unreasonable" (*People v. Scott*, p. 72).

The court then found that the instruction the defendant had requested should have been given:

A person is justified in the use of force against another when and to the extent that he reasonably believes that such conduct is necessary to defend himself or another against such other's imminent use of unlawful force. However, he is justified in the use of force which is intended or likely to cause death or great bodily harm only if he reasonably believes that such force is necessary to prevent imminent death or great bodily harm to himself or another, or the commission of a forcible felony. (*People v. Scott*, p. 72)

CONCLUSION

Self-defense is a justification. It is a defense that, successfully employed, declares that the defendant was justified in acting as she did. In a homicide case, it can operate as a complete defense, resulting in acquittal. Self-defense is the defense most often employed on behalf of battered women who kill their batterers, but it is a difficult defense to use in these cases and it rarely produces an acquittal; more likely, the fact finder declares the defendant guilty of some lesser degree of murder or manslaughter. In nonconfrontational cases, self-defense is even less likely to succeed and, in those cases, the court sometimes refuses to allow the jury to even consider it.

As it is traditionally understood, self-defense requires a finding that the defendant reasonably believed she was threatened with death or serious bodily harm. Most jurisdictions measure reasonableness objectively, by a reasonable man standard. So, as self-defense is traditionally understood, the question for the jury is: Would a reasonable man have thought he was threatened with death or serious bodily harm? On this issue, the law of self-defense is developing in a fashion that is favorable to battered women; courts are beginning to allow more evidence of what the battered woman perceived and more evidence of the battering relationship. That approach is moving the standard somewhat from a strictly objective/reasonable man standard to one allowing a more subjective element that allows us to consider what a reasonable person in the defendant's situation would have believed.

As it is traditionally understood, self-defense further requires a finding that the defendant was in imminent danger of death or serious bodily harm. This has always been a difficult issue, especially in those cases in which the battered woman kills when the batterer is sleeping or otherwise incapacitated. If imminence is understood as a time-bound variable, the nonconfrontational cases are lost. If imminent harm is not bound by immediacy, but is more closely related to the reasonableness requirement, the battered woman who kills may be able to make more expansive arguments about the battering relationship and the threat it posed. Courts that are beginning to focus more on the necessity of self-defense (as opposed to relying on the more traditional concepts of reasonableness and imminence considered as separate entities) are creating more meaningful opportunities for battered women to get to the jury, even in nonconfrontational cases.

Whatever definition of self-defense is employed in the state in which the battered woman is tried, these trials often require the services of expert witnesses. An expert will generally be allowed to testify if that person's specialized knowledge will assist the trier of fact to understand evidence or will help the jury to determine a fact in issue. Experts may be used to help establish the reasonableness of the defendant's belief in the necessity of self-defense; they may be used to dispel myths lay people often have about battered women; they may be used to help the jury understand typical emotional and behavioral responses of battered women. Expert testimony is generally not allowed to establish the defendant's state of mind at the time of the murder.

Beyond expert witnesses, battered woman cases often rely on lay testimony to corroborate the defendant's testimony. The testimony is generally restricted to what the lay witnesses actually observed and, only rarely, will their opinions be allowed.

The state law of self-defense will finally be reduced in summary form at trial in the jury instructions. Jury instructions vary from state to state, reflecting the different understandings of self-defense. These instructions generally track statutory language and they may specifically reference the battering relationship. When the battering relationship is referenced in jury instructions, the jury is generally told that it may consider the battering relationship along with every other fact in considering whether the defendant acted in self-defense. In some instances, the instruction will be more helpful to the battered woman defendant and the jury will be instructed that it may consider the battering relationship in determining whether the defendant honestly believed she was in imminent danger, and in determining whether she acted reasonably.

There is no uniform criminal law in the United States. In this chapter, we have attempted to survey state law as inclusively as possible to illustrate the dominant themes that appear in cases in which battered women who killed their batterers were tried for murder and claimed that they killed in self-defense.

NOTES

1. Although Ohio clearly claims to utilize a subjective test, it is a curious claim because it does not represent the law as it existed in Ohio at the time these cases were decided. In each of these cases, the Ohio Supreme Court cited and quoted from its opinion in *State v. Koss* (Ohio 1990), a case containing some untidy language that may create some of this uncertainty. Specifically, the *Koss* case approved an instruction directing the jury to determine if the defendant "had reasonable grounds for an honest belief" that she was about to be killed. The "reasonableness" language as it appears may lead some to think this is at least a hybrid instruction. Having said that, however, we are not prepared to argue with the members of the Ohio Supreme Court. Although their test seems to allow for both objective and subjective elements, they place themselves in the subjective ballpark and there they shall remain.

2. In one sense *Frye* illustrates the "common law" of evidence, because there were no federal statutory rules of evidence at the time it was decided. The "common law" rules as inherited from England likely had no rule at all on novel scientific evidence.

3. The *Daubert* standard for determining reliability instructs the court to consider these factors:

1. Testability of the scientific theory or technique;

2. Whether the theory or technique had been subjected to peer review and publication;

3. The known or potential rate of error;

4. The existence or nonexistence of maintained standards;

5. Whether the theory or technique has general acceptance in a relevant scientific community. (*Daubert v. Merrell Dow Pharmaceuticals, Inc.*, p. 590)

4. Arizona (*State v. Tankersley*, 1998); California (*People v. Kelly*, 1976); Kansas (*Armstrong v. City of Wichita*, 1995); Illinois (*Harris v. Croptmate Co.*, 1999, acknowledging guidance of *Daubert* as well); Indiana (*Sears Roebuck and Co. v. Manuilov*, 1999), but *Daubert* was acknowledged as guidance and relied upon heavily); Maryland (*Reed v. State*, 1978); Minnesota (*State v. Alt*, 1993); Mississippi (*Gleeton v. State*, 1998); Nebraska (*State v. Houser*, 1992); Pennsylvania (*Wack v. Farmland Industries, Inc.*, 1999); Washington (*State v. Jones*, 1996).

5. Iowa (*Johnson v. Knoxville Community School Dist.*, 1997); Kentucky (*Mitchell v. Commonwealth*, 1995, but not for experienced-based testimony in a pre-*Kumho* case, according to *Collins v. Commonwealth*, 1997); Montana (*Gilkey v. Schweitzer*, 1999, but only for novel scientific testimony); New Mexico (*State v. Albercio*, 1993); Oklahoma (*Taylor v. State*, 1995); Tennessee (*State v. Collier*, 1998, not actually adopting *Daubert*, but relying on it in interpreting its state rule of evidence); Wyoming (*Bunting v. Jamieson*, 1999).

6. The only exceptions to this rule of inadmissibility are cases in jurisdictions using a subjective test of reasonableness. See, e.g., *State v. Daws* (Ohio 1994) in which the expert was allowed to opine on the mental state of the defendant, the reasonableness of her beliefs, and the reasonableness of her use of force. See also *People v. Rossakis* (N.Y. 1993) where the expert on Battered Woman Syndrome was allowed to testify to her opinion of the defendant's state of mind. But note: In that case the court held, over strong objection by the defendant, that Battered Woman Syndrome went to a claim of mental disease or defect, not self-defense.

7. There is a general rule against introducing character evidence of past aggression by the victim in a homicide case, but there is an exception to that general rule when it is not clear which party initiated the aggression that led to the fatal blow.

REFERENCES

Cahn, N.A. (1992). The looseness of legal language: The reasonable woman standard in theory and practice. *Cornell Law Review*, 77, 1398.

Colorado Revised Statutes (1988).

Corrado, M. (1991). Note on the structure of a theory of excuses. *Journal of Criminal Law and Criminology*, 82, 465.

Fed. R. Evid. 702.

Gillespie, C. (1989). *Justifiable homicide: Battered women, self-defense, and the law*. Columbus, OH: Ohio State University Press.

Greenawalt, K. (1984). The perplexing borders of justification and excuse. *Columbia Law Review, 84*, 1897.

Heller, J. (1998). Beyond the reasonable man? A sympathetic but critical analysis of the use of subjective standards of reasonableness in self-defense and provocation cases. *American Journal of Criminal Law, 26*, 1.

Johnson, K.C. (1994). Note, exiting the twilight zone: Changes in the standard for the admissibility of scientific evidence in Georgia. *Georgia State University Law Review, 10*, 401.

Kansas Statutes Annotated.

Kentucky Revised Statutes.

Kinports, K. (1988). Defending battered women's self-defense claims. *Oregon Law Review, 67*, 393.

Maguigan, H. (1991). Battered women and self-defense: Myths and misconceptions in current reform proposals. *University of Pennsylvania Law Review, 140 (December)*, 379–487.

Model Penal Code, Tent. Draft 1958.

Model Penal Code, Official Draft 1962.

Murray, M. (1997). Note, *People v. Humphrey*: The new fuels of self-defense for battered women who kill. *Southwest University Law Review, 27*, 155.

Official Code of Georgia Annotated (Revised 1993).

Ohio Revised Code.

Pattern Instuctions for Kansas, Crim. 2d. (1985–86 Supp.)

Rosen, R.A. (1993). On self-defense, imminence, and women who kill their batterers. *North Carolina Law Review, 71*, 371–411.

Saitow, S.J. (1993). Battered woman syndrome: Does the "reasonable battered woman" exist? *New England Journal of Criminal & Civil Confinement, 19*, 329.

Schopp, R.F., B.J. Sturgis, and M. Sullivan (1994). Battered woman syndrome, expert testimony, and the distinction between justification and excuse. *University of Illinois Law Review, 1994*, 45.

Schullhofer, S.J. (1990). The gender question in criminal law. *Society, Philosophy and Policy, 7*, 105.

Singer, R.G. (1987). The resurgence of mens rea: Honest but unreasonable mistake of fact in self-defense. *British Columbia Law Review, 28*, 459.

Singer, R.G., and M.R. Gardner. (1996). Crimes and punishment: Cases, materials, and readings in criminal law (2d ed.) New York: M. Bender.

Vanderbraak, S.B. (1979). Note, limits on the use of defensive force to prevent intramarital assaults. *Rutgers-Camden Law Review, 10*, 643.

Wagners, J.F., Jr. (1989). Annotation, *Standard for Determination of Reasonableness of Criminal Defendant's Belief, for Purposes of Self-Defense Claim, That Physical Force Is Necessary—Modern Cases*, 73 A.L.R. 4th 993.

Walker, L. (1984). *The battered woman syndrome*. New York: Springer.

Wyoming Statutes.

Cases Cited

Armstrong v. City of Wichita, 907 P.2d 923 (Kan. App. 1995).

Bechtel v. State, 840 P.2d 1 (Okla. Crim. App. 1992).

Bonner v. State, 740 So.2d 439 (Ala. 1998).

Brooks v. People, 975 P.2d 1105 (Colo. 1999).

Buhrle v.State, 627 P.2d 1374 (Wyo. 1981).

Bunting v. Jamieson, 984 P.2d 467 (Wyo. 1999).

Collins v. Commonwealth, 951 S.W.2d 569 (Ky. 1997).

Commonwealth v. Rodriguez, 481 Mass. 1, 633 N.E.2d 1039 (1994).

Commonwealth v. Stonehouse, 521 Pa. 41, 555 A.2d 772 (1989).

Daubert v. Merrell Dow Pharmaceuticals, Inc., 509 U.S. 579 (1993).

Dow Chemical v. Mahlum, 970 P.2d 98 (Nev. 1998).

E.I. du Pont de Nemours & Co. v. Robinson, 923 S.W.2d 549 (Tex. 1995).

Fielder v. State, 756 S.W.2d 309 (Tex. Crim. App. 1988).

Fishback v. People, 851 P.2d 884 (Colo. 1993).

Frye v. United States, 293 F.1013 (D.C. Cir. 1923).

Gammill v. Jack Williams Chevrolet, Inc., 972 S.W.2d 713 (Tex. 1998).

General Electric Co. v. Joiner, 522 U.S. 136 (1997).

Gilkey v. Schweitzer, 983 P.2d 869 (Mont. 1999).

Gleeton v. State, 716 So. 1083 (Miss. 1998).

Harris v. Croptmate Co., 706 N.E.2d 55 (Ill. 1999).

Hawthorne v. State, 408 So.2d 801 (Fla. Ct. App. 1982).

Hawthorne v. State, 470 So.2d 770 (Fla. Ct. App. 1985).

Ibn-Tamas v. United States, 407 A.2d 626 (D.C. 1979).

Johnson v. Knoxville Community School Dist., 570 N.W.2d 633 (Iowa 1997).

Kumho Tire Co., LTD. v. Carmichael, 526 U.S. 137 (1999).

Mitchell v. Commonwealth, 908 S.W.2d 100 (Ky. 1995).

People v. Aris, 215 Cal.App. 1178, 264 Cal.Rptr. 167 (Cal. Ct. App. 1989).

People v. Beasley, 622 N.E. 1236 (Ill. App. 5 Dist. 1993).

People v. Garcia, 1999 WL 459470 (Colo. App. 1999).

People v. Goetz, 66 N.Y.2d 96, 506 N.Y.S.2d 18, 497 N.E.2d 41 (1986).

People v. Humphrey, 13 Cal.4th 1073, 921 P.2d 1, 56 Cal. Rptr.2d 142 (1996).

People v. Kelly, 549 P.2d 1240 (Cal. 1976).

People v. Rossakis, 159 Misc.2d 611, 605 N.Y. Supp.2d 825 (1993).

People v. Scott, 424 N.E.2d 70 (Ill. App. Ct. 1981).

People v. Torres, 488 N.Y.S.2d 358 (N.Y. App. Div. 1985).

People v. Wilson, 194 Mich. App. 599, 487 N.W.2d 822 (1992).

People v. Yaklich, 833 P.2d 758 (Colo. Ct. App. 1991).

Reed v. State, 391 A.2d 364 (Md. 1978).

Rogers v. State, 616 So.2d 1098 (Fla. Dist. Ct. App. 1993).

Sears Roebuck and Co. v. Manuilov, 715 N.E.2d 968 (Ind. App. 1999).

Smith v. State, 277 S.E.2d 678 (Ga. 1981).

Smith v. State, 268 Ga. 196, 486 S.E.2d 819 (1997).

Smith v. Albercio, 116 N.M. 156, 861 P.2d 192 (1993).

State v. Allery, 101 Wash.2d 591, 682 P.2d 312 (1984).

State v. Alt, 504 N.W.2d 38 (Minn. App. 1993).

State v. Anaya, 438 A.2d 892 (Me. 1981).

State v. Anderson, 785 S.W.2d 596 (Mo. Ct. App. 1990).

State v. Bowen, 532 A.2d 215 (N.J. 1987).

State v. Brown, 687 P.2d 751 (Ore. 1984).

State v. Burtzlaff, 493 N.W.2d 1 (S.D. 1992).

State v. Collier, 1998 WL 42487 (Tenn. Crim. App. 1998).

State v. Cramer, 17 Kan. App.2d 623, 841 P.2d 1111 (1993).

State v. Daws, 104 Ohio App.3d 448, 662 N.E.2d 805 (1994).

State v. Eagle Thunder, 226 N.W.2d 755 (Neb. 1978).

State v. Gallegos, 104 N.M.247, 719 P.2d 1268 (1986).

State v. Gartland, 694 A.2d 564 (N.J. 1997).

State v. Goldberg, 12 N.J.Super 293, 79 A.2d 702 (1951).

State v. Griffiths, 610 P.2d 522 (Idaho 1980).

State v. Hazlet, 16 N.D. 426, 113 N.W. 374 (1907).

State v. Hodges, 239 Kan. 63, 716 P.2d 563 (1986).

State v. Houser, 241 Neb. 525, 490 N.W.2d 168 (1992).

State v. Hundley, 236 Kan. 461, 693 P.2d 475 (1985).

State v. Jones, 922 P.2d 806 (Wash. 1996).

State v. Koss, 49 Ohio St.3d 213 551 N.E.2d 970 (1990).

State v. Leaphart, 873 S.W.2d 870 (Tenn. Crim. App. 1983).

State v. Leidholm, 334 N.W.2d 811 (N.D. 1983).

State v. Necaise, 466 So.2d 660 (La. Ct. App. 1985).

State v. Norman, 324 N.C. 253, 378 S.E.2d 8 (1989).

State v. Peters, 534 N.W.2d 867 (Wis. App. 1995).

State v. Pisciotta, 968 S.W.2d 185 (Mo. 1998).

State v. Richardson, 189 Wis.2d 481, 525 N.W.2d 378 (1994).

State v. Riley, 500 S.E.2d 524 (W.Va. 1997).

State v. Sallie, 81 Ohio St.3d 673, 693 N.E.2d 267 (1998).

State v. Stewart, 763 P.2d 572 (Kan. 1988).

State v. Tankersley, 956 P.2d 486 (Ariz. 1998).

State v. Thomas, 423 N.E.2d 137 (Ohio 1981).

State v. Thomas, 77 Ohio St.3d 323, 673 N.E.2d 1339 (1997).

Taylor v. State, 889 P.2d 319) Okla. Cr. 1995).

United States v. Gaviria, 804 F.Supp. 476 (E.D.N.Y. 1992).

Wack v. Farmland Industries, Inc., 1999 WL 1251844 (Pa. Super. 1999).

Wahl v. American Honda Motor Co., 181 Misc. 396, 69 N.Y.S.2d 875 (1999).

Wieand v. Florida, 732 So.2d 1944 (1999).

Witt v. State, 893 P.2d 132 (Wyo. 1995).

Chapter 5

The Traditional Test Case Revisited

When we began, we summarized a case that was tried in a traditional fashion, relying on Battered Woman Syndrome to understand the battering relationship, and in a jurisdiction that has a traditional understanding of self-defense. We now take the opportunity to revisit this case, focusing on presentation of the facts developed at trial, as those facts would be argued using the theory of battering introduced in this book. As noted in Chapter 1, the information we rely upon for this chapter is taken from the trial transcript, pretrial motions, sentencing hearing, pretrial depositions, police reports, the presentence investigation, and the Illinois Court of Appeals opinion. We also critically examine the law under which this case was tried, and discuss how an expanded understanding of self-defense may have influenced the outcome of the decision.

PEOPLE V. BEASLEY (1993)

Facts

The facts do not change. The facts are those that were developed at trial and set out in some detail earlier.

If defense counsel is going to rely on the theory presented here to help the jury understand the battering relationship, how it is influenced by the socialization of the parties, and how it escalates to the point of threatening homicide of one or the other party, the jury will need to be alerted to the general idea of the theory in the opening statement. Thereafter, factual development will proceed to address each element of the theory, and the final argument will be an effort to discuss the elements as an integrated whole in light of the jury instructions that will be given.

The most critical issue in self-defense is persuading the jury that it was reasonable for the defendant to use deadly force. That is especially true, and particularly difficult, in a nonconfrontational case such as *Beasley*. It is the focus of our attention here.

The theory of the battering relationship developed here understands battering as a homicidal process, supported by socialization differences and feeding on imposed isolation and control of the battered woman, and the absence or failure of resources to allow her to escape; these factors are compounded by an unrelenting escalation of violence. Each of these variables is summarized here, accompanied by facts developed at trial that relate to each of them.

In cases in which battered women kill their batterers, the fact finder must be helped to understand the process that led to this homicidal encounter. And the fact finder must understand it fully enough to be able to appreciate the argument that under these circumstances it was reasonable for the battered woman to believe that her own preservation required the use of deadly force. This section summarizes the variables that define the deadly battering relationship, and the arguments that would be made to justify the reasonableness of defendant's actions. Using *Beasley* as the case study, we focus specifically on how the actions of Sheila Beasley were justified when she shot Glen Beasley.

Socialization Differences

Socialization is a critical element in this theory because it conditions both individuals' responses to the situation. It also helps to determine how individuals interpret and then react to the actions of the other person. These reactions are the heart of the interaction process and its escalation.

Women, in general, are socialized against the use of aggression and into relationship maintenance, particularly the maintenance of marriage, family, and home. Women do not generally learn violence or aggression as a way of solving problems or as a way of maintaining relationships. Consequently, women are unlikely to attempt self-defense until they have exhausted their other alternatives for survival. Men, however, are socialized into the limited use of aggression to achieve goals or to solve problems. Additionally, men who grow up in domestic violence learn that violence is a direct and easy way to solve problems and get their way.

These facts in *Beasley* relate to socialization of Glen and Sheila and helped to condition them for the abusive relationship that developed: Glen was about five years older than Sheila. They began dating when Sheila was 15 years old. Her parents tried to end their relationship because of Glen's violent reputation; in response to that attempt, Glen told them that if they interfered, he would run away with Sheila and marry and they would never see her again. The parents relented and allowed the couple to continue seeing one another. When Sheila came of age to marry (18 years old), she and Glen did run away, and married a few months later.

Almost immediately after their marriage, Glen established rules for Sheila to follow. Sheila testified that she did not think those rules were extraordinary. Rather, she thought she had a lot to learn about being a good wife. She thought the things that enraged Glen were partly her fault (after all, for example, she *had* forgotten to buy Ding Dongs for his lunch and she knew he liked those), and she tried to placate him by doing everything the way he wanted.

The psychologist testified that Sheila viewed women as sex objects who are used by men and then must bear the burden of guilt, shame, and embarrassment. She expected close relationships to be upsetting and to be violent. She was fearful of males in close relationships because they are destructive influences. In other words, what she had in her marriage was disappointing, but it was not necessarily unexpected. She was a woman; Glen was a man. She was subservient; Glen was dominant. She was a wife who, if she did a better job, would have a better life; Glen was a husband who established the rules and punished her for her failure to follow them.

Sheila's traditional belief system comported well with Glen's experiences and with his view of the domestic world. Perhaps none of us, Glen included, realize just how powerfully our family and early experiences shape our actions and beliefs; but Glen came as close as anyone on the night of the shooting, when he asked Sheila why she was shaking and she said it was because she was scared. He replied: "I ain't done half to you what my dad done to me." Glen had been beaten by his father when he was a child; his mother had been beaten by his father and he had observed that; and now he beat his wife.

Glen had grown up in a violent home and he had incorporated violence into his own persona early on. His mother described him as the "group bully," a characterization confirmed by his sister and friends. According to his mother, Glen's father was a batterer and that problem had prompted their divorce. Despite that early and sustained association with battering in his home, Glen contended that his family did not have problems. Indeed, he always maintained greater allegiance to his family of origin than to

Sheila and his children, as evidenced by the fact that she was beaten virtually every time she made any comment that he found critical of his parents or siblings. Glen denied any negative influence caused by this battering in the home; his mother denied it as well, as illustrated by her testimony that although Glen had witnessed and experienced his father's domestic violence, Glen was still a good and loving husband and father.

Sheila's socialization was such that she was in for the long haul. Her parents had taught her that people marry for life. That moral value had serious consequences for Sheila. She knew she could not return to her parents if she divorced Glen, because they did not believe in divorce. She also feared they would not support her in that decision; indeed, she testified that she not only feared they would not support her, but she feared that she would lose their support if she left her husband. At one point, when the violence was obvious to her mother, her mother asked the family pastor to talk with Glen and Sheila. Her mother apparently did not discuss domestic violence with the pastor (which makes sense, given her own denial of it and Sheila's reluctance and failure to admit it to her) and he most likely did not know it was present in the relationship, nor did he inquire to determine if that might be a problem. At any rate, this traditional value of marrying for life was confirmed when the pastor met with Glen and Sheila one time and encouraged them to do what was necessary to stay together and work out their problems.

Although Sheila recognized that she was abused by Glen, she did not share that fact with her family or friends. Instead, she hid the evidence of physical abuse. Bruises were covered by long sleeves and slacks. Black eyes were explained away by a child hitting her in his sleep. A broken tailbone was attributed to a fall on the ice. These lies allowed Sheila to maintain the facade of normalcy. They also contributed to her isolation in a way that made it more difficult for others to help her, had they been so inclined.

Physical Size and Strength Differences

As a result of their smaller size and lower muscle mass, women generally are not as strong as men. The size and strength differential between men and women is critical because it allows the stronger male to use aggression/violence without becoming apprehensive about physical retaliation. Some men, batterers in particular, may feel that physical dominance is their primary or only asset for control as a male. Consequently, they may perceive intimidation and physical violence used to control their opponent as a reflection of their manhood and/or superiority. It doesn't take long for the batterer to realize that his physical dominance is the easiest and quickest way for him to get what he wants and maintain complete control of his physically smaller and weaker partner. Additionally, a few experiences of his physical dominance is generally enough to convince the female partner that she lacks the size and strength to adequately protect herself physically or others he may threaten.

The facts in *Beasley* that relate to the size and strength differential are relatively clear-cut. Female Sheila Beasley was five feet one inch tall and weighed 105 pounds, while male Glen Beasley was six feet tall and weighed 195 pounds. So, Glen possessed both a clear size and strength advantage in this relationship. When this advantage was combined with the socialization differences and Glen's apparent routine use of aggression in all aspects of his life, it set the stage for complete physical domination of Sheila Beasley.

Isolation

Isolation is an important factor to consider in the battering relationship because it affects both the battered woman and the batterer. In particular, it reduces or limits each party's resources and behavioral options. A batterer isolates his victim because it reduces his risk of exposure, which could have negative consequences, and it increases his chances of maintaining control in the relationship. It reduces the battered woman's access to resources that might provide support or assistance, and it increases her reliance on the batterer. Isolation forces the victim to take the route that her socialization encourages, which is to appease and placate the batterer in order to survive rather than confront or leave him. It reduces the involvement of outside resources that might convince her there is a problem, forcing her to rely on her own stressed assessment of the situation and its escalation.

The following facts in *Beasley* contributed to Sheila's isolation and therefore to the homicidal battering relationship that developed: When Sheila and Glen were first married, Sheila had only Glen's family to reach out to for support; but no family relationship developed to include her and support was not forthcoming. Sheila had run away from her home in Illinois and gone with Glen to Indiana, where his family lived. When she was pregnant with their first child, they lived with Glen's sister and her husband; then, when that arrangement became too strained, they moved to Glen's mother's apartment where another of his sisters and her husband also lived. Sheila tried to establish a good relationship with Glen's mother and one of his sisters, but those efforts were not successful. At trial, one of Glen's brothers-in-law testified to what a poor wife Sheila was and how Glen worked to please her at every turn. By 1984, when they were still in Indiana, Sheila still did not know anyone except Glen and his family. She was afraid of Glen's father. That fear was fostered by Glen, who told her that, if his father should come to the door, she was not to open it, but should call the police because his father was dangerous.

In March of 1985, when Glen was unemployed, Sheila persuaded him to move back to Illinois and to the town where her parents lived. She testified that she begged Glen to make this move so she could be closer to her family and friends. They moved and reaped some financial benefits from Sheila's parents, who contributed financially by providing cars and other things to help them get started. A price was extracted for the move, however, in terms of more stringent rules that Sheila was to follow.

When Sheila was not working, Glen did not allow her to leave the house or to leave the baby with anyone when she ran errands. He required her to wait until he was home in the evening, and to do errands at that time, taking the baby with her.

Glen removed himself from the family somewhat as the children's health problems became apparent, leaving Sheila with the entire responsibility for dealing with those difficulties. After Amanda's cystic fibrosis was discovered and while Sheila was pregnant with Nathan, Glen rejected Nathan because there was a high probability that he would also have cystic fibrosis. Glen did not participate in activities related to the pregnancy, nor would he go to the hospital when Sheila delivered Nathan. In 1990, when Amanda's cystic fibrosis and leukemia required extended periods of hospitalization in Memphis, Tennessee, Sheila took her for these treatments. She had to take the other children along because Glen would not care for them at home; the responsibility for the children was entirely Sheila's.

In one sense, this cut both ways. It increased the isolation because it severely reduced any time Sheila might have to spend with family or friends, or to work outside the home; but it also allowed her time away from Glen because he would not accompany her to doctor's appointments for the children, either in town or in other cities where they were required to go for treatment.

By 1990, just months before the shooting, Sheila was confined to the marriage. She was in the same city but not in close association with her parents; she was separated from her friends by her silence about what her life was really like. She had withdrawn from Glen as much as possible, trying to escape the beatings at home by sleeping with the children. She focused virtually all of her attention on the children. It was during this period, however, that she had an affair that lasted for a few months, an affair that neither partner hoped to, nor sought to make into, a long-standing relationship. Sheila testified she engaged in the affair as an attempt to find some affection to substitute for the severe physical abuse she suffered at home.

Perhaps there were resources out there to help Sheila, but when she tentatively reached out for any of them, none proved to be a source of support or a means to alleviate the increasingly dangerous situation in which she found herself.

Resources

When human beings face stress as a result of strain (personal or structural strain), they experience negative affect. When they experience negative affect, normal people respond by utilizing their personal resources to either cope with or end the negative feelings. This is what battered women do as well. However, often their personal resources fail to end the violence (sometimes these resources do not even recognize the level of danger involved) and even abandon the victims by pushing them toward management of the violence; or these resources may be successfully blocked by the batterer. For example, a woman might not call her mother for advice anymore if the batterer says that such calls will result in the death of the family dog or of a child. When personal resources fail or are blocked, it is natural for the victim, as she sees the violence escalating, to reason that she will have to seek external social resources to help her end the violence.

Battered women reach out to a variety of external resources for assistance if they have knowledge of them (e.g., crisis centers, ministers, employers, police, friends, attorneys, shelters, courts). The problem is that most of these resources are failure-prone. For example, they do not recognize the level of danger involved; they do not want to believe it; they recommend conciliation for the sake of the family; they allow ideological requirements of the system to interfere with efforts to end the violence; they put roadblocks in the way of the battering victim's use of services. When resources are utilized by the victim and fail to end the violence, they place the victim in greater jeopardy because she must face an even angrier batterer who feels he must increase the violence to block her use of that resource in the future and regain control of the relationship. This results in a steady escalation of the violence over time.

The following facts in *Beasley* relate to blocked and failed resources, which contributed to the abusive relationship that was sustained over the years: Sheila Beasley had virtually no one and nothing to rely on for support during the earliest stage of her marriage. She and Glen lived near, and literally with, his family members who did not care for Sheila. Her parents were in another state and further distanced in a personal sense because Glen and Sheila had run away together to be married. It was not until March of 1985, after she and Glen moved back to Illinois, that Sheila began to reestablish her relationship with her parents. There are facts developed in the record that illustrate ways in which her parents provided meaningful assistance: They began to visit with Sheila and Luke occasionally; they bought Sheila and Glen cars, clothes, and groceries; when Sheila was ready to give birth to Amanda, her mother took her to the hospital and stayed with her when Glen refused to be there. In these respects, Sheila's family operated as a resource to which she could turn for help. This resource had been blocked initially, when Sheila was separated from her parents. And it was a resource that eventually failed. Although Sheila's parents helped to provide material goods when Glen was unemployed, they did not recognize, or else they ignored, clues of the abuse Sheila suffered at Glen's hand. When they were most needed as a resource to relieve the abuse, the parents were not there. Or, to put it more charitably, they were there in the only restricted way they knew to be there: Sheila's mother walked in on an abusive encounter—she saw her son-in-law throwing a coffee table at her daughter—and she responded by leaving the children there and going home. Later, she followed up by asking the pastor to counsel the young couple, but she apparently did not alert him to the fact that her daughter was a victim of physical battering. That was what Sheila's mother knew to do: seek a pastor's help to keep the marriage together.

Sheila's mother witnessed other evidence of abuse, but she did not pursue it. And Sheila lied about what was happening, so her mother had a reason to continue to ignore what may well have been signs of battering. In early 1990, Sheila's mother helped with the children for over a week when Sheila was in bed with a broken tailbone. Sheila told her mother that she had slipped on the ice, and her mother accepted that. Not long after that, Sheila explained her black eye as having happened when Luke hit her in his sleep, and her mother accepted that.

Sheila's mother was not the only one who witnessed evidence of abuse and did nothing to help. Sheila's employer at Baby World inquired about Sheila's health one day when Sheila was unable to stand and lift without obvious pain. Sheila, approximately five months pregnant with Amanda, showed the employer her bruised belly and explained that Glen had kicked her because he did not want her to be pregnant. The employer also testified that she had seen bruises on Sheila's arms and then understood why Sheila typically wore long-sleeved blouses even during the heat of the summer. But that was it. No offer to help was forthcoming. This is not to say that it was the responsibility of any third party akin to a co-worker or employer to step in and intervene, or even that it was the responsibility of Sheila's mother to get her to a shelter, or even to tell her about a shelter. It is simply to say that, even in the face of facts that people understood to be evidence of abuse, no one helped. Why? Because Sheila did not ask for help? Probably not. Because these are uncaring people? No. Help did not come because domestic violence is an awful thing to know about. And when we know about it, we do not know what to do. Domestic violence invites what we might understand best as willful blindness, an unwillingness to discover the facts that will force us to confront the reality we want to avoid.

The record developed at trial reflects that Sheila reached out a few times to traditional resources that may be expected to be the source of real help, resources that could offer protection from further abuse. Each of these attempts had brutal consequences. On two occasions, Sheila contacted a lawyer to pursue divorce. The first time, in 1988, Glen found out and, in retaliation, he raped her and he threatened to kill her. That was really the first time Sheila had taken a step of seeking help outside and, arguably, it increased the risk for Glen. Her action increased the risk that his abuse of Sheila would be found out, and it increased the risk that she really would get away. It became an impetus for increased violence toward Sheila.

Sheila nonetheless contacted another lawyer about a divorce in 1989. That time, the lawyer had to change the appointment and someone from his office called Sheila's home to make that change. Sheila was not at home when the call came in and the office person left a message with Glen. When Sheila got home, Glen told her that he knew of her attempt to see a lawyer and upped the ante. He told her that if she ever tried to get a divorce again, he would kill her, the children, and her parents. Divorce was not an option.

The last time Sheila sought outside help was in the fall of 1990, just three months before the last and fatal encounter. For the first time in almost eight years of marriage, for the first time in almost eight years of abuse, she actually called the police for help. This beating was especially harsh; Glen was especially enraged because Sheila had flushed his drugs. She escaped into a closet and called the police for help. Initially, the police officers just told Glen and Sheila to work things out. It was apparently treated like an old-time "domestic call." As the officers were leaving, Glen attacked Sheila in their presence. The officers arrested him and took him to the station. That evening, Amanda suffered a cystic fibrosis attack requiring emergency care, so Sheila took her to the hospital. When she returned, Glen was home; he had been released from jail. Nothing further came of that appeal for police protection—except that Glen was angrier than he had been before.

By this time, Sheila understood that she could not get a divorce without risking her life and the lives of her children, perhaps even the lives of her parents. She could not depend on the police for help, or at least when she did that, no help was forthcoming. Private counseling from the pastor produced only the admonition to stay together and find a way to work out the problems. There were significant expenses associated with the three children, two of whom were seriously ill, and the only source of financial assistance in that regard was the health insurance Glen had through his employer. Sheila could not depend on her parents for support, because her parents felt so strongly about keeping a marriage together for life. She did not have money to leave and establish a home for herself and her children elsewhere; the record revealed that by 1990 Glen had limited Sheila's money to $20 per week—and that to cover food and utilities. Glen's violence was escalating, not only toward her but toward others as well. In September 1990, he was arrested for battery, his seventh offense for a crime against the person.

Where do you go with no money? With two seriously ill children? How do you get away from an aggressive husband with a history of violence, who says he will hunt you down and kill you if you leave him? How do you separate yourself from him or find a way to diffuse the violence when the police have not been of assistance? When the pastor has counseled you to stay together? When his family supports him and believes he is not doing anything wrong but, on the contrary, you are entirely too demanding? And your family ignores evidence of battering?

At this point, in late 1990 just before the shooting, virtually all coping resources had been blocked or had failed. The tension continued to build. Contrition had been abandoned long ago. The violence now was more frequent and more intense.

Control

It is natural for human beings to want to feel in physical and emotional control of their bodies and environment, although we rarely have complete control of either. Batterers go beyond this natural want. They want complete control of their partner and the relationship as well. Most research indicates that batterers can use violence successfully to achieve complete control by getting what they want and thus reducing their anxiety.

A batterer attempts to get and maintain complete control of a partner and of the relationship through the use of degradation, intimidation, threats of violence against the battered woman and others she cares about, sexual violence, general physical violence, and blockage of the victim's coping resources that might threaten his control.

The following facts in *Beasley* relate to control and contributed to the abusive relationship: Glen's control of Sheila was exhibited in three arenas: financial, social, and physical. One of the first rules Glen set for Sheila involved his control of the money. Even when Sheila worked outside the home, she turned her check over to Glen. She was not allowed to cash his check, to write checks for cash, or to write checks for more than the amount of a purchase. Sheila had no independent access to money. By 1990, Glen had restricted her to $20 per week and, on that, she was expected to buy food for the family of five and pay the utilities.

Early in their marriage, Glen controlled Sheila socially by restricting her to the house while he was at work and insisting that she take the children with her when she ran errands. By 1990, when Glen's domination was more obvious and public, he reacted violently when she talked with someone who prompted his jealousy. When Glen saw Sheila talking to a man (who had simply inquired as to Glen's whereabouts), Glen responded by pulling Sheila away and picking a fight with the man. In a different sense, Glen controlled Sheila by threatening her with serious harm if she contacted an attorney to establish herself apart from him.

Finally, on the physical front, Glen's control was most effective. The record is replete with evidence of his physical control and abuse. The major incidents were detailed in the earlier factual account of this case, and they are simply listed here. In a closing argument, each would be detailed as they were in our initial discussion in Chapter 1:

Event Precipitating Abuse	Abuse Inflicted
1. Food not in bowls as he preferred	Hit Sheila in the head with a pan
2. No Ding Dongs in his lunch	Verbal abuse; pushed and choked her
3. Sheila criticized his family	Beat her
4. No reason apparent	Slapped, then beat her and Luke got hurt in the fray
5. Sheila criticized his family	Beat her
6. Hangers in closet turned the wrong way	Abuse reported, not specified
7. Keys left in outside door lock	Abuse reported, not specified

These last two incidents were astoundingly trivial. But this was right after Glen and Sheila had moved back to Illinois from Indiana, and Glen had initiated new rules as the price extracted for that concession of moving. For example, toilet paper had to be hung as he prescribed, shower doors cleaned immediately after use, and all clothing ironed. This was also a time when Sheila had taken a job outside the home because Glen had been unemployed for some time prior to their move and, although her parents were helping them, money was tight. That show of independence may have sparked the increased show of control.

8. Sheila did not socialize as Glen preferred	Beat her
9. Sheila not attentive enough	Beat her
10. Sheila talked with another man	Pulled Sheila away by the hair, knocked her to the floor, and kicked her in the sides
11. Sheila had contacted an attorney	Beat her and threatened to kill her, their children, and her parents
12. No reason apparent	Hit her, forced intercourse and oral sex; forced her outdoors in the winter elements when she wore only underwear
13. Sheila talked with another man	Threw a table, dragged Sheila outdoors; punched and knocked her over a chair, breaking her tailbone
14. Sheila criticized Glen	Backhanded her across the face, blackening and scratching her eye
15. Sheila flushed Glen's drugs	Beat her in isolation and then again in presence of police
16. Glen thought Sheila ignored him	Beat and raped her
17. No reason apparent	Beat her until she agreed to lie for him
18. Sheila not at home	Beat her multiple times; threw a table at her; grabbed her by the neck and beat her head against the window frame; threatened to beat Nathan

Just a glance at these battering incidents demonstrates the extent of Glen's efforts to physically control Sheila. His tactics were harsh, even brutal, and they were prompted by the most trivial of reasons.

Escalation of Violence

It is the interaction between the two individuals that changes over time and creates the escalation. Escalation can be identified in two ways: short-term from incident to incident, and long-term from the beginning of the battering relationship to its end. Within each battering cycle of the relationship, we can identify the interaction process that escalates the violence.

1. The victim's actions to use resources of some type to manage (survive) or end the violence, usually during periods of tension building;
2. Resources fail to end the violence;
3. The batterer feels threatened so he acts to block coping resources, especially the one tried by the victim;

4. The batterer then increases the frequency and intensity of the violence to regain control of the victim and the relationship, which creates escalation.

Over the long term, we can see escalation of the violence as a change from
the batterer's use of contrition to keep the victim in the relationship, to intimidation, to threats of violence, to actual physical and sexual violence
with more frequency, to extreme forms of violence and those with serious
injuries, and the increasingly uncontrolled use of violence.

The following facts in *Beasley* demonstrate the severe escalation of violence up to and including the night of the shooting: The record developed
at trial in this case does not contain actual instances in which Glen report-
edly apologized or promised not to hurt Sheila again. Contrition is only inferred from Sheila's testimony that by early 1989, Glen was no longer
contrite, primarily because he was generally so drunk that he did not re-
member the next day that he had abused his wife the night before.

The actual physical and sexual violence included intimidation, and
those episodes were accompanied by threats of violence. There is virtually
no instance in which a threat of violence was not accompanied by actual
violence. There are numerous instances in which actual violence was accompanied by threats of greater violence if Sheila ever misbehaved again.
For example, when Glen found out Sheila had contacted an attorney, he
beat her. Beyond that, he threatened to kill her, the children, and her parents if she should ever offend in that fashion again.

By 1990, Glen had escalated threats to the children. These threats took
a particularly simple and ugly form: Glen threatened to quit his job, hence
to lose the health insurance that assisted in payment of medical expenses
for Nathan's cystic fibrosis and Amanda's cystic fibrosis and leukemia.

The actual physical violence in this relationship began just weeks after
the wedding. It was not preceded by intimidating and threatening behavior
that was short of physical violence. Instead, in this relationship, physical
violence began as fairly minor (at least relatively speaking), and then escalated dramatically in intensity for the next seven years.

Glen's violent outbursts were consistently directed at Sheila. She was
the object of his beatings for the entire period of their marriage. In 1986
and in 1987, however, Glen's violence was more obviously directed at people outside the home, as well as toward Sheila. Specifically, Glen was convicted for disorderly conduct and battery, attempted sexual assault, and
sexual assault. Victims of these assaultive behaviors testified at trial. Each
described Glen Beasley as a strong man, out of control when he was drunk,
and capable of inflicting serious physical damage to another person.

The physical and sexual violence against Sheila increased after Amanda's diagnosis of cystic fibrosis (April 1988) and after Nathan's birth (June 1988). Sheila had begun sleeping with Amanda, in part to avoid Glen who by this time was often so drunk that he urinated in the bed. He also had begun sexually assaulting her. While that separation may have stifled some of the violence directed toward Sheila, it did not eliminate it. By 1990, Glen's violent rage was apparent in other forms, most often exhibited in ruining cars, as well as more frequent physical violence and sexual assaults directed at Sheila.

In 1989 and in 1990, Glen seemed to become more comfortable with his battering and less concerned with the fact that it might be noticed. For example, he dragged Sheila out of a bar on two occasions. On another, he sent her out of the house and into the night when she was not fully clothed. Beyond that, he inflicted injuries that were obvious to third-party observers: a black eye, a broken tailbone, fingerprints up and down her arm.

The violence was worse. It was more obvious. It was more severe. And it was more frequent.

The violent episodes began coming closer and closer together in 1990. Intervals of a month or so between beatings were reduced to intervals of just a few weeks (three weeks between the seventeenth and eighteenth incidents, and the nineteenth coming just two weeks after those and just three weeks before the last, fatal encounter). Perhaps as significant is the fact that these last episodes were all extremely violent.

Sheila noted, however, that there were identifiable patterns. These lent an element of predictability that allowed her to survive. The pattern was this: Glen would drink heavily. Then he would beat her and perhaps sexually assault her. Then he would pass out and that would be the end of it for that night. It was just a matter of surviving the beating and the sexual assault.

On the night of the fatal shooting, that pattern did not hold. That night, nothing happened the same way.

As we examine the events of January 18, 1991, the question is this: Given this history of battering, abuse, and violence, was it reasonable on January 18, 1991, for Sheila Beasley to believe she needed to use deadly force to defend herself?

Glen came home drunk. It was 1:30 A.M. when he dragged Sheila from bed and into the living room. He began talking about killing her. He told her not to close her eyes, because if she closed them, she would never open them again. This was a new tactic.

Glen pulled Sheila by the hair out of the chair and into the bathroom, where he forced her to her knees and pushed her head into the toilet bowl.

He had never done this before, either. Then he forced her into the kitchen with him, where he undressed and told her to think about what he was going to do to her. He had never done this before. Finally, he fell asleep.

This should have been the end of it. Glen generally beat Sheila when he was drunk, then fell asleep, and it was over until the next day.

While Glen slept, Sheila checked to see if his gun was in the bedroom where he always kept it. It was gone. Now she was more afraid, afraid that he was armed.

Luke was sleeping in the house. Sheila was afraid to awaken him and try to leave, for fear that Glen would also awaken and discover she was trying to get out. She had to stay in the house, with a drunken and angry husband who had a gun for which she could not account.

Sheila called Kevin Rice and arranged for him to bring a gun. She took it into the house and then went to bed, having done nothing to ensure it was loaded or ready to fire. She simply put the gun in the closet.

That still should have been the end of it. Glen was sleeping. Sheila had armed herself in the event she needed to be armed, but she had done nothing more because nothing more was necessary.

Later, in the early morning hours, Glen awakened Sheila to continue the threats of violence. "How can you go to bed when you know you ain't going to wake up?" And then, stroking the bridge of her nose with his finger: "Dead bitch. Dead bitch." This was a different situation. He had never before awakened Sheila for a second round of threats of violence. He had never before talked this way to her.

Glen ordered Sheila from her bed, into a chair in the living room. Again he warned her not to close her eyes. Again, he went to sleep.

Sheila was afraid of what Glen would do when he awakened again. She slipped into the bedroom, called Kevin Rice, and asked him how to fire the gun. She cocked it as he instructed, then put it back in the bag and back in the closet. Then she returned to the living room chair as she had been told. Sheila did not shoot Glen.

As she sat there and watched Glen sleep, and thought about what he had done and what he had said that evening, knowing that he had his gun somewhere although she had no idea where, she got more and more afraid. She retrieved the gun from the closet and placed it, still cocked, under her chair. Sheila did not shoot Glen.

A car sounded outside. Sheila got up to look and Glen awakened. He told her to get back to the chair and to think about living in a casket. He said he was going to kill her and her parents, and he would bury them all together. They argued, and he told her to get back to bed.

On her way to the bedroom, Sheila went to the kitchen for a drink of water. She saw a picture of a baby in a casket. She went back to the living room and asked Glen what that was. He said the little girl in the picture reminded him of Amanda. When Sheila protested that Amanda was going to be all right, he said simply, "No, Amanda's not going to be okay and neither are you." Then he threw a blanket at her and said, "I have something for you." "What?" "A bullet through the heart."

At this, Sheila begged Glen to let her take Luke and leave. She said she would pay for a divorce, he could be rid of her. But Glen would have none of that and told her she would not get off that easily. Then he jumped up and tilted her chair back, claiming he would kill her and make it look like suicide. When the chair was tilted, he saw the gun. When she purported not to know anything about it, he slapped her and called her a lying bitch.

Glen asked what she intended to do with the gun and Sheila said she had it for protection. He told her that "Beasleys don't die easy," then he forced the cocked gun into her mouth and said "bang." He put the gun down and told her the next time he would fire it in her mouth. He left the room. Sheila did not shoot him.

Glen went to the bathroom and ordered Sheila to come in there. She did. He forced her to the floor and shoved her face into the toilet bowl where he had just urinated. Then he pulled her to her feet and wiped her face with a used sanitary napkin from the wastebasket. Then he dragged her by the hair back to the living room.

Sheila broke loose from Glen and ran to the door. He caught her, pulled her back, and pushed her into the chair. When he released her, she grabbed the gun and ran for the door again. He told her she would have to shoot him and Luke would hear it. She sat down in the doorway and cried. She did not shoot Glen.

Dawn was breaking. Glen ordered Sheila over to the couch where he was, and she complied. She tried to touch him, to calm him in ways that had worked before, but this time was different. Her attempt did not work. He told her not to touch him, ordered her to stop. She returned to the chair and he ordered her to go to bed.

At this point, Sheila did not know where the gun was. She went to bed as ordered. Glen was on the couch. He should go back to sleep. It would be over until the next day. But it was not over. This time was different.

Glen came back to the bedroom, carrying the gun. He laid it on the floor next to her and he said, "Here's your protection." And he went back to the living room. She waited. Then she cracked the door to see if he was asleep. He reacted immediately, and when she told him it was hot in the bedroom, he said she could open the door.

Sheila went into the living room. Glen told her she was going to get what she deserved. He said that he had been hearing things, that she had been to the bar. She denied it and began to cry. He told her that he liked to see her cry. Then he went to sleep.

Sheila sat in the living room chair and cried. At some point she went into the bedroom and called her friend who was scheduled to come over and pick her up. Sheila told her not to come. She called the woman who was scheduled to take Luke to school and told her not to come. She retrieved the gun from the bedroom. She returned to the living room chair.

Nothing resembled the other incidents of battering. Glen looked different, wilder than ever. He had made threats that he had never made before. He had abused her in ways he never had before: He had pushed her face into the toilet; he had put a cocked gun in her mouth; he had shown her a picture of a baby, ostensibly their daughter, in a casket. He had beaten her, and then gone to sleep, and then beaten her again, and then gone to sleep, and then beaten her again. He had never done that before, had never inflicted multiple beatings punctuated by sleep. He had threatened to kill her when he awakened. And now he was asleep.

Then he stirred. She believed he really would kill her when he woke up. He seemed to be awakening. She shot him.

The question is: Was it reasonable for Sheila Beasley to believe—that night, after almost eight years of a violent marriage—that deadly force was necessary for her defense?

Jury Instructions

The *Beasley* case was sent to the jury with traditional self-defense instruction. In order to find that the defendant's actions were justified and that she acted in self-defense, members of the jury were instructed that they must find that the threat of death or great bodily harm was imminent. Beyond that, they were instructed that they must find that Sheila Beasley's belief in the need to use deadly force was reasonable.

The argument summarized in this section, based on the theory proposed in this book, would be admissible under the most traditional self-defense instruction. It would be even easier to make, and would be more likely to succeed, under more expansive instructions on self-defense, such as those discussed earlier as "blended" tests of reasonableness.

Battered Woman Syndrome was not an enormous help in resolving these two most critical issues of imminent harm and reasonableness. That testimony helps the jury understand battering but it invites a psychological focus, a concentration on the mental state of the defendant. That is not necessarily the way the theory is designed, but it is the way it often works on its feet. Indeed, that invitation was strengthened by the expert's testimony in *Beasley* that Battered Woman Syndrome is a subcategory of post-traumatic stress disorder. The testimony allowed the prosecutor to argue that Battered Woman Syndrome is not a mental illness included in the most widely respected manual of mental illnesses. That is a facetious argument, but one that flows easily from the evidence.

The approach proposed here moves the focus away from the psyche of the defendant, and toward the dynamics of the battering relationship which is characterized by violence uncontrolled and uncontrollable by the battered woman. Violence that may well have been nurtured by the socialization of both parties, as in this case. Violence that finds a more secure spot in the relationship as one party is isolated and controlled by the other. Violence that is not eliminated or even reduced by reliance on outside resources. Violence that escalates during the course of the marriage, toward the inexorable end of death. One or the other will die.

Sheila Beasley shot Glen at a time when she could, and at a time after she had endured violent beatings and threats of death. Would it have been reasonable for Sheila to have shot Glen when she ran from him that night, gun in her hand, and reached the door? She was still armed. Would that have been self-defense? What was different about shooting an unarmed man then, and shooting him an hour later? The fact that he was awake? He was as dangerous to her on the couch as he was across the room when she was armed and he was not. We would have found self-defense when he was across the room, and we would have found it with little difficulty. We would have found self-defense because Sheila Beasley was threatened with serious bodily injury or death and she was justified in defending herself from that, with the same amount of force as that used to threaten her. When Sheila Beasley shot Glen, the threat was still present. As was the justification.

REFERENCE

Case Cited

People v. Beasley, 622 N.E. 1236 (Ill. App. 5 Dist. 1993).

Chapter 6

Application of These Theoretical Ideas to Gay and Lesbian Battering

Anne Garner and Robbin S. Ogle

In everyday speech, and even in most social science discourse, domestic violence, according to Ferraro (2000), is about men beating women. Historically, women have fallen victim to battery at the hands of husbands and boyfriends who desire to control and subordinate their partners in intimate relationships through the use of violence. This cultural narrowing of the violence spectrum has failed to address violence in same-sex relationships.

Throughout history, the crime of intimate battery has been shrouded in secrecy and deemed a private matter (Muraskin 2000). Only in recent decades has said phenomenon been characterized as a social problem, with both social and legal institutions emphasizing a hands-off approach to domestic violence. In the contemporary arena, according to Coleman (1990), the battered women's movement and domestic violence theory has concentrated on heterosexual battering and the perpetration of violence by men. Women perpetrating violence against their partners challenges traditional gender-based, socio-political theory on domestic violence.

In this chapter, violence in gay and lesbian partnerships is addressed and examined in the context of Ogle and Jacobs' (1998) theoretical perspective. Definitions of such battery types are proffered, in addition to prevalence rates, myths regarding the occurrence of domestic violence in lesbian and gay partnerships, and a summary of current research examining the topic.

WHAT IS SAME-SEX DOMESTIC VIOLENCE?

In all intimate relationships, the perpetration of domestic battery is essentially about power and control, notwithstanding the label attached to describe the relationship (Vickers 1997). Lundy (1993) defines both heterosexual and homosexual domestic violence generically as nothing less than the systematic exercise of illegitimate coercive power by one partner over another. These elements are also identifiable in Hart's (1986) work, in which lesbian battering is described as a pattern of violent and coercive behaviors whereby a lesbian seeks to control the thoughts, beliefs, or conduct of her intimate partner or to punish the intimate for resisting the perpetrator's control over her (Vickers 1997).

Contextualized under the genre of gay male domestic violence, Island and Letellier (1991) define that violence as any unwanted physical force, psychological abuse, material or property damage inflicted by one man on another, including, but not limited to, physical, psychological, and/or emotional abuse; isolation; threats and intimidation; sexual abuse; property destruction; or economic abuse.

Various researchers (Renzetti 1988, 1992; Renzetti and Goodstein 2001; Renzetti and Miley 1996; Meyer 1988; Hammond 1989; Gardner 1989; Hart 1986; Island and Letellier 1991) have identified variant forms of abuse that remain exclusive to lesbian and gay relationships. These forms arise as an unequivocal result of the heterosexist and homophobic nature of our society, and they are used as a means of control over a partner. Such abuses include:

1. Telling the partner that he/she will receive no assistance from the police and that the justice system is homophobic.

2. Outing or threatening to out a partner to employers, police, family, church or the community.

3. Telling a partner that he/she will not be believed because of society's belief that homosexuals do not abuse or rape their partners.

4. Making his or her partner believe that he/she deserves what he/she gets simply because he/she is homosexual, playing on the internalized homophobia and self-hatred of the abused.

5. Due to the pervasiveness of domestic violence in heterosexual partnerships, attempting to convince a partner that the abuse is normal and that the abused just does not understand gay or lesbian relationships.

6. Relying on heterosexist and sexist stereotypes to hide abuse and thus increase the power and control over a partner by portraying such abuse as mutual or consensual combat (Vickers 1997).

MYTHS AND STEREOTYPES REGARDING LESBIAN AND GAY DOMESTIC VIOLENCE

Much of the research on battery in lesbian and gay relationships demonstrates that, in large part, societal viewpoints regarding violence in said couplings are based on preconceived myths and stereotypes. Indeed, many of these widely held myths serve to sustain and closet the problem of same-sex domestic violence. Vickers (1997), for example, suggests that

men are encouraged to conform to the heterosexual, stereotypical definition of masculinity which venerates aggression and dominance as desirable male characteristics. (p. 3)

Hence, the fact that men are violent and controlling of their male partners would be understandable, based on the internalized norms of what is appropriate in male behavior. Moreover, suggests Vickers (1997), internalized homophobia may be further augmented in such relationships in an attempt to be characterized as more masculine or male.

Regarding violence in lesbian relationships, societal beliefs suggest that the incidence would be substantially lower than evidenced in male couplings because of the absence of the male-female gender dynamics inherent in traditional patriarchal unions and the associated power and size differentials. Additionally, socially constructed female gender attributes emphasize females as caring, passive, nonaggressive, and desirous of mutuality. As a result, intimate partnerships among women are viewed as being more equal and nonviolent. Other myths include:

1. Lesbians do not engage in violent behavior against their partners, because women are not violent.
2. Domestic violence is more prevalent among those gay and lesbians who frequent bars, or are poor or members of racial/ethnic minorities.
3. A batterer must be physically larger than the victim.
4. Women in relationships have equal power.
5. Lesbian battery occurs only in relationships where a butch/femme or sado-masochist (S/M) dynamic exists.
6. Lesbian and gay domestic violence is nothing more than "mutual combat," not an exercise of power and control by one partner over the other. The violence is an equal fight.
7. Violence is a normal aspect of same-sex relationships.
8. Violence among gay male partners is merely boys being boys.
9. Lesbian and gay domestic violence is merely "sexual behavior," a form of S/M in which both partners take pleasure.

Such stereotypes and flawed perspectives are summarily refuted by existing research, as we shall see.

LITERATURE REVIEW

Research on domestic battery, notwithstanding research regarding domestic violence in gay and lesbian relationships, remains elusive. Only since 1987 have statistics regarding violent incidents in gay and lesbian domestic partnerships been empirically tabulated. According to Schilt et al. (1990), this was in no way due to a lack of calls for assistance by victims of said violence. For example, the San Francisco Police Department, beginning in 1987, has evidenced no less than 100 calls per month by victims of gay and lesbian violence. Additionally, the Lesbian Anti-Violence Project has reported that between 12% and 15% of its clients have sought assistance in dealing with a battering partner, with others reporting figures in excess of 35% (Schilt et al. 1990).

Many scholars who study gay and lesbian battering have indicated that it is a very similar phenomenon to heterosexual battering (Gardner 1989; Hammond 1989; Hart 1986; Island and Letelier 1991; Meyer 1988; Renzetti 1988, 1992; Renzetti and Goodstein 2001; Renzetti and Miley 1996). For example, these studies reflect similar levels of prevalence, a similar cycle of battering, resource difficulties, and similar victim responses.

The "scanty pre–1960s literature," according to Renzetti (1996), contains an inherent heterosexism bias. That, taken with the general paucity of studies, has compromised the reliability of existing research. Krieger (1982) notes that this literature presented a depiction of homosexuals as pathologically sick, inverted, deviant, and narcissistic, propagating the assumption that homosexuality itself was the problem in battering relationships. Yet, while much of the subsequent three decades of literature has continued to manifest a level of homophobic bias, some new work has emerged that offers more realistic perspectives and understanding. However, even this new research has been plagued with difficulties concerning sampling, interpretation, stereotyping, and a general fear or reluctance by the gay community and researchers to participate.

Not infrequently, the gay community and feminist writers have idealized gay relationships as "egalitarian, noncompetitive, and free from the power struggles that plague heterosexual relationships" (Renzetti 1992, 28). While such gay affirmative literature has not been free from criticism, it has been instrumental in traditionalizing myths regarding the "utopic" nature of homosexual dyads. Problematic here is the lesbian and gay community's acceptance of these myths, resulting in denial that such relational violence exists. This, in turn, has resulted in few resources to address the issue, little research, and increased pressure on homosexual battering victims not to report the violence for fear of further stigmatizing an already marginal community. However, some contemporary research is now avoiding the worst of the old biases and focusing on the influence of a homophobic environment, heterosexist socialization as part of a patriarchal relationship model, violence desensitization, inadequate social and gay community support mechanisms creating negative self-concept, and a host of other social and psychological issues (Nicoloff and Stiglitz 1987; Renzetti 1992; Hamberger and Renzetti 1996; Halberstam 1998).

In contrast to the wealth of research available regarding heterosexual domestic violence, a deficit of comparable data on same-sex relationships exists, making generalization concerning patterns of violence extremely difficult. Much of this research is based on non-probability sampling or anecdotal data, making generalization a problem. Such samples generally have a low response rate and fail to include those who are closeted, housebound, handicapped, or unwilling to participate for any number of reasons. This creates a sample selection bias which (1) skews the quality of results toward the experiences of those who voluntarily participate and (2) may be equated with response bias. Additionally, as with all survey research, there are serious concerns about question construction, sampling, methodology, data analysis, and interpretation.

However, this absence of data on same-sex battering should not be attributed to a lack of violence in these relationships. The limited research available suggests that the nature, prevalence, frequency, and severity of violence in homosexual relationships is proportional to what is evidenced in heterosexual dyads (Renzetti 1996). According to the fourth annual report on lesbian, gay, bisexual and transgendered (LGBT) violence completed by the National Coalition of Anti-Violence Programs (National Coalition of Anti-Violence Programs 2000), the number of reported incidents of domestic violence among gay couples in 1999 grew 23% from those recorded in 1998. However, the National Coalition of Anti-Violence Programs (1998) cautions that, while significant, this rise in case numbers should not be solely attributed to absolute increases in incidences of such violence, but that enhancements in staffing, improved outreach efforts, and program capacity may have contributed to the higher totals.

The report determined that incidences of domestic violence were largely equal between gay men and women. However, race was less significant in that 45% of abuse victims were Caucasian, 17% Latino, 11% African American, 14% Asian/Pacific Islander, and 13% other. Age differentials were as follows: 44% of victims were between the ages of 30 to 44,

21% were 23 to 29, 12% were 45 to 64, 4% were 18 to 22, 1% were under 18 years old, and the remainder were over 65.

Straus and Gelles (1986) determined the rates of violence in heterosexual relationships to range from 28% to 55% (see also Gelles and Straus 1979). Similarly, Gardner (1989) and Brand and Kidd (1986) established that the prevalence rate of violence in lesbian relationships ranged from 25% to 48%, and Island and Letellier (1991) have noted similar rates (15% to 20%) in gay couples, estimating that approximately 500,000 gay men per year are battered by a violent partner.

Brand and Kidd (1986) in their frequency of violence studies posit that rates of heterosexual and homosexual women physically abused by their domestic partners were 27% and 25%, respectively. In noncommitted relationships, they concluded that only 5% of lesbians, as compared to 19% of heterosexual women, were victims of violence. Analyses revealed no significant differences when they controlled for age, race, class, socioeconomic status, or education between the groups.

Some studies further suggest that the rates of violence may be higher in same-sex relationships. In 1991, Lie and Gentlewarrior, in a study of 1,109 lesbians, reported that in excess of half of the respondents indicated that they had been the subject of abuse by a female partner. Coleman (1994), in her study of 90 lesbians, determined that 46.6% had experienced repeated acts of violence. Finally, Ristock's (1994) analysis of 113 lesbians reported that 41% articulated that they had been abused in one or more relationships.

A caveat to all of the above prevalence studies is that most researchers believe that the actual number of cases of lesbian and gay domestic violence may be higher than those reflected in the findings due to fear of outing, fear of the police or courts, and/or lack of appropriate services to assist victims.

An exploratory study by Kelly and Warshafsky (1987) utilized a survey instrument to measure factors associated with homosexual partner abuse. The 98 participants (48 females and 50 males) were all openly gay, professional, white, middle-class, and politically active volunteers. The researchers, using a version of Straus's 1979 Conflict Tactics Scale (CTS), determined that verbal abuse and assertiveness tactics were prevalent in 95% and 100% of the cases, respectively. Moreover, respondents reported that use of physical aggression occurred about 50% of the time, with violent tactics occurring on less than 5% of the occasions.

In a comparison study, which examined correlates of domestic abuse in both gay and straight partnerships (43 heterosexual, 43 lesbian, and 39 gay couples), Gardner (1989) used the CTS in an effort to assess levels and prevalence of physical aggression over a one-year span. The author found no significant differentials in prevalence among the three groups. Lesbian couples evidenced the highest rates (48%), while heterosexual couples had the lowest rate (28%) and gay couples fell in between the two (with a rate of 38%). Coleman (1991) reported similar findings concerning domestic violence among homosexual couples. Consequently, the current research literature would support the position that prevalence rates and severity levels of violence are very similar in heterosexual and homosexual relationships.

Hammond (1989) suggests that there is a common perception that women are incapable of perpetrating serious harm to others, and that the range of violence experienced between homosexual couples may differ in form or severity from heterosexual couples. She notes that this fallacy serves to promote misunderstanding, denial, and a minimalization of the impact of such abuse, and the invisibility of alternative forms of abuse. Renzetti (1988, 1992), in a study of 100 self-identified battered lesbians, ascertained that violence in said relationships increased in both severity and frequency over time. This analysis revealed that of the participants, 77% had experienced an initial incident of violence within the first six months of the relationship, with 71% reporting an increase in both the frequency and severity of said violence as the relationship progressed. Renzetti (1992) determined that high victim independence, combined with elevated levels of batterer dependence correlated to higher levels of abuse in homosexual couples, mirrors findings in the research on heterosexual couples. Renzetti (1992) asserts that this research supports the similarity of variables involved in homosexual and heterosexual battering, and it supports the universal existence of a cycle of battering as identified by Walker (1979). This research further supports Gardner's (1989) findings indicating little difference in the variables or cyclical nature of battering in lesbian, gay, and heterosexual couples.

Hammond (1989) also suggests that much of the literature on heterosexual battering points to the significance of a size differential as a primary factor in battering, indicating that because one partner is larger and thus more physically powerful, battering is possible. The perception in the current literature is that women, in general, are not likely to display aggressive behavior. Chodorow (1978) posits that the socialization of women takes place in a culture where both women and their prescribed social roles are devalued. The author suggests that, as with homophobia, sexist values become internalized and consciously, or unconsciously, affect how a woman views herself and her partner. Whether violence occurs or not depends on contextual factors inherent in the situation (i.e., perceived utility of the behavior, rewards associated with partner compliance, control of resources, etc.) (Chodorow 1978). Additionally, Island and Letellier (1991) have noted that size is a poor predictor of whether an individual will become a batterer or a victim. Other researchers have noted that size is not the issue, but rather physical and social strength or power are the relevant concerns (Hammond 1991; Island and Letellier 1991; Renzetti 1992). Hence, researchers surmise that the incidence and prevalence of abuse in lesbian couples should be no different than that among heterosexual couples.

Further, it has been argued that violence is sometimes used instrumentally in same-sex couples to create distance and autonomy in a relationship perceived to be becoming overly "fused" (Kaufman, Harrison, and Hyde 1984). According to Burch (1982), this fusion occurs because stricter relationship boundaries may be necessary in such a tight, closed community where many past and potential lovers reside. These stricter boundaries can result in higher levels of closeness, but also in higher levels of isolation and control, which may improve the contextual conditions necessary for battering.

It has been postulated that in lesbian and gay couplings the partners are of relatively equal size and are mutually capable and/or willing to engage in violence as "mutual combatants" (National Coalition Against Domestic Violence 1986). Yet, according to Island and Letellier (1991), size and strength, while they may make violence a more effective tool for the batterer, are poor indicators of whether a person will become a victim or a batterer. In fact, many researchers have noted that the perception of "mutual" violence in same-sex relationships is incorrect and represents a misinterpretation of the self-defensive efforts of the physically equal victim (Hammond 1989; Island and Letellier 1991; Renzetti 1988, 1992). While the victim's response may be more likely to be aggressive because of the belief that he or she can defend himself or herself, it is nonetheless self-defensive.

The sociopolitical stance on domestic violence contributes to our understanding of how cultural beliefs, social systems, and politics serve to facilitate and perpetuate the occurrence of domestic battery (Hamberger and Renzetti 1996; Hart 1986; Lie and Gentlewarrior 1991). Renzetti (1992) suggests that "social stress, social isolation, low socio-economic status, and rigid sex roles" (p. 80) are factors that tend to serve as precipitators for increases in the incidence of violence among couples (see also Weidman 1986). Furthermore, the influence of dwelling in a patriarchal society that condones female subordination and the control of women (Dobash and Dobash 1978) facilitates relationships that tend to fit a model that is hierarchical in nature with a tolerance for the use of violence as a means to exert and maintain power (Gamache 1991; Hamberger and Renzetti 1996). Additionally, some scholars believe that the internalization of society's negative image of homosexuals creates internal shame and lower self-worth which may serve to increase aggressive behavior and tolerance of aggression directed at oneself (Coleman 1990; Lobel 1986; Planck 1998). This finding is not incompatible with discussions of the socialization of women into devalued self-images in the literature on heterosexual battering.

Hart (1986) has articulated the role of power in intimate relationships. She contends that "lesbians, like their non-lesbian counterparts, are socialized in a culture where the family unit is designed to control and order the private relationships between members of the family and where a social desensitization toward or acceptance of violence is promulgated" (p.174). Partners in a dyad of any type often desire control over the resources and decisions in family life that power brings and that violence can assure when control is resisted. Hart (1986) further suggests that the same elements of hierarchy of power, ownership, entitlement, and control exist in same-sex relationships, where partners have also learned that violence, coercion, and intimidation will likely enhance one's power in the relationship. This literature suggests that both members of a gay or lesbian relationship are likely to have been socialized similarly to each other and to heterosexuals with reference to relationship roles and the use of violence; consequently, their relationships are likely to reflect the same types of adaptive difficulties. Hamberger and Renzetti (1996) have further articulated this position with their analysis of the influence of a patriarchal relationship model. They note that the hierarchical nature inherent in social structures and the patriarchal values espoused in society have produced a relationship model that is predominantly based on domination through subordination, a norm which is internalized by both men and women regardless of sexual partner preference. Hence, even in homosexual dyads, there is a heightened potential for one partner to seek to control and dominate the other.

As a result of homophobia, heterosexism, and a general lack of support from the gay community, Coleman (1994) suggests that lesbian and gay victims are faced with discrimination, social isolation, and a lack of available resources or social support mechanisms to deal with battery. Consequently, such victims may have absolutely nowhere to turn for assistance in coping with the violence or the resulting feelings of powerlessness, low self-esteem, internalized homophobia, and inferiority. Gamache (1991) even argues that this situation may provide the very foundation for the maintenance of battering in same-sex relationships, which mirrors Ogle and Jacobs' arguments concerning the significant role of social resources in heterosexual dyads. Others have noted that the propagation of the myth of same-sex relationships as egalitarian and devoid of violence, as well as the gay community's acceptance of these myths, has made social acknowledgment and efforts to address these issues almost nonexistent (Coleman 1994; Gamache 1991; Hamberger and Renzetti 1996; Lie and Gentlewarrior 1991; Renzetti 1992).

Hammond (1989), in her analysis of violence in lesbian couples, posits that relationship violence does not happen in a vacuum. Friends, family, and social resources all play a direct or indirect role in the interaction dynamics. For example, she notes that choices regarding whether to confront the abuser, get help, try to discuss the problem or simply ignore the problems are often influenced by comments of others and have a direct impact on the integrity and self-esteem of the persons involved. The author suggests that factors sustaining victim contact with the batterer also create problems, such as fear of escalation should the victim attempt to leave; fear of being alone or incapable of establishing a new intimate relationship; the close, small, and closed nature of the gay community; a lack of specific resources; and a fear of being "outed" if one attempts to utilize mainstream resources. All of these problems can make the victim reluctant to seek outside assistance (Hammond 1989; Lobel 1986; Robson 1992). Additionally, threatened by outside friendships or resources, the batterer may have sabotaged victim efforts to maintain individual outside linkages or efforts to forge new ones, again similar to difficulties identified in heterosexual battering (Meyer 1988). Meyer notes that the maintenance of such a network of outside supports drastically increases autonomy and lowers a couple's closeness, isolation, and the batterer's power and control (1988). The provision and utilization of social helping resources for gay and lesbian victims has come under scrutiny in recent years. The research indicates that few services specific to same-sex battering exist. Most of the services available exist in programs designed for heterosexual victims, where usage is minimal because of homophobic workers, workers refusing to identify same-sex intimate violence as battering both to protect the gay community and their resource funding, as well as the general belief that battering is caused primarily by sex role inequity that can only exist in heterosexual relationships (Hammond 1989; Lie and Gentlewarrior 1991; Renzetti 1992).

In a survey of 100 battered lesbians, Renzetti (1992) determined that the majority of the study participants had not sought assistance from domestic violence hot lines, shelters, or similar agencies because they believed these services were only for heterosexual battering victims. Moreover, they expected to be turned away or made to feel uncomfortable by the help providers.

In a subsequent study, Renzetti (1996) examined the perception of service providers with regard to services for lesbian victims. Ninety-six percent answered affirmatively when asked if their agency welcomed lesbians.

However, when asked how they would make such a welcome clear, 90% left the answer blank. Only 9.7% of these agencies reported any efforts that were actually designed specifically for lesbian and gay victims.

The apparent reluctance of homosexual battering victims to utilize community services may be directly attributed to real or perceived homophobia and heterosexism within mainstream community service units and providers, rendering such services unresponsive and insensitive to the needs of gay and lesbian victims. Mainstream services also pose a risk to the victim of being "outed," which can then affect every other aspect of his or her life (i.e., custody of children, job, friends, family, etc.) (Hammond 1991; Lobel 1986; Robson 1992). This may be particularly salient if Renzetti's (1996) findings about social service agencies and their attitudes are correct. Additionally, some victims will fear that reporting the violence will further stigmatize the already marginal gay community; or, in the case of gay men, the men may believe that in reality they should be able to take care of themselves and helping resources are only for women (Island and Letellier 1991; Lie and Gentlewarrior 1991).

Finally, to further complicate matters, 21 states and the District of Columbia still have sodomy laws, and seven of these jurisdictions specifically target the behavior of homosexuals (Bull 1999). This may discourage reporting of same-sex domestic battery because reporting may require "outing" oneself and admission of felony sodomy activity (National Coalition Anti-Violence Programs 1998). Moreover, seven states have criminal statutes that define domestic violence in such a way as to specifically exclude same-sex unions (Bull 1999).

In sum, available research has demonstrated the existence of homosexual battering, and that the prevalence, severity, causality, and partner responses are similar to findings in the research on heterosexual battering. Although some differences have been identified (i.e., little strength differential and little use of outside helping resources), given the identified similarities, it seems reasonable to attempt to apply Ogle and Jacobs' (1998) theory to lesbian and gay battering.

The goals here are twofold: first, to apply this sociological perspective to lesbian and gay battering and examine areas where the application may vary from heterosexual battering; and second, in raising these questions, to create new avenues for examination in both areas of battering research.

Ogle and Jacobs' (1998) sociological perspective on battering utilizes three social elements that influence the battering relationship, in addition to the actual interaction between the two individuals. These three elements are socialization differences, strength differential, and the failure of social coping resources. Ogle and Jacobs explain the influence of these ele-

ments on the maintenance, progression, and escalation of the battering interaction within the framework of the cycle identified by Walker (1979).
Basically, they posit an interaction process where the victim's efforts to
cope with the violence elicit an aggressive response from the batterer to
maintain the status quo. As the battering cycle progresses, they argue that
the victim will seek coping resources outside the relationship. Each time
those resources fail to end the violence, this will precipitate an increased
response from the batterer to regain control through the use of increased
violence, and blockage of outside resources that threaten control, thus reducing the increased risk of exposure. Ultimately, the better the batterer,
the more likely the victim is to find himself or herself exposed to increased
violence and ever decreasing coping options.

On the face of things, it seems reasonable that such a sociological perspective would apply to gay and lesbian battering. However, this application is admittedly limited because of the scarcity of research on gay and
lesbian battering.

APPLICATION OF OGLE AND JACOBS'
PERSPECTIVE TO LESBIAN AND GAY BATTERING
AND BATTERING ESCALATION

According to this sociological perspective, in order to examine the battering relationship realistically as a battering process we have to understand some of the social, cultural, and structural elements that make this
ongoing confrontation different than that traditionally recognized in
self-defense law. Ogle and Jacobs (1998) put forth three elements inherent
to the battering relationship that influence the existence, maintenance,
and process of the interaction: the role of socialization differences, the
strength differential, and the role of social resources that, if failure-prone,
may unintentionally do more to maintain the battering interaction than to
end it.

Three Elements That Influence the Battering Interaction

The First Element

Ogle and Jacobs (1998) identify first the role of socialization differences.
This first element indicates that women tend to be socialized into relationship maintenance and avoidance of aggression (Bernardez-Bonesatti 1978;
Lerner 1980). This fact is not only consistent with lower levels of violence
by women, but also with the cultural/social message that women are responsible for the success or failure of relationships and with the theoretical
prediction of initial responses primarily directed at appeasing the batterer.

Application of this element in gay and lesbian battering relationships may be difficult, but it may well add significantly to our understanding. The first difficulty in applying this element to gay and lesbian relationships is that there would appear to be two individuals in the relationship with similar gender socialization. On the surface, it would appear that such partners would view and approach the relationship in similar ways, producing a more egalitarian partnership than heterosexuals.

However, this conclusion ignores two issues that may well offset this equitability: a non-dichotomous conceptualization of gender, and socialization into a "patriarchal relationship model." The former involves a misconception that gender is dichotomous (feminine or masculine). Some scholars indicate that gender can realistically be understood as a continuum, running from extreme femininity to androgyny at the center, to extreme masculinity at the other end of the spectrum (Halberstam 1998; Kessler and McKenna 1978). If we view gender in this manner, it is not unreasonable to expect that some gay men may develop a gender identity that falls on the feminine side of androgyny, while some lesbians may develop a gender identity that falls on the masculine side of androgyny. This is not to say that such gender identities do not develop among heterosexuals, but rather that they may impact partner choices in a way that makes them fit a dominance/subordination *relationship* model that we are all socialized into in a patriarchal society.

Consequently, even gay and lesbian partnerships—because of this relationship model socialization—are likely to involve similar role divisions that influence the battering interaction. Examples of this can be seen in studies of the butch/femme phenomenon (Halberstam 1998; National Coalition Against Domestic Violence 1986) and gay male battering dyads (Island and Letellier 1991). Studies on lesbian and gay battering indicate that, even in these relationships, batterers and victims display similar relational attributes to those seen in heterosexual battering relationships (i.e., jealousy, control issues, dependence, struggles for autonomy, etc.). This similarity might well reflect efforts to mold partnerships into this kind of patriarchal relationship model (Chodorow 1978; Kessler and McKenna 1978; Renzetti 1988; Hamberger and Renzetti 1996).

Other socialization factors that may affect the battering interaction involve the internalization of negative societal images of homosexuality. Hence, the resultant shame and lowered self-esteem may lead to the necessity to make the relationship work at all costs—not unlike heterosexual women who believe that they are responsible for, or deserving of, their victimization (Hamberger and Renzetti 1996; Hart 1986; Island and Letellier 1991; Planck 1998; Renzetti 1988).

It is also noteworthy that lesbians and gay men, like heterosexuals, are socialized into a society with high desensitization to violence in general and the devaluation of feminine attributes. There still exists the patriarchal socialization to devalue attributes considered feminine (Chodorow 1978; Halberstam 1998; Planck 1998; Renzetti 1988) and promote the rewards associated with violence and partner compliance. This situation seems to exist, even given the caveat that gay men and lesbians may well be more independent individuals than average because of the difficulties associated with, and the effort required to adopt and maintain, a lifestyle not only outside of the mainstream but, in some instances, in opposition to it.

In summary, scholars who have studied lesbian and gay battering relationships have indicated that there appears to be little difference in relational and battering dynamics between homosexual and heterosexual couples (Gardner 1989; Renzetti 1988; Renzetti and Miley 1996). Socialization differences that Ogle and Jacobs (1998) found to be significant in battering interactions in heterosexual relationships are similar to those evident in homosexual battering relationships because, rather than being individualistic, socialization differences are part of gender role identity and socialization into the patriarchal relationship model.

The Second Element

The second element that Ogle and Jacobs (1998) state influences the battering interaction is the strength differential. They indicate that in the heterosexual relationship women are simply not as physically strong as men and are not socialized into the use of aggression, but rather into relationship maintenance. Therefore, women are likely to initially appease the batterer, use self-defense minimally, and suffer significant injuries in the process. Ogle and Jacobs (1998) imply that this is one explanation for why it is reasonable for heterosexual battered women to realize self-defense will require the use of a weapon to equalize the power differential. Yet, the variable of size or strength differential takes on a different role when applied to gay and lesbian battering. It is possible that less size or strength differential and the potential for nearly physically equal retaliation or self-protection in lesbian and gay battering relationships may mean that there is less success achieved through aggression, and thus fewer rewards for the batterer for the use of violence.

In gay and lesbian relationships, victims—because of a lesser size and strength differential—may well view the battering as less threatening because they possess the wherewithal to physically protect themselves. This wherewithal increases the likelihood that victims will view the violence more as fighting than battering, and will be less likely to identify it as escalating beyond their ability to control. This appearance may be why some researchers have identified gay and lesbian battering as involving more "mutual combativeness" (Walker 1989). Many researchers have indicated that this is a misconception, because even in these relationships there is an identifiable batterer as a primary aggressor and a victim whose responses are clearly self-defensive (Chodorow 1978; Hamberger and Renzetti 1996; Lie and Gentlewarrior 1991; Renzetti 1988). Taken together, these variables may reduce the likelihood that the interaction will escalate to the level of homicide because there are fewer rewards for the batterer; and victims, over time, are less likely to be paralyzed by fear of death in a fight, and more likely to view fighting as an unacceptable element of the relationship. Thus, the likelihood that lesbian and gay victims would leave the relationship before it escalates to the level of lethal violence may well increase.

The Third Element

The final element that Ogle and Jacobs (1998) believe affects the battering interaction concerns social coping resources. The authors contend that social coping resources are often failure-prone and, because of this, the resources may do as much to maintain battering as they do to eliminate it. Ogle and Jacobs base this on two misconceptions: (1) the misconception that social resources for battering victims are plentiful and successful, and (2) the misconception that there is easy access to these resources and social support for their use. The authors note that these resources are neither plentiful nor successful. They also note that the scarcity of crisis centers, shelters, training and financial assistance in the United States, when compared to the millions of women and children who need these services each year, is dramatic. They question the success of the criminal justice system's methods and resources for addressing battering and point out how the lack of successful assistance from such programs may well assist the batterer in maintaining the battering relationship.

Additionally, Ogle and Jacobs note that social support for the use of resources is less than adequate. For example, police, clergy, and counselors sometimes encourage reconciliation, rather than exposure. The medical community, and social and child welfare agencies, fail to directly address battering and insurance companies often maintain the right to cancel life and health insurance on women and children if the battering is reported. They contend that when victims attempt to utilize social resources, and those fail, this reinforces the batterer's power and control and further isolates the victim. Given the existence of these kinds of problems with resource adequacy and utilization, there are significant reasons for victims to feel alone and resigned to self-help (Ogle and Jacobs 1998).

The problems concerning the adequacy and availability of social resources are compounded with regard to lesbian and gay victims. There are
few social support resources designed specifically for these victims
(Coleman 1992; Hammond 1991; Island and Letellier 1991; Lie and
Gentlewarrior 1991; Renzetti 1992, 1996). The methods of shelters and
crisis centers may be less useful to lesbian and gay victims because of the difficulty men have identifying themselves as victims and, in the case of lesbian battering, the reduction of protection that can be provided when the
batterer, because she is also female, may have as much access to these resources as the victim. Police, courts, and counselors often view violence in
homosexual couples as a fair fight, rather than as battering, and exhibit homophobic attitudes or refuse to render assistance. Often lesbian and gay
victims seeking help must accept services designed for the heterosexual
community, and they may be required to deny the nature of the relationship to obtain services (Lie and Gentlewarrior 1991; Renzetti 1996).
Renzetti (1996) determined from her research that less than 10% of social
battering resources report any services designed specifically to meet the
needs of the homosexual community. Many researchers have found that
most resource providers have not even taken the simplest of steps, such as
anti-homophobic training, possibly because of a lack of funding or fear of
jeopardizing existing funding (Coleman 1992; Hammond 1989, 1991; Lie
and Gentlewarrior 1991; Renzetti 1996; Renzetti and Miley 1996).

Other issues that affect the availability and support of resource use involve the homosexual community's overall denial of the existence of battering, in all likelihood based upon a fear of backlash against the gay
community in general. The gay community is a relatively small, close-knit,
and often closed entity. This can present a problem for victims because
they are unlikely to completely avoid contact with their batterers and may
likely share the same support mechanisms. It may then be difficult for victims to actually separate themselves from their batterers and still maintain
some semblance of a support system. It should also be noted that if victims
choose to go outside that small community to obtain assistance—not designed for their use—they face the additional risk of being "outed." Being
outed carries tremendous risk in terms of the loss of job, children, and reputation, as well as being forced to face a homophobic system alone. Further,
it has been noted that many gay and lesbian victims indicate that they do
not report battering because being abused by a partner is far less frightening
than being abused by the system (Island and Letellier 1991; Hammond
1989; Hart 1986; Lobel 1986; Robson 1992). Consequently, resources for
gay and lesbian victims are even less available, usable, or successful than

those available for heterosexual victims, and they may well leave victims feeling that self-help is their only option.

The Battering Cycle as an Interaction Process

Ogle and Jacobs (1998) claim that battering is often a long-term homicidal process, regardless of the batterer's intentions. They note that several thousand homicides each year are the result of battering, and that victims are most often killed at the point at which they attempt to utilize social resources to end the relationship and end the violence. They note that the typical self-defense scenario involves a single incident between two relatively equal combatants with only superficial knowledge of each other, in a short-term confrontation in which both parties recognize a foreseeable end. However, battering is a long-term, ongoing confrontation wherein the parties have developed an intimate knowledge of each other over time, where there is no foreseeable end to the interaction. Consequently, the authors develop a sociological perspective on battering as a long-term interaction process involving the three elements discussed above: socialization differences, strength differential, and failure of social resources as integral parts of the interaction in the relationship.

Ogle and Jacobs (1998) use Walker's 1979 battering cycle (tension building phase, acute battering phase, and contrition phase) as a broad framework in which to set the interaction. They posit a repetitive cycle where periods between the extreme violence do not represent a return to "normalcy," but rather the beginning of the next cycle of tension development leading to the acute violence. Thus, over time—after contrition disappears—violence is not just *one* characteristic of the interaction, but rather the *primary* characteristic of the relationship.

The authors claim that battering creates negative affect (i.e., fear, anger, etc.) for victims and high chronic arousal for both parties which is periodically relieved for the batterer through the use of violence, but is never relieved for the victim. Consequently, the victim functions in a constant high state of arousal under conditions of tension development. When *normal* people face negative affect and chronic arousal they use their coping mechanisms to either manage the situation or end it. Since women are socialized against the use of aggression and into relationship maintenance, they are likely to begin by attempting to manage the battering situation by utilizing their personal coping mechanisms to appease the batterer. When these efforts fail, and the cycle continues, the victim will reasonably recognize the necessity for outside assistance to end the violence and eventually no longer believe the batterer's promises of desistance that make up the contrition phase. Once the victim no longer believes the batterer's efforts at contrition, the batterer will discontinue those efforts because they are no longer useful to keep the victim in the relationship. Ogle and Jacobs claim that once contrition disappears, violence is the primary control method, and the interaction is constantly potentially homicidal.

When the victim attempts to utilize social resources to end the battering, she places herself at even higher risk because social resources are failure-prone and the batterer will perceive these coping efforts as an even greater threat to his control. The batterer will respond to this threat by blocking those coping resources and increasing the frequency and intensity of the violence in an effort to regain control. The authors note that desistance by the batterer becomes less and less likely because successfully regaining control is self-reinforcing and the cost of exposure becomes greater for the batterer as the level of violence increases. Consequently, there are no *nonconfrontational* periods because the victim is constantly experiencing negative affect and high chronic arousal, which the batterer seeks to maintain as tension building once contrition has disappeared. After social resources have failed to end the violence, and the batterer consistently regains control, the victim would reasonably perceive herself to be isolated, with fewer and fewer coping options in an increasingly lethal situation.

Application of this interaction portion of the theory to homosexual relationships should be very similar to its application in heterosexual battering relationships. Much of the research on lesbian and gay battering indicates a battering cycle similar to that identified by Walker in 1979 (Gardner 1989; Hart 1986; Island and Letellier 1991; Renzetti 1988, 1992; Renzetti and Miley 1996). Additionally, these studies indicate an increase in the frequency and severity of violence over time, as well as similar response patterns by victims and batterers. For example, Renzetti (1988) found that increasing victim independence and batterer dependence led to increased abuse and violence in lesbian couples as they did in heterosexual couples. Island and Letellier (1991) report similar findings concerning gay male couples. Consequently, this explanation for the cyclical nature of the battering interaction seems to apply to gay and lesbian battering as well as to heterosexual battering.

Battering creates negative affect (fear, anger, etc.) for lesbian and gay victims as well, and high chronic arousal for both parties, which is never relieved for the victims, but is periodically relieved for the batterers through the use of violence. We would expect that gay and lesbian victims, just like heterosexual victims, would initially utilize their personal coping mechanisms to manage or end the violence by appeasing the batterer. Ogle and

Jacobs (1998) posit that heterosexual women appease because they are socialized against the use of aggression and into relationship maintenance. Since this victim response is similar in gay and lesbian battering relationships, Ogle and Jacobs may be incorrect in focusing on sex socialization differences between heterosexual couples. Rather, the issue may well be related to the intersection of gender socialization and gender identity as part of a non-dichotomous perspective on gender and gender socialization. Thus, it is possible to speculate that same-sex relationships will likely involve couples wherein one partner will exhibit more masculine traits, while the other more feminine traits on a spectrum of gender. Additionally, as noted in earlier discussion, lesbians and gays are socialized into a patriarchal relationship model, just like heterosexuals, and therefore it is not unexpected that they would set up relationships that are reflective of the patriarchal roles in that model. If this is the case, then we would expect to see similar gender-related differences in same-sex couples and similar responses by victims and batterers in the interaction process. Consequently, we speculate that the element of gender differences will be the same for lesbian and gay couples. The differences may not be so extreme as those seen in heterosexual relationships, although they may well be more rigid. Therefore, one partner in the lesbian or gay relationship is likely to exhibit more feminine gender socialization resulting in responses to the violence involving appeasement and relationship maintenance, as opposed to aggression.

Ogle and Jacobs indicate that when the use of personal resources aimed at relationship maintenance fails, and violence continues, victims will attempt reactive self-defense. If reactive self-defense fails, victims will resort to social coping mechanisms to end the violence. This may vary when applied to gay and lesbian battering relationships because of the absence of an extreme strength differential. It may be expected that reactive self-defense for gay and lesbian victims might be at least somewhat more successful. This may be why much of the research on gay and lesbian battering indicates that these victims more often utilize reactive self-defense that is often misinterpreted to be mutual combativeness (Hammond 1989; Island and Letellier 1991; Renzetti 1988, 1992). With this limited success at reactive self-defense, gay and lesbian victims may be less likely to view theirs as a lethally dangerous situation that is escalating beyond their ability to protect themselves. Additionally, limited success at reactive self-defense may reduce the effectiveness of the use of violence for the batterer, thus moderating the escalation of the violence. The possibility should also be noted that since gay and lesbian victims might not see the violence as so lethally dangerous or beyond their ability to protect themselves, this might make them less likely to seek outside resource assistance, which would also reduce the escalation of the violence as predicted in this theoretical perspective. This possibility would reduce the escalation of violence, according to Ogle and Jacobs, because it is the risk that outside social resources pose for the batterer that creates the escalating fear of loss of control, defiance, and exposure resulting in increased efforts to block such resources and increased violence to regain control. We would speculate under this theoretical perspective that more lesbian and gay victims would leave the relationship before it would escalate to the point of homicide, because these victims might be more likely to identify the violence as mutual fighting that was "sick" or counter to the egalitarian ideal they were seeking in a relationship. Additionally, it might be that gay and lesbian couples face much less social pressure to stay together and work it out at all costs, because society denies the relationship's existence or devalues its significance to the participants.

Ogle and Jacobs indicate that contrition disappears when the victim no longer believes it, and thus it is no longer an effective tool for the batterer in maintaining control and keeping the victim in the relationship. A victim, after this occurs, becomes more fearful of the violence and is more likely to seek outside resources to end it, thereby increasing the risk for the batterer, resulting in increased violence to regain control. This process might vary in gay and lesbian battering relationships because, not only are social resources failure-prone, they are almost nonexistent for gay and lesbian victims, as noted earlier (Coleman 1992; Gamache 1991; Hammond 1991; Island and Letellier 1991; Renzetti 1988, 1992; Renzetti and Miley 1996). Therefore, victims may be more likely to feel alone in their efforts to cope with the violence long before it escalates to a point where it becomes lethal. This, of course, is speculative because data available on gay and lesbian battering, especially battering homicides, is too limited to determine how long these couples stay intact or how often these relationships end in a homicide.

CONCLUSION

Given the caveat of very limited research in gay and lesbian battering and battering homicides, it appears evident that Ogle and Jacobs' (1998) sociological framework is universally applicable to such partnerships. This is in part true because the research indicates far more similarities than differences between heterosexual and homosexual battering. Specifically, prevalence rates and severity of violence research findings appear to be equivalent, and problems concerning social resources also affect these interactions. Research indicates that the same type of cyclical process exists in lesbian and gay battering relationships as that identified by Walker (1979) in heterosexual dyads. Additionally, socialization appears to play a similar role in lesbian and gay battering, although we posit that Ogle and Jacobs (1998) may have restricted the usefulness of this variable by concentrating only on sex socialization rather than the broader issues of gender socialization and the influence of a patriarchal relationship model into which we are all socialized.

Two minor differences that affect the course of the interaction predicted in Ogle and Jacobs' (1998) framework appear evident: the strength differential and resource availability and usage. This sociological perspective predicts that the strength differential makes violence a more effective tool for the batterer and a significantly more dangerous situation for the victim than that commonly perceived in self-defense. The differential also makes reactive self-defense by the victim less useful to counter the violence. However, this pattern may vary when applied to gay and lesbian battering because the potential for nearly equal self-defense is likely to reduce the effectiveness of the violence for the batterer, reduce the likelihood that the victim will see the violence as particularly dangerous or lethal, and increase the likelihood that the victim will view the violence as fighting rather than battering. If the violence is viewed in this way, it seems more likely that the victim will perceive it as "sick" or counter to the egalitarian relationship being sought. This might well make the victim more likely to leave the relationship before the violence escalates to the level of homicide, rather than relying on outside social resources to end the violence. Application of the theory in this way would lead us to predict that gay and lesbian victims would be less likely to resort to the use of outside social resources that, if they failed to end the violence, might actually escalate the interaction towards homicide. Therefore, this theory would seem to predict fewer homicides in gay and lesbian battering relationships. However, it is impossible to support or refute this outcome at present because of the dearth of available data on homosexual battering homicides.

We might suggest that homosexuals, in the process of understanding and accepting their own homosexuality, may actually develop a level of self-insight beyond that generally experienced by heterosexuals. Such insight might increase the likelihood of the individuals having more clearly identified what it is they want and do not want in relationships, and therefore increase the likelihood that they will leave relationships wherein they feel threatened or devalued. This might be particularly true if they were seeking a more egalitarian relationship as some of the literature indicates. Additionally, it is possible that homosexuals are generally more independent individuals because such independence is likely a necessity, possibly even a result of living a lifestyle outside of or in opposition to the mainstream society. It seems reasonable that more independent individuals would be more likely to seek egalitarian relationships wherein their independence would be maintained and nurtured, and identify violent relationships as contrary to their egalitarian ideals. It is also possible that such independent individuals might be more likely to simply leave a relationship before it escalates to a homicidal level because they fear their own exposure in a homophobic society and fear the resultant backlash that might further devalue an already marginal gay community. Although all of the above involve pure speculation, with further research we believe such issues might be identified as significant to our understanding of both homosexual and heterosexual battering.

REFERENCES

Bernardez-Bonesatti, T. (1978). Women and anger: Conflicts with aggression in contemporary women. *Journal of American Medical Women's Association, 33*, 115–219.

Brand, P.A., and A.H. Kidd. (1986). Frequency of physical aggression in heterosexual and female dyads. *Psychological Reports, 59*, 1307–1313.

Bull, C. (October 27, 1999). Scene of the crime: Laws against gay sex can block everything we want. *The Advocate, 771*, 36–40.

Burch, E. (1982). Psychological merger in lesbian couples: A joint ego, psychological and systems approach. *Family Therapy, 9(3)*, 203–208.

Chodorow, N. (1978). *The reproduction of mothering: Psychoanalysis and the sociology of gender.* Berkeley: University of California Press.

Coleman, V.E. (1994). Lesbian battering: The relationship between personality and the perpetration of violence. *Violence and Victims, 9(2)*, 139–152.

———. (1991). Violence in lesbian couples: A between groups comparison. Doctoral dissertation. Abstract in *Dissertation Abstracts International, 51*, 5634b.

———. (1990). *Violence between lesbian couples: A between groups comparison.* Ann Arbor, MI: University Microfilms International.

Dobash, R.E., and R.P. Dobash (1978). Wives: The "appropriate" victims of marital violence. *Victimology: An International Journal, 2(3–4)*, 426–442.

Ferraro, K. (2000). Woman battering: More than a family problem. In C. Renzetti and L. Goodstein (Eds.), *Women, crime, and justice: Original feminist readings* (pp. 135–153). Los Angeles, CA: Roxbury.

Gamache, E. (1991). Domination and control: The social context of dating violence. In B. Levy (Ed.), *Dating violence: Young women in danger* (pp. 69–83). Seattle, WA: Seal Press.

Gardner, R. (1989). Method of conflict resolution and characteristics of abuse and victimization in heterosexual, lesbian and gay male couples. Doctoral dissertation. Abstract in *Dissertation Abstracts International, 50*, 746B.

Gelles, R.J., and M.A. Straus (1979). Determinants of violence in the family: Toward a theory of integration. In W.R. Burr, R. Hill, F.I. Nye, and K. Reiss (Eds.), *Contemporary theories about family* (vol.1) (pp. 549–581). New York: The Free Press.

Halberstam, J. (1998). *Female masculinity*. Durham, NC: Duke University Press.

Hamberger, L.K., and C. Renzetti (1996). *Domestic partner abuse*. New York: Springer.

Hammond, N. (1991). Lesbian victims and the reluctance to identify abuse. In K. Lobel (Ed.), *Naming the violence* (pp. 10–198). Seattle, WA: Seal Press.

———. (1989). Lesbian victims of relationship violence. *Women and Therapy*, 8, 89–105.

Hart, B. (1986). Lesbian battering: An examination. In K. Lobel (Ed.), *Naming the violence* (pp. 173–189). Seattle, WA: Seal Press.

Island, D., and P. Letellier (1991). *Men who beat the men who love them: Battered gay men and domestic violence*. New York: Harrington Park Press.

Kaufman, P., E. Harrison, and M. Hyde (1984). Distancing for intimacy in lesbian relationships. *American Journal of Psychiatry, 141(4)*, 530–533.

Kelly, C.E., and L. Warshafsky (1987). *Partner abuse in gay male and lesbian couples*. Paper presented at the National Conference for Family Violence Researchers, Durham, N.H.

Kessler, S.J., and W. McKenna (1978). *Gender: An ethnomethodological approach*. New York: Wiley.

Krieger, S. (1982). Lesbian identity and community: Recent social science literature. *Signs: Journal of Women in Culture and Society, 8(1)*, 91–108.

Lerner, H.G. (1980). Internal prohibitions against female anger. *The American Journal of Psychoanalysis, 40*, 137–147.

Lie, G.W., and S. Gentlewarrior (1991). Intimate violence in lesbian relationships: Discussion of survey findings and practice implications. *Journal of Social Service Research, 15*, 41–59.

Lobel, K. (Ed. 1986). *Naming the violence*. Seattle, WA: Seal Press.

Lundy, S. (1993). Abuse that dare not speak its name: Assisting victims of lesbian and gay domestic violence in Massachusetts. *New England Law Review, 28 (winter)*, 273–294.

Meyer, C.J. (1988). Social support and couple closeness among lesbians. Doctoral dissertation. Abstract in *Dissertation Abstracts International, 50*, 2667A.

Muraskin, R. (2000). *It's a crime: Women and justice*. Upper Saddle River, NJ: Prentice Hall.

National Coalition Against Domestic Violence (1986). Fact Sheet. www.vaw.umn.edu/finaldocuments/glbtdv/htm.

National Coalition of Anti-Violence Programs (NCAVP, 2000). Fact Sheet. www.lambda.org/dv99

———. (1998). Annual report on domestic violence from 1996. *American Bar Association Journal, 84*.

Nicoloff, L.K., and E.A. Stiglitz (1987). Lesbian alcoholism: Etiology, treatment and recovery. In Boston Lesbian Collective (Eds.), *Lesbian psychologies* (pp. 283–293). Urbana: University of Illinois Press.

Ogle, R.S., and S. Jacobs (1998). Battered women who kill: A sociological perspective on the battering process and the use of self-defense. A paper presented at the Annual Law and Society Conference in St. Louis, MO, June 1998.

Planck, C. (1998). Same gender domestic violence. *Lesbian News, 24(3)*, 17.

Renzetti, C. (1996). On dancing with a bear. In L.K. Hamberger and C. Renzetti (Eds.), *Domestic partner abuse*. New York: Springer.

———. (1988). Violence in lesbian relationships: A preliminary analysis of causal factors. *Journal of Interpersonal Violence, 3*, 381–399.

———. (1992). *Violent betrayal: Partner abuse in lesbian relationships.* Newbury Park, CA: Sage.

Renzetti, C., and L. Goodstein (2001). *Women, crime, and justice: Original feminist readings*. Los Angles, CA: Roxbury.

Renzetti, C., and H.C. Miley (1996). *Violence in gay and lesbian domestic partnerships*. Binghamton, NY: Harrington Park Press.

Ristock, J. (1994). And justice for all: The social context of legal responses to the abuser in lesbian relationships. *Canadian Journal of Women and the Law, 41(5)*, 135–155.

Robson, R. (1992). *Lesbian (out)law: Survival under the rule of law*. New York: Firebrand Books Publications.

Schilt, R., G.W. Lie, and M. Montague (1990). Substance use as a correlate of violence in intimate lesbian relationships. *Journal of Homosexuality, 19*: 57–65.

Strauss, M.A. (1979). Measuring interfamily conflict and violence: The conflict tactics (CT) scales. *Journal of Marriage and the Family, 41(1)*, 75–88.

Strauss, M.A., and R.J. Gelles (1986). Societal change and change in family violence from 1975–1985 as revealed by two national surveys. *Journal of Marriage and the Family, 48(3)*, 465–479.

Vickers, L. (1997). Second closet: Domestic violence in lesbian and gay relationships: A Western Australian perspective. *ELAW-Murdoch University Electronic Journal of Law, 3(4)*, pp. 1–16.

Walker, L. (1989). *Terrifying love: Why battered women kill and how society responds*. New York: Harper & Row.

———. (1979). *The battered woman*. New York: Harper & Row.

Weidman, A. (1986). Family therapy with violent couples. *Social Casework, 63*, 259–265.

About the Authors

ROBBIN S. OGLE is Associate Professor of Criminal Justice at the University of Nebraska at Omaha.

SUSAN JACOBS is Associate Professor of Criminal Justice at the University of Nebraska at Omaha.